THE GIRL IN THE GRAVEYARD

Sharon O'Rourke

Copyright © 2025

The moral right to be identified as the creators of the work has been asserted by them in accordance with the Copyright, Designs and Patents Act 1988. All rights reserved.

No part of this book may be reproduced, stored in a retrieval system or transmitted in any form or by any means, electronic, mechanical, photocopying, recording or otherwise, without the prior permission of the authors.

Book Cover by Ven Visual

www.venvisual.com.au

Designed by Red Feather Publishing

www.redfeather.com.au

ISBN for print: 978-1-7643681-0-0

ISBN for E-Book: 978-1-7643681-1-7

Certain names and places have been changed to protect myself and my family.

CONTENTS

Acknowledgements	1
Author's message	4
1. 1975 – 1979	5
2. 1979 – 1981	9
3. 1982 – 1985	15
4. 1986 – 1988	38
5. 1989 – 1991	70
6. 1991 – 1994	96
7. 1993 – 1996	119
8. 1997 – 1999	157
9. 2000 – 2002	168
10. 2002 – 2005	192
11. 2005 – 2010	197
12. 2010 – 2015	209
13. 2015 – 2017	228
Epilogue	264
Afterword	266

ACKNOWLEDGEMENTS

My best friend, the father of our amazing kids, my soul mate, the love of my life. I love you with all my heart and soul. Your healing touch grounds me and makes me feel safe and loved always. Words cannot express what you mean to me. You saved me from myself many times. You acknowledged the good things. You have acknowledged all the things I have achieved over the years, no matter how small. You have supported me through this tough, exhausting journey. So many would have given up long ago, but you believed in me. You are my rock. We were told we saved each other all those years ago. I don't know if that is true for you, but I know for a fact you saved me. I will love you always and forever, my darling Norman. Xxxx

To my gorgeous kids. You both make me proud each and every day. You have grown into the kindest human beings I know. Conor, you work hard in everything you do. You have such a caring nature and gentle healing hands. Catherine, you are such a beautiful, gentle soul. You have worked hard to get where you are today. You will one day find your path in life and be great at it, I know it. I love you both with all my heart. xx

To my beautiful baby sister, I love you more than words can say. You have made me the proudest big sister ever. I am proud of everything you have achieved. You are amazing! I'm glad you have found love. You deserve the world, honey. xx

My gorgeous niece, you are such a special girl. You have had a tough life, but please keep talking about your past. Believe me, it helps in the long run. You will live a life full of love. Love you loads. Xx

Hege and Jen thank you for a great 5 ½ years in beautiful Kongsberg, Norway. You are both beautiful, amazing women, and I am grateful to have known you. Much love to you both. Xx

Dear Robyn, I was grateful for everyday you were my daughter's Grade One teacher. We met and became good friends. Volunteering with you for 10 years were some of the happiest times in my life. Thank you for introducing me to your parents, too. They took me into their home and lives like I was one of their own. Love you, Mum and Dad xx

To my good friend Judy, thanks to you and your family for taking me in when my family were in Vietnam, and I needed to come home for therapy. You made me feel welcome, and I will be forever grateful. You are one in a million. Love you, my friend. xx

To my friend Helen, because of our gorgeous girls, we met and became good friends. You have been there through some of my toughest times with an ear to listen and a shoulder to cry on. Thank you, my dear friend, love you big time. xx

Dr Robbins, thank you for being my doctor these last 16 years. You gave me faith in doctors again. Thank you for sticking by me and for sending me to Danielle. x

Dear Yajna, thank you for introducing me to EMDR and imagery therapy. Because of you, I no longer have nightmares about my grandfather. I wish you and your family all the happiness in the world. Thank you. x

Dearest Danielle, what can I say, thank you, thank you, thank you. I have been seeing you for six years now, and I think I am the happiest, strongest I have ever been. We have talked, laughed and even cried together. We have done EMDR and imagery, which has worked amazingly. I can honestly say you have saved my life multiple times over. Thank you for being you, Danielle. I wish for you all the happiness in the world, you deserve it, and more. xx

Dr Liana, thank you for taking me on as one of your patients. You made me feel heard and important. You didn't just feed the symptoms with medication, you listened to my story. Thank you so much. x

ACKNOWLEDGEMENTS

Nikki, having an eating disorder has been a 30-year battle for me. I have struggled mentally because of it. Thank you for continuing to work with and encouraging me along the way. I am eternally grateful. x

To all the beautiful people at Perth Clinic. Thank you to each and every one of you. From the beautiful office staff to the amazing kitchen staff, all the therapists and of course all the amazing nurses. I am grateful to each and every one of you. My stay at the clinic multiple times over the last three years have always been positive ones. I learned so much through my time in Purple Group with Laura and Prachi, DBT with Tash, Red Group with Ingrid and Caz and my favourite, art therapy with Ingrid. From the bottom of my heart, I thank you all. xx

Thelma, Winnie, Jo, Joanne, Tiffany, Jasena, Brenda and Chido thank you. xx

Dearest Ingrid, you are such a beautiful soul, and I want to thank you from the bottom of my heart. Art therapy has given me a way of expressing myself. I have come a long way thanks to you. The Thursday group is amazing, and individual therapy has helped me in my healing journey more than you know. I want to thank you for asking every time we meet for that promise, because of you I'm still here today. Please don't stop asking. Thank you, Ingrid. Xx

Dear Megan, we have known each other only a short time but the work we have done together is so significant. We have been angry, we have laughed, and we have cried heaps. Thank you for being you, Megan. My life is blessed for having you in it. Much love xx

Thanks to my editor, Karen Peradon-Alaga. Thank you for getting me through the editing process and for getting me to publishing, Karen. I wish you all the happiness in the world. xx

AUTHOR'S MESSAGE

This message is to everyone out there that has been abused either emotionally, physically, mentally or sexually. This book is proof you can overcome your trauma. You can live a life full of happiness and love. You will always carry your scars, and they will come back to bite you on the backside from time to time, but you will learn to not let them control your life. You will one day control them instead. Please go out there and get the help you so desperately need. Believe me, there are really good therapists waiting and willing to help you. Take the leap, I did.

Much love,

Sharon O

X

This book contains content that refers to sexual abuse, child abuse, suicide, drug-taking, domestic and physical violence.

Chapter One
1975 – 1979

I was born in Glasgow, Scotland, on 18th June 1975, to Margaret and John O. My earliest memory—or one that was planted by my parents talking about it over the years—was at the age of 2 ½ years.

I was riding my little red tricycle on the landing. We lived on the fifth floor of a 21-storey block of flats in Thomas Street. My great-gran lived next door with her cat Smokey, a beautiful silver-grey tabby.

Mum and Dad were 21 and 19 at the time. Mum was on the landing with me, watching me ride up and down on my tricycle, when Granny called on her, and she left me alone while she went to see what Gran wanted. The elevator stopped on our floor, and I rode my tricycle in. The doors closed behind me.

I have no memory of what ensued and only know from the stories told. Mum returned to find I was no longer there. Then they started searching for me. Mum phoned Dad's work to let him know he was needed at home, that his daughter was missing.

The search started on the bottom floor. The concierge said no child had come past their station on a tricycle, but they would look at the cameras covering the entrance. There were no cameras in elevators in those days.

Dad searched floor by floor in the elevator while Mum stayed on our floor in the hope I would turn up.

They found me on the 18th floor, riding up and down on my tricycle, not a care in the world. I was later told it took almost an hour to find me.

Thinking about that story now sends chills down my spine. A feeling of panic and fear all at the same time. Anything could have happened to a child so young. I guess now that I have kids of my own, I know the fear I would have felt in me if one of my own disappeared from my sight at such a young age.

I can now put myself in my parents' shoes and feel the panic and fear that would have run through them that day. The guilt my mum would have felt; not knowing if she would get her child back, and in one piece.

Luck be it, I was found safe and sound and unaware of the danger I was in and how much fear I had placed on my parents that day.

My New Baby Sister

A year later, in January 1979, my baby sister (Wendy) was born. I was 3 years old. Mum was taken into hospital for a caesarean. There were complications.

While on the operating table, Mum suffered what doctors considered to be a stroke. The left side of her face, her mouth and eye had dropped. She never did get an answer why from the hospital. To this day, she believes they left her on the operating table too long before administering the anaesthetic, making her panic at the sight of the operating instruments.

Dad dressed me in a lemon dress and put my hair up in a ponytail. I looked pretty. He took me to the hospital to see Mum and my new baby sister. Mum was holding Wendy in her arms when we arrived. She was beautiful and tiny, with dark curly hair and beautiful blue eyes. I fell in love with her.

Mum didn't look right. She didn't look like my mum. Her face looked strange. Dad said she was a little sick. It took her many months before she was well again. To this day, when she looks in the mirror, she can still see her face droops slightly.

Hide and Seek

My cousin Ronald is a month older than me. I loved it when his mum, my auntie Joan, would bring him over for a play. He was my friend, the only person I got to see who was my age.

I remember us going to Nannie's house (my dad's mum), and we loved it when her youngest son, Uncle Joshua, was home, and we got to play hide and seek. Uncle Joshua, my dad's little brother, was only 9-years-old, and he was the baby of the family. Ronald and I were 3 years old at the time. One day we played hide and seek and found a great hiding place in the coal bunker, which was in the hallway. It had a small door, maybe two-by-two feet. Uncle Joshua was always the one who counted, while we hid. Ronald and I opened the small door to the coal bunker and climbed in. We could hear Uncle Joshua coming towards us, calling out our names as he searched. Ronald and I were giggling, thinking he would never find us.

Minutes later he found us because we were giggling so much. We climbed out of the bunker, black as coal, covered in soot. We giggled as we climbed out. Nannie could hear Uncle Joshua gasp, then laugh. She came out into the hallway, gave us a good serving and a hard smack on the backside. The soot flew everywhere. She was angry and put us into the bathtub fully clothed, stripped us and scrubbed us from head to toe. We were both crying by the end. It wasn't fun being scrubbed clean by Nannie. She was rough.

Uncle Joshua

On Easter Sunday 1979, when Wendy was just 3 months old, Mum and Dad took me and Wendy to Dad's Auntie Cathy and Uncle Joe's. Auntie Cathy is Dad's dad's stepsister. She had six kids, all older than me. She had boiled some eggs, and my cousins and I painted them in reds, blues, greens and yellows in different patterns.

Auntie Cathy took us to the local park, and we rolled our eggs down a hill until the shells came off, then it was time to go back to Auntie Cathy's to get Dad and go home on the big double-decker bus.

This specific Easter Sunday would stay branded in my family's minds forever. My Uncle Joshua asked if he could come with us that day, and for whatever reason, my dad said no. He called my dad a fat bastard and ran off. Because he wasn't coming with us, he decided to take his fishing net to the loch and fish instead. Two boys crept up on him, pushing him in the water. He couldn't swim, and the divers said his legs were tangled in the reeds next to an old car that had been in the loch for many years. He had no chance. That sunny afternoon, while we rolled our Easter eggs down the hill with our cousins, my Uncle Joshua drowned. He was only nine years old.

He wasn't found until Easter Monday. A lady walking her dog saw his hair and thought it was a doll floating in the water. It alarmed her enough, though, to call the police.

That Monday, as we were on our way home on the bus, we noticed the loch was cornered off with police tape. When we got to Nannie's house, there were many people there. Nannie told Dad, 'The police think Joshua is in the loch.'

Dad ran from the house and didn't stop until he reached the loch. The body had just been laid in the undertaker's van, and Dad was taken by the police to the mortuary to identify the body. His baby brother was lying on the cold slab. Just a child. Dad would be haunted for the rest of his days.

That day broke and changed my dad in so many ways. He would never be the same again.

Chapter Two

1979 – 1981

Wendy and I got the same dolls for Christmas. We played inside a pop-up house Dad had put together for us. We must have been in that house for hours and hours. Wendy got a little kitchen, which we put inside. We would pretend it was our house, and we had to look after the babies.

Mum wrote our initials on the backs of the doll's necks, so that they didn't get mixed up.

One day, Wendy's doll's leg got caught in the door and broke in a way it couldn't be fixed. She cried and cried for her doll. Dad asked me to give her mine, but I said no, 'she is my baby not Wendy's'. He told me again to give her my doll. I refused, crying, and screaming.

He grabbed me tightly by the arm and told me to get my doll. He asked where it was. It was in my room, and he dragged me into the bedroom to get it. She was tucked up under my sheets sleeping, and he grabbed her, throwing me on the floor. I sobbed for hours. I hated Dad and Wendy for taking my doll.

Dad told me to put my nightdress on and get to bed, but still crying, I told him, 'It's not bedtime yet'. He stood on my fingers and said I would lose them if I didn't stop whining. I tried hard to stop crying, to be a good girl. He left the room telling me he would be back in 10 minutes and, if I was not in my bed and still crying, he would give me something to cry about.

When I had stopped crying, I was allowed to get up out of bed. Wendy had my doll and was happily playing with her when I went into the living room. Dad told me I had to keep my mouth shut about the doll. No more talk about it, or I'd get another beating. I hated watching Wendy play with my doll.

She would go to bed with the doll, and as soon as she was asleep, I would sometimes take the doll just to hold her. I had to make sure to put her back before she woke up. I fell asleep one night with the doll in my arms, and Wendy screamed I had stolen her doll and ran into Mum and Dad's room, crying that I had taken her. Mum said Wendy was just a baby, but at five, I was young too.

Dad didn't like being woken. He hated mornings and didn't want his sleep disturbed. He jumped out of bed and grabbed my hair, blaming me for waking him. He pushed me against the bedroom door. I was crying, begging Mum to help me, but she just lay there. He dragged me into our bedroom, sat on my bed, put me over his knee and slapped my backside until it was red raw. I couldn't sit on it for ages, so I lay on the floor or bed. Dad had big hands, so when he would hit me, he covered most of my backside.

I was ordered to stay in bed until told to get up. My bottom stung, and the pain was horrible. I don't know how long I had to stay there, but it was a long time.

Nannie gave Wendy and me dolls for Christmas. I got the newborn baby doll with no hair. Wendy got one with beautiful long hair. My doll looked so real, I loved my baby. I adored dressing her and taking her for walks on the landing in her pram. But I was warned over and over again not to go in the lift if it stopped on our floor, so I learned not to do that again. Wendy had a buggy for her doll as hers was much bigger than mine.

My baby would sleep on my bed when I wasn't playing with her, so when I found her on the floor in one of the corners of the room one day, I got angry at Wendy for touching her. She started crying and shouting for Mum. I picked up my doll only to find her face was drawn all over with coloured pens, I started screaming. My baby was destroyed.

Mum came into the room and saw the state I was in, and the state of my baby. She asked me what the hell had happened. I told her' I didn't do it. Wendy did it. She drew all over my baby.' Mum told Wendy off, but she screamed she didn't do it. Mum believed me but asked how Wendy managed to get into the tin of markers. That one was my fault. I didn't put the lid on after I used them earlier. I tried to clean her, but the marker wouldn't wipe off. Mum tried too. She said, 'Dad will be crazy if he sees her like that.'

I had to hide her when Dad was around in the afternoons and bring her out to play when he was sleeping. Only I forgot to hide her one afternoon, and Dad walked into the living room holding the baby up and shouting, 'What the hell did you do to this?'

I burst into tears. I knew I was in trouble. He walked over to me and pushed her into my face. I told him I didn't do it. 'Wendy did it.'

He screamed, 'Why are you lying? You did it. You are not getting another toy if you are going to destroy it.' He ripped my doll's head off and threw her on the floor. I bent to pick her up, and he smacked me, grabbed the doll and grabbed me by the arm and walked me out onto the landing where he opened the bin chute, threw her in and closed it. I heard her fall into nowhere, and I screamed for my baby. He grabbed me harder and dragged me back into the house, threw me onto my bed and told me to stay there. I fell asleep after a while and woke when it was dark outside. Mum was tucking Wendy into bed. Very quietly I said, 'Mummy, I'm sorry for being a bad girl. I promise I will be good now.' She came over and gave me a piece and butter. (A piece is what we called a slice of bread.)

I wanted her to hold me, tell me I wasn't a bad girl, not give me a piece and butter. She left the room, and I silently wept and nibbled at my piece, finally falling asleep again. She always wanted to please Dad, not make him angry.

A few weeks before Easter that same year, Mum took me and Wendy shopping. Wendy was in her pram. We went from shop to shop picking up clothes, books, and Easter eggs and putting them in the basket under the pram. We were stopped on the way out the door of one of the shops. A security guard wanted to see what was under the pram. Mum refused, so we were escorted to a room where the manager came in and said he had called the police. The police escorted us to the station. Mum looked scared, but we went in a police car, which I loved. I had never been in one before; it was exciting. Wendy's pram was put in the boot. At the station, we were led into a room. Wendy was placed in her pram, where she stayed sleeping. The only thing I remember from that day is a police lady taking me to the kitchen where she gave me milk and a biscuit. Again, I don't know if this is another memory I have, or it could have been planted in my brain due to the story being told by my parents later on and many times over the years.

I had no idea at that time what was going on. I only knew Mum was in trouble. She was given a fine for stealing the items but didn't have to go to court. Dad had to come and get us. He was mad at her for getting caught and going home with nothing. I could hear him screaming at Mum from my bedroom. What happened that day didn't stop her from stealing again and again, though, I don't ever remember her getting caught again.

Dad had a few jobs that didn't last long over the next few years—building a bridge over the motorway, working in the sewers. He was such an angry man. In the end, he stopped working because he wasn't coping with the death of his brother. He repeated this many times over the years. He blamed himself for what happened because he didn't allow him to come with us that day. He started drinking, often 4 times a week in the beginning. My parents were getting money from the social security, and child support, so money was pretty scarce. Mum had a few small jobs at times, cash in hand mostly, working as a cleaner in offices, or in a tie factory.

I started nursery when I was 4 years old. I met and made my first friends at that school. Karen and Helen will stay with me forever. We were close and spent so much time together. Helen lived in the third block of flats from me, and Karen stayed in the fourth. My mum was friends with their mums, so we spent a lot of time together both inside and outside of school.

There was a playground between the second and third block of flats. We would often meet there after school. Our mums would sit and chat while we played on the swings, slide and roundabout. We loved that because it went fast, but the seesaw was our favourite. I loved the feeling of being up in the air. We would scream as our feet left the gravel. Our mums would help us with the seesaw because the three of us would want to be on it at the same time. We could have played at the park all day and would often cry not wanting to go home. It was the only freedom I had to have fun.

We found some money in the sand one day and felt rich. There were 1s 2s 10s and 20 pence pieces. Our mums took us to the shops, and we got ice poles. That was a great day. I went to their houses a lot, but they never came to my house. Mum never invited them.

A boy in my class, John Brown, played in the sand with me a lot. One day, he asked me to take down my knickers so that he could see my flower. He said he would show me his peewee. I did what he asked. I thought this was okay but was surprised at what I saw. He didn't have the same as me. I had never seen what a boy had. I thought we were all the same. Our teacher gave us a telling off. She said we shouldn't show our private parts to each other. We cried, and our mums were called. My mum smacked me hard and told me to stay away from John and to never do that again.

Halloween 1981

It was Halloween; I was 6 years old, and I was looking forward to going trick or treating with my friends. My costume was ready: I was going to be a pumpkin.

I had to see the dentist that morning to have four of my teeth out. My mouth wasn't big enough to house all my teeth, so I was given gas that put me to sleep. When I came to, I was groggy, and so Mum had to borrow a buggy to take me home. I slept on the couch all morning. When I woke, I was ill and wouldn't stop throwing up.

Mum and Dad said I couldn't go trick or treating, and I cried so much that day. I wanted to go trick or treating with my friends and their mums. Back in those days, we got more fruit from people and not so many sweets. We also had to sing or do a trick to get the treats. At some homes, we had to duck for apples to get one. This was a basin full of water and apples bobbing in it. We would put our heads in the water and try to grab an apple with our teeth. If we managed to do this, we got the apple. We would get soaked doing it, but it was so much fun. We didn't think about germs back then. My friends came to visit me after they had gone door-to-door trick or treating. They shared their apples, oranges, monkey nuts and some sweets with me. I felt lucky that day.

My baby brother was born in June 1983. He was the cutest baby, so tiny. I used to love watching him while he slept. He very seldom cried. I looked after Colin a lot while Dad was drinking, and Mum was working in a bookbinding company. I was seven years old but had to grow up fast. I gave Colin his bottle and changed his nappy. I didn't complain though; I loved being the big sister, although I pretended I was his mum. He had blond hair and blue eyes. He smelt like a newborn baby should. I put him in his pram and took him onto the landing, where I pretended I was playing house. I had Wendy holding onto the side of the pram, and she walked with us, too.

It broke my heart when we moved from the flats in Thomas Street. I didn't want to leave my friends or Granny behind.

Chapter Three
1982 – 1985

Everyone loved our Wendy. At just three years old she was a little entertainer. Auntie Grace and Uncle Robert, Dad's brother and sister-in-law would take her to Auntie Grace's mum's house. She would sing and dance for them and get some pocket money from them for singing. She was always chosen to go places with family members. I guess she was bubblier than me. She had cute little dimples and a little button nose. I don't ever remember a time I was chosen to go somewhere nice. I was jealous of her. She could do no wrong. I would get smacked all the time. Even when Wendy did something, I would somehow get the blame for that, too. God, I envied Wendy. I wanted and wished I was her.

We moved from the flats into a three-bedroom block house in Carway Street when I was 7, closer to Dad's parents. A block house consists of four houses—two upstairs and two downstairs. We lived in one of the upstairs three-bedroom houses. Two families lived on the bottom floor houses—the Calders lived below us and the Stevens next door on the top floor. All that separated us from our neighbours was a thin wall. We could hear the neighbours when they argued, played music and we even heard them when they had sex. It was awful. I am pretty sure they could hear us too.

We had a football pitch beyond our back garden and a graveyard beyond that. This separated us from my dad's mum and dad, my nannie and grandad.

I don't ever remember Nannie coming to visit us when we lived in Carway Street. She changed so much after Uncle Joshua died. She never smiled or laughed, was always angry. I don't remember her ever leaving her home after he died. Grandad did all the shopping and paid the bills at the post office. He would visit us often to collect money from my parents. They were paying him back for a loan they got at Christmas time to pay for presents, food and of course lots of alcohol for New Year. They would borrow money often. I remember them being in debt and arguing about it constantly. A man named Millard worked for a company called Prudential. He would come and collect the money from Grandad every week.

Mum was at work and Dad was in a drunken sleep as usual these days. He seemed to be drinking most nights now. He was happy when drinking. I had to light the fire for him around eleven every morning. He liked the living room warm for when he got up out of bed. I never forgot eleven o'clock. Dad made sure of that. One morning I played in my room too long and didn't put the fire on before he got up. He stormed into my room spitting and shouting.

'You didn't put the fucking fire on, you bastard.' He dragged me into the living room and pushed my face towards the clock. 'What is the fucking time?'

'I don't know... (crying) Is it eleven?'

'No.'

He took his slipper, put me over his knee and beat me with it across my bare backside. I screamed, 'Please Daddy, I promise I'll remember next time. I will be a good girl from now on.'

He threw me on the floor and left the room. I very quickly lit the fire, ran into my room, and lay on my bed crying for Mum. Knowing Mum wouldn't and couldn't do anything, but still wanting her there. Mum was scared of Dad too, I'm sure of it.

Colin was crying in his cot in Mum and Dad's room. Mum usually brought him into me in the morning before she left but didn't on this particular morning. I heard him cry and very quickly and as quietly as possible went into their room to pick him up, grateful Dad didn't wake up. I carried Colin into the living room, placed him in his bouncy chair and put the fire on. Wendy had also woken with Colin's cries. She came in as I put him in his bouncy, came behind me and put her arms around my neck. I hugged her back and put the cartoons on for them both. I told her to sit on the floor beside Colin while I made breakfast. I very quietly put cornflakes and milk in a bowl for Wendy, and warmed Colin's bottle. I sat Wendy at the coffee table and picked Colin up, sat on the couch with him and fed him his milk. Colin started blowing raspberries after his bottle. I tickled him, and he laughed, making me and Wendy laugh along with him. He was so adorable. I heard a bang on the wall. Dad was awake. I quickly put Colin back in his bouncy and told Wendy to sit by him. I turned the cartoons up a little as I heard Dad stomping down the hallway towards us. I told Wendy, 'No matter what you hear, stay looking at the TV, okay?'

'Okay, Sharon,' she replied.

I didn't want her to witness anything that Dad might do to me. Dad came in with anger on his face. I knew I was going to get it. He slapped my face so hard, I fell and hit my head off the wall as I hit the floor. I lay there holding my head and silently crying. I thought if I stay down long enough, maybe he will stop hitting me, but he told me to get up. I didn't. He kicked me one, two, three times. I screamed out in pain. Colin started to cry, and Wendy turned around and looked at me. I signalled her with my eyes to turn back to the TV. I couldn't bear her seeing what I went through. She took Colin's little hand in hers. Dad stormed out of the room and into the bathroom. I struggled to get up off the floor. The pain in my chest was unbearable; I don't know if he cracked a few ribs. I went into Mum and Dad's room, praying he wouldn't come in and hit me again. I grabbed Colin's nappies, his dummy and romper suit. As I got back to the living room, the toilet door opened. I felt scared. I heard Dad go back to his room and slam the door, and I sighed with relief.

Wendy's eyes were watery. I held her close to me, whispering in her ear, 'I'm okay.' I could see the worry in her little face.

I decided to take them out for a walk. I picked Colin up, and as I did, I winced with pain. I changed his nappy on the couch and put his little romper suit on. I picked him up and sat him on my hip. Wrong side, I almost dropped him with the amount of pain I was in. I took him to my room and helped Wendy get ready. Put her shoes and little red coat on. I had to take it really slow going down the stairs. Having Colin on my hip and holding Wendy's hand was really challenging. I went to the shed behind the house to get Colin's pram, and we walked out onto the street. I wasn't sure where to go, so I walked up the hill to the entrance of the graveyard. Just inside the gates on the left-hand side were giant rocks. Colin was sound asleep, so I put the brake on his pram and got Wendy to climb the rocks. I told her to lie down beside me and look up into the sky and asked her what she could see in the clouds.

She took my hand and said, 'I can see a horse and a dog.'

I didn't want to go home. As we walked back down the road, I could see Mum at the other end of the street, so we passed the house and went to get Mum. Wendy was so excited to see her. Ran to her and hugged her tightly. I was relieved she was home. Mum didn't speak to Dad about what had happened earlier. She could see the bruises so knew what he had done. It was just forgotten.

I was told to look after Wendy one Sunday afternoon, so I took her onto the football pitch behind the house. She took her shoes off and started climbing the football post but slipped halfway up. As she hit the ground, she cut her foot open on broken glass and started screaming. I tried hard to calm her by talking to her. I took her sock and covered the cut, but there was too much blood. I knew I would get it for not looking after her properly.

Mr Calder climbed over our fence and picked Wendy up. He carried her through the field and out through the gate of the graveyard. When he carried Wendy upstairs, Mum and Dad came running to see what all the commotion was all about. Mum wrapped Wendy's foot in a towel. Dad slapped me and told me, 'Get to bed, you fucking idiot, you were supposed to look after her.'

He would deal with me later. He put Wendy up on his shoulders, and they left to catch the bus, taking her to hospital. She got 10 stitches.

God, did I get it when Dad got home. He spat in my face. It was all my fault for not looking after her properly. He hit me with his belt over and over on the backside and legs. It was my fault. I tried to say sorry to Mum and Dad later. I promised I would be a good girl from now on. He threw me on the bed and told me to stay there. No dinner for me tonight. I was scared to leave my room. So I stayed in there until Mum and Dad said I could come out. Which felt like days, I don't know how long it took until I was allowed to join them again.

I started primary school in August 1982. My first teacher was Miss Wilkinson, and she taught me for the next few years. They say you always remember your first teacher; that one teacher teaches you how to read and write, how to act, react to situations both in the classroom and on the playground even outside of school. That one teacher who lays the foundations that will help you through your school journey. I believe this to be true.

Miss Wilkinson saved me in many ways. It was because of her I found my love of art. She taught me how to hold and shade with my pencil. She asked questions when she saw bruises, but I always had an answer—I fell down the stairs, I crashed my bike, I fell out of bed. My answers were always well rehearsed, Dad had taught me well. It didn't stop her from continually asking, though. I loved her for that.

Miss Wilkinson played a trick on us one morning. We arrived at school as usual, took our bags and coats off, hung them up on our pegs. Took our shoes off and put them on the shelf underneath our coats and put on our indoor shoes. We sat on the carpet in front of her so that she could tell us what we would be doing throughout the day.

This specific morning as we sat on the carpet in front of her, she started to tell us what the day held for us, but something didn't seem right. The way she said certain words like 'Good morning, boys and girls' wasn't right. 'This morning, we will start off with a story.' This didn't usually happen until after recess or lunch.

She started reading the story 'Hansel and Gretel' to us. She had read this book before. It was my favourite story book, but it sounded different to the way she usually read it. We sat captivated as she told the story, then the cupboard door opened, and Miss Wilkinson stepped out. We sat with our mouths wide open and gasped in astonishment. Miss Wilkinson had an identical twin sister. It was hard telling them apart. We were all amazed.

Mum enrolled Wendy and me into a summer holiday club. I loved the club because they took us out on great outings. I remember we went on a trip to a place called 'Saltcoats'. Saltcoats was near the beach. It was pebbly near the waterfront. The pebbles would cut your feet. Mum came along sometimes and brought Colin. He slept a lot of the time. I filled my bucket with sand and turned it over, but the sand wouldn't compact enough to make a castle. I took my bucket down to the waterfront, screaming as I went with the pain of the pebbles under my feet, but I was too excited to get water in my bucket. I filled the bucket with water and headed back to where Mum was sitting feeding Colin. I dug a little moat and put the water in there. I could then compact the sand into my bucket. Turn it over and a great castle started to form. I loved my castle. That had to be one of my happiest trips with the holiday club.

I was happy at the beach. I wished we could stay in that time forever. The weather was nice, and Mum seemed happy looking after Wendy and Colin. I gave Mum some seawater from my bucket for Wendy to use. Wendy loved the sand but loved the water more. One of the leaders looked after Wendy while Mum fed Colin.

We got battered sausage and chips from the chippie for lunch and sat on the beach while we ate. I reckon we ate as much sand as we did chips. I hated when it was time to leave the seaside.

We headed to the very large rocks to pick whelks and mussels. They were attached to the rocks. We filled all our buckets with them and then it was time to head home on the big bus again. I dreaded it. Dad put a massive pot of water on to boil and added the whelks. You could hear them scream while being boiled. The house stunk like a racoon letting off, but they tasted amazing.

Grandad (Dad's dad) was a well-dressed man; always wearing formal trousers, a clean shirt and a tie. He started visiting more and would rub against me as he moved past. It was at this time he started touching me. I was 8 years old. He asked me to sit beside him and stroked my hair and back. He put his hand on my leg when he was talking to Dad. I felt so lost and alone. I couldn't tell anyone, because no one would believe me. Was this love from Grandad? Was what he was doing normal? Did everyone's Grandad do this? He told me I was his special girl. He spoiled me with little gifts like money, a small locket, a little ornament, etc. He told me not to tell anyone about the gifts. He said they would get jealous because they didn't get presents. He gave me a little ornament of a white rabbit sitting amongst green grass that he told me to put under my pillow, that way he would always be with me. He loved me more than anyone in the world. He loved me more than Mum and Dad did; I was special. I got all his attention when he came to visit. Another time, he gave me a tiny locket. I was only to wear it when no one else was around. He whispered in my ear; I would be his special girl forever. I loved him because I was his special girl. I never felt those feelings before. It was nice to hear someone say they loved me, that maybe I was a good girl after all.

The Graveyard

We didn't have any playgrounds around us. Not like they do these days.

I played in the graveyard behind our house almost every day after school. Most of the time, on my own. It was quiet and peaceful. When the weather was okay and not too cold, I would sometimes climb onto the rocks just inside the gate of the graveyard, lie down and look up into the sky and make pictures out of the clouds, like I had with Wendy.

I felt sad when I walked past graves that didn't have flowers. I picked wildflowers from the tall grass and placed them on the graves. Sometimes when a grave had lots of flowers, I took some, thanked the person/people for allowing me to do so, and as I placed the flowers on a grave that had none, I said a few words to each of the people buried there.

I would often walk past the stones, reading the names and ages of the people buried there, and imagine what they looked like. I would then sit in front of the graves and talk to the person buried there.

I came across an old stone with a seven-year-old girl's name on it, Rose. She was just one year younger than I was at the time. After a time, I visited Rose most days. On the days I couldn't make it, I would still tell her I was thinking of her in my head, tell her how my day was. She became my best friend.

I told her I was sorry she was no longer here, and I hoped she was happy in heaven. I pictured her free to dance and sing. I imagined the feeling of being free to do so. Sometimes I wished I was there with her. Especially when Dad was angry at me for the umpteenth time that day. Rose grew up with me, well at least in my mind and heart. I could see her as we aged together. I loved her; she was my best friend and the only person that knew me and everything about me. For the next ten years, I visited Rose four or five times a week. I always picked wildflowers and replaced the ones from the previous day.

One summer's day around June or July, Dad had beat me badly. He punched me so hard in the chest, I fell to the floor, and he kicked me in the back. I struggled to walk and couldn't catch my breath. I made my way to see Rose. God, I hurt all over. I lay beside Rose's grave crying and telling her why had Dad beaten me again for the umpteenth time that week. After a time, I fell asleep. When I woke up, it was getting dark. I hurried home as fast as I could, opened the door and crept up the stairs. Mum was in the kitchen. She put her finger to her mouth and told me to go into my room. I lay on my bed paralysed with fear that Dad would come in and kill me. Mum opened the door a short time later and gave me some beans on toast for dinner. She said to stay in my room, and all would be okay, and it was.

I loved it when my cousins would visit—Ronald, Katy, Steven, and Nicole. I was the same age as Ronald and Nicole. Katy and Steven were a few years younger.

We played hide and seek in the graveyard, and swing tarzies from the trees. Tarzies were thick ropes we hung from the trees. We tied a large knot at the bottom, sat on it and swung. We took our fishing nets and ice cream containers to fish for tadpoles. We spent hour upon hour in the graveyard. Nicole and Katy loved picking rose petals to make perfume.

There was a warehouse called B&Q. It was a hardware store and sold everything you needed to do a project in your home or garden. At the back end of the store, there were wooden pallets. Ronald and I climbed the fence and passed some pallets over to the others. We had a special place in the graveyard we called the witch's circle. It was a tall hedge in the shape of a circle. In fact, it was a circle inside a circle. We took the pallets we had gathered and built a cubby house inside the witch's circle. We gathered in there sometimes and told ghost stories to scare each other. As I got older, I spent a lot of time in the circle, drinking and smoking on my own and sometimes with friends. We sat in there for hours upon hours. I never wanted to go home when I spent an afternoon with my cousins; I felt alive and free. Those were the best days.

The graveyard was my safe place. I loved it in there. I never felt safer than when in the graveyard. It was peaceful with people walking around visiting loved ones. Some people just went for a stroll.

Dad was now drinking more and more throughout the week, having whiskey and beer. On occasions he would smoke a cigar. He got angry and aggressive with Mum at times. I never saw him hit her back then. Wendy and Colin could do no wrong, but he beat me most days. He would find any excuse; he could be very scary. It seemed I was always doing the wrong thing. Five minutes late coming home. Not washing the dishes properly. Not heating the food through properly. Not saving the outsider of the bread for him. The outsider was the end piece of the bread. The list was endless. The beatings became more frequent. On the odd occasion I found peace was when Mum would get it instead. He would get angry at her, and once or twice he slapped her face. It was nice when he had been drinking during the day and fell asleep on the couch for a few hours. I tried to be out as much as I could in all weathers. It rained and still does rain a lot throughout the year in the UK. I went out in all weathers to see Rose. If I missed a day, I was upset and prayed to Rose to forgive me for not seeing her that day.

My parents had many parties over the years. They would use any excuse to hold one. Mr Calder downstairs often came, but it was mostly family—Dad's brother and sister-in-law, Robert and Grace, and sister Jane. Mum's family; her three brothers, William, Johnny and David, sister Sarah and her husband Michael.

I loved Auntie Grace being there, though. She often took me and Wendy into our room to put together a dance routine that we then showcased in front of everyone. I loved it when parties were held. I got attention from Auntie Jane, Uncle Robert and Auntie Grace. They would give us pocket money, something I never got from Mum or Dad.

Now, keep in mind the graveyard was between us and my Nannie's house. One night when everyone was arriving for a party, Dad's record player wasn't working. So he and Uncle Robert decided to go through the graveyard to Nannie's house to borrow her radiogram. It was sunset and getting dark outside when they started their return. Now picture this scene. The radiogram was in a long wooden box with two men carrying it through a graveyard at night. It looked like they were carrying a coffin. Lucky the police weren't called—that would have been tough to explain! That story was told many times over the years. Everyone got a kick out of it. It had to be told at every party.

The only problem with having parties was that everyone got drunk and fights broke out. They were usually between Dad and Mum's brothers. Dad's brother Robert usually jumped in on Dad's side. The fights were like something out of an action movie—lots of blood and gore. Sarah and Michael left early before a fight broke out between Dad and Mum's brother Johnny.

Dad punched Johnny so hard he fell against the wooden fireplace. The whole thing fell apart with the TV landing on top of him. That made Dad even angrier. Uncle Michael and Uncle Robert pulled Dad back to let Johnny up, but Dad wasn't ready to stop. He broke free and grabbed Johnny by the shirt and threw him down the stairs. Charles then punched Dad. The only problem with that was Dad was a very large man. Charles was barely five foot and skinny. He had no chance. They all ended up out in the street, fighting each other. The police were never called. I guess the neighbours were too scared to phone them. Dad could be a very scary man.

Usually when the fights started, I took Colin from his cot into mine and Wendy's room, where we would huddle in a corner hoping the banging and shouting would stop.

Sometimes when the party was over, and Dad was still pissed and angry, he would take it out on Mum. Sometimes we heard her scream. I would get Wendy to sit with Colin on my bed. Hug them and tell Wendy it will be okay. 'Just stay here—everything will be okay. I'm just going to see Mum.'

I could see Wendy was worried, so I gave her bear to her and told her to hold him close. 'He will protect you, I promise.' I was always scared I wouldn't be able to keep that promise.

I crept down the hallway just to see if Mum was okay. She was sitting on the bed crying. I went to her, not seeing Dad behind the door. I took her hand and asked if she was okay. I heard a noise behind me and turned quickly to see Dad standing there with a drink in one hand and a cigar in the other. He just screamed, 'You fucking bastard. What the fuck are you doing up?'

I said, 'I heard Mum.'

He threw the glass he was holding at my head. It missed and hit the wall. I ran from the room expecting him to run after me, but he didn't. He told Mum to heat the curry through because he was starving.

I quickly went back into my room to see if Wendy and Colin were okay. Colin was sound asleep with a pillow either side of him. Wendy was very sleepy, lying on my bed with her head on my pillow. I lay beside her and put my arm around her as she fell asleep. I lay awake for some time, still scared Dad would come for me.

When I woke in the morning, Colin was gone, and Wendy was sitting on her bed playing with her doll. Dad stayed in bed most of the day, only to get up ready to start drinking again that evening. I had to help Mum clean, although I got all the shit jobs. The floor was covered in food, drink and blood. The hallway wall was also smeared in blood, and halfway down the stairs. It was really hard cleaning white artex (textured plaster on the walls) when stained in red blood. I couldn't clean it all off with the Jiff. Mum told me to use bleach, but it not only took the blood off, it took the paint off too. There was no way to hide it. I knew I would get it from Dad when he saw it. He was going to the social security to sign on for his social money, something he had to do every week. He saw the wall on his way downstairs was no longer peach but grey. He screamed, 'Who the fuck took the paint of the fucking wall?'

I froze when I heard him. I knew right away what he had seen.

Mum said there was blood on the wall and that I had cleaned it with bleach. She didn't mention that she was the one who told me to use it. He shouted my name, and I knew what was coming.

He said, 'Get the fuck down here, you bastard.'

I said, 'Please, Dad, no.'

He said it with much more force, 'Get fucking down here.'

I very slowly crept down the stairs, and when I was on the step above, he grabbed me by the arm and pulled me down to him. Mum went further down the stairs and opened the front door. Dad grabbed my hair and pushed my face against the wall, saying, 'Look what the fuck you've done, you stupid cunt. You fucked the colour, and I don't have any paint left. I should fuckin kill you. I'm going to have to paint the whole fuckin thing again, you fuckin bastard.'

He dragged me down the rest of the stairs on my front and left me lying at the foot of the stairs as he kicked my legs out of the way for him to pass.

I lay at the bottom of the stairs for what felt like hours. My head was throbbing. I could feel it pulsing. The pain was intense. I crawled upstairs and lay on my bed. I cried myself to sleep only waking when I heard the front door open. They were back. I asked Mum if I could go out. Dad had started drinking early, and I was terrified he would go crazy at me again. I put my coat on as it was raining lightly outside. The sky was grey, but I walked through the graveyard to Rose's grave. I sat in front of her and told her what Dad had done.

'I hate him, Rose. I am always such a bad girl. He hates me. I am trying hard to be good, I promise. I wish I was dead. If I was dead, I wouldn't get hit again. I made a real mess of the wall. All the paint came off. Can I come visit you? I promise I'll be good. I just want to come with you. Please come and get me. PLEASE'

I lay down on the wet grass and prayed for her to come. I thought maybe God wouldn't let her come and visit me. 'You are my best friend,' I told her.

Nannie told Dad for months to send Wendy and me to church on Sunday mornings. Dad was too drunk or hungover to go to church. Therefore, Mum took us for a few Sundays. After that, I had to take Wendy on my own. We spent the first 20 minutes at the Sunday service, while the minister, Mr Moodie, gave his sermon and then excused the children, who were taken to another hall where we attended Sunday school. We talked about the bible. The younger kids drew or coloured in pages to do with God, Jesus, etc. I personally hated bible class. As I got older, we had to read from the bible. I found it boring. I preferred to sit in on the service and sing the hymns. I loved listening to the choir and singing along with them. I wanted to be in the choir. When I was older, I loved going to church on Christmas Eve from 11 p.m. to 12 a.m., we sang lots of Christmas songs and hymns. My favourite was *the 12 Days of Christmas* and *Oh Holy Night*. The advent candles were lit for the last evening. It was going to be Christmas soon. When the clock struck midnight, we all turned and wished each other a very merry Christmas and went downstairs into the big hall where we ate hot soup and a roll. Christmas was my favourite time of year.

I don't ever remember Mum and Dad sitting around the tree giving us our presents. We were told to open our selection boxes and have chocolate for breakfast. We then opened the presents while Mum and Dad stayed in bed.

I did love going to the Brownies. On a Sunday early evening around 5.30 p.m., we met at the church hall with our Brownie uniform, a brown dress with a mustard scarf. We had to do special tasks to receive merit badges, like carry an elderly person's shopping, help them cross the road, do shopping for someone, etc. The badges were then sewn onto the arms and chest of the dress.

I loved the Brownies; it gave me an escape from home.

Mum loved dressing Wendy and me the same way. I didn't mind at first, but it went on year after year. I was three and a half years older than Wendy, so thought this weird. Sometimes the colour would be different, but the clothes were the same—white dress with black polka dots and yellow cardigans, white socks and black polished shoes. I got the lime green jacket, and Wendy got the pink one. Even when school pictures came around, our hair had to be the same. I think I was 12 when it stopped.

Mum used ripped cloth (usually from an old bed sheet) to make tight ringlets in our hair. When we woke in the morning, she took the strips of cloth out, resulting in a mass of tight curls. Mum always did this to our hair the night before school pictures were taken. She liked to leave our hair down, but head lice went around the class so much back then, we usually wore it up.

I loved bath times. We had a bath on Sunday afternoons. We all shared the same bathwater. Mum went in first; Colin often went into the bath with Mum after she had washed. Being the youngest, he went to bed earlier than Wendy and me. Wendy was next, or we went in together. The bathwater was black by the time we had finished. Sometimes when Dad was in a shitty mood, he came into the bathroom while I was in the bath. He screamed that my neck and behind my ears were black and he had to clean it because I was doing a shit job of it. He got the nail brush lathered it with soap and scrubbed my neck and ears with it. I screamed and splashed, only infuriating him to the point where he grabbed my hair and slapped me around the head and face. I hated him so much by that point. When I climbed into bed at night, I cried myself to sleep, and I always asked God, 'Why am I bad? Why can't I be good like Wendy? Why does Dad hate me so much? I'm trying to be a good girl. I promise, God, I will be good tomorrow.'

The next day I would go to Dad and say, 'I'm sorry, Daddy, I will be a good girl today.'

He just turned to me and said, 'You don't know how to be fucking good.' He then dismissed me to make him tea or feed Colin or dress Wendy. I didn't complain when having to look after Wendy and Colin. I stayed in my room with them if possible or took them for a walk. The graveyard became a place I visited not only with Wendy and Colin but also a place I could escape to when trying to stay out of Dad's way.

On Sunday afternoons, the rag and bone man came around the streets with his horse and cart. We took any old clothes and shoes to him for a lollipop or a sweet. Sometimes we scrounged around the street asking the neighbours if they had any old clothes or shoes they didn't want anymore. When I think of that now, a lollipop or sweet isn't much, but back then it was amazing.

It was summer holidays, and Dad and Mr Calder downstairs built a bike and spray painted it royal blue. Dad told me to take the bike up the hill and ride it down to see how it ran. I climbed on the bike and started riding it down the hill. I was going faster and faster. I tried to slow down, but I couldn't. There were no brakes. I started to panic. The bike wobbled with me trying to find a way of stopping it. I was getting more and more out of control. I avoided a car parked on the street but crashed into a lamppost. I was badly cut up all over. My clothes were ripped and bloody. I grazed all down the side of my face and had a deep cut in my head. There were tiny bits of gravel embedded in my head. Screaming out, I was in pain all over. A few neighbours came running to help me. Dad didn't move from our gate. Uncle George was one of the people who came to help. He lived a few blocks away from us. He and Mrs O'Neil helped me up. both taking an arm. I screamed out. My arm was grazed from my shoulder down to my hand. I had sprained my ankle. One of the other neighbours picked up the broken bike and carried it to our gate. Dad just looked at me.

Mum cleaned my cuts with methylated spirits. It stung like hell. She screamed at me to stay still. I couldn't; I was in so much pain and crying uncontrollably. Dad screamed from the living room, 'SHUT THE FUCK UP! Stop being a baby.' They didn't take me to the doctors or the hospital, not like they did with Wendy. Just rubbed me over with some Germolene and sent me to my bedroom. I lay on my bed crying all afternoon. I stayed home from school for a few days, and I hated that, not knowing what sort of mood Dad would be in.

When out playing with Ronald and Nicole one afternoon, we witnessed a girl running in the street with no shoes on. She was carrying something in her arms and screaming, 'Help me, help me. My baby's dead. Help me, please.'

Neighbours came running from every direction to help. Someone took the baby from her arms, and another got the girl to sit on the pavement. The ambulance and the police arrived. I had never seen so many people in our street before. The girl had given her baby girl a bottle, then fallen asleep. She had rolled on top of her, and the baby died. Baby Dawn was buried at the top end of the graveyard where my maternal grandmother was buried. The funeral was on a Saturday afternoon. All the neighbours were there, and the girl's two sisters held her up as she couldn't stand. The poor girl was in bits. I think the image of her and her baby in her arms will stay with me forever. I never saw anyone visit Dawn's grave, so I started taking wildflowers for her too. I never saw fresh flowers or a visitor when I visited her grave.

After the funeral, the girl was admitted to a hospital for the mentally insane where she remained for some years. I saw her years later in the pub.

Elizabeth Walsh

As long as I live, I will never ever forget Elizabeth Walsh. I met her in primary three.

In 1982, at just 7 years old, she always came to school dirty; her clothes were filthy and ripped, her hair was matted. 'Like rats' tails' as we said back then. It was always knotted, never brushed, and tied up. She smelled bad.

I felt bad for her because some of the girls picked on her. The kids bullied her every day. They called her smelly, pushed her around and threw mud at her. When she came to school the next day, she still had the mud smeared on her clothes. She was always sad. No one sat next to her in class because she smelled of urine and sweat.

One day I decided to sit next to Elizabeth in class. The smell was awful—I felt quite sick, but I tried not to show my reaction. The other girls in the class looked at me with disgust, as if I had done something wrong.

That is when Jessica and Emily started bullying me instead.

Elizabeth and I became good friends that day. She was a quiet, shy girl like me, but she was really funny. We got on so well, I think, because we were similar in a way. We didn't see each other outside of school because my mum wouldn't allow me to.

Her parents didn't have much money, but her dad could always afford his tobacco and skins (cigarette papers) but not clothes for his daughter. Sometimes they couldn't afford food either. They lived on the same street I was born, on the second floor of the close (a close has six apartments). I knew her parents were not the most caring people. Apart from Elizabeth and Joseph, Elizabeth's big brother, there were another two siblings, but we never saw them. I guess they were younger than Joseph and Elizabeth. They kept themselves to themselves.

Elizabeth told me she and Joseph were sent to the chapel to beg the nuns for food and clothes. Most of the time, the nuns would give them a bag of stale bread and soup. Usually, there wasn't enough to feed the six of them. Elizabeth said she and Joseph had to eat some of the food before they got home as their dad took most of the meal, and what was left was shared amongst the other five of them. That is why they were all skin and bones.

I caught head lice many times over the few years I was friends with Elizabeth. I scratched like crazy, sometimes my head bled. Mum went crazy at me. She swore at me, 'You fucking stay away from Elizabeth. I'm sick of you getting lice.' God, I hated the bone comb. It hurt like crazy. It would scrape through the scabs and make my head bleed. I had such thick long hair that it would take hours to comb after Mum put the head lice treatment in my hair. It smelled like ammonia, and it would sting from the cuts I had from scratching.

I hated going to school the day after Mum put the ointment on. My hair looked greasy and stank. Jessica and Emily would have fun teasing and pushing me around.

Nannie told my mum to shave my head if I didn't stay away from Elizabeth. After two years of having head lice on and off, Mum's friend Katie cut my hair into a bob. I cried—I hated my hair and myself after that. It didn't sit nicely because my hair was thick.

Joseph Walsh

Elizabeth's older brother Joseph was 10 years old. He growled at people like a dog. Most of the kids feared him. I must say, I was scared of him myself.

He used to sit in class or in the playground or walk home with his hands wrapped around his neck and squeezing. He blacked out sometimes. It was terrifying to watch. He turned blue then purple and fell to the floor. So still. On many occasions, the janitor was called out to the playground because Joseph had fainted again due to strangling himself.

He was a skinny boy; you could see his bones. His face was sunken, and his legs were like sticks. He had matted hair, and his clothes were in tatters.

The janitor was a huge man but a gentle giant. Joseph was small, he looked about six or seven. The janitor scooped him up in his arms. and caried him into the First Aid room. We didn't usually see Joseph for the rest of the day. Sometimes his mum or dad came to the school and take him home.

They lived close to school. Only a five-minute walk. The janitor went to their house, and if they answered the door, they walked back to the school with him to pick Joseph up and take him home.

There was a fire in their house one day. It started in the kitchen. We heard later that a pot of oil had caught on fire. They didn't have a fire alarm. The kitchen was close to the front door therefore the exit was blocked. Neighbours gathered outside.

Elizabeth's dad threw two mattresses out the window. The neighbours screamed for him to throw the kids down. They grabbed blankets so that they could catch them, but he was more interested in saving his TV. He threw that out first, but it didn't survive the fall.

He then dropped the kids from the window. Each one was caught in the blankets. Elizabeth's dad then jumped before his wife. She was terrified to jump after him. One of the neighbours pleaded with her to jump. She eventually did and they caught her. I didn't see Elizabeth again after the fire. She and her family moved out of the area. I missed her.

I can tell you that Mum was grateful I was no longer getting headlice.

The bullying got worse though, and Mum was called to the school many times.

Emily and Jessica

I had a pencil case in the shape of a pencil that Mum had stolen for me along with some pencils. It was one of the best presents I got. No one else in the class had one like it and I felt really special. Emily had had her eyes on it for ages. When I got home one day after school, I took my tin of words out of my bag. These were pieces of paper with words on them I had to learn—I, am, so, you, do, etc. My words were inside a tobacco tin, but my pencil case was gone. I looked through the bag many times, but it was gone. I was terrified to tell Mum and Dad.

Dad gave me the biggest beating for losing the pencil case. I told them I was sure Emily took it. Mum told me to put my jacket on. She was taking me to Emily's house. I was terrified. Emily's mum looked big and scary. She screamed, 'My daughter wouldn't take your fucking pencil case. We're not that hard up. We can afford to buy a pencil ourselves.' She then slammed the door in our faces. I didn't see that pencil case again.

Another girl in my class, Jessica, brought £10 into school one day, and the money disappeared. Miss Wilkinson was furious. She had a huge talk to everyone about how bad it was to take someone else's things without their knowledge.

'I know someone in this class has taken Jessica's money. I need whoever took it to give it back.'

Everyone looked scared as Miss Wilkinson spoke. We had never seen her angry before. It was that day, I found out Emily had taken my pencil case. She broke down after Miss Wilkinson gave us the talk about stealing. Crying, she said she was sorry and that her sister Sharon had the pencil case.

Miss Wilkinson said to the class. 'If you have taken Jessica's money, I want you to return it tomorrow morning. I will allow the person to do it quietly. All you have to do is place it in an envelope and put it on the shelf at the back of the classroom, no one will ever know, and the matter will be resolved.' I couldn't believe it, but by the next morning, there was an envelope on the shelf. Miss Wilkinson said thank you for returning the money to whoever took it.

Emily and Jessica picked on me more after Elizabeth left the school. On a few occasions, they chased me out the school gates. They caught me at times and pulled my hair, kicked and punched me. At lunchtime one day, I didn't stop running until I got home. They stopped chasing me eventually, gave up and went back to school. When I got home, my parents were mad at me for leaving school. 'What the fuck are you doing home at this time of day?'

I told them what happened, and my dad took off his shoe and hit me with it. He said he would toughen me up, that I needed to fight those girls back, and if I didn't, he would beat me more and more until I fought them back.

This also got me in trouble with Mrs Angel, my principal. She could be very scary and intimidating. She never smiled and always looked and sounded angry. She got mad at me for leaving the school grounds. She stood over me at lunchtime and shouted at me for not eating my veggies. I never got veggies at home, so I wasn't going to eat them at school. I hated the taste. My favourite was the pink custard; it tasted like strawberry milkshake. That was the best.

Emily caused a fight between me and another girl, Ellen. I liked Ellen. She was tiny. I don't know what Emily said to Ellen, but Ellen called me out and said she wanted a 'square go' (a fight) in the playground at lunchtime. I told her I wouldn't fight her, but she pushed. By lunch time all the class knew there was going to be a fight. Again, I told Ellen I didn't want to fight her, but she ran at me arms all in the air. I didn't know what to do as she was so much smaller than me. I was scared I'd hurt her. Then Jessica picked Ellen up, held her and came running for me. Ellen grabbed my hair and held on tight. As Jessica dropped her, Ellen pulled my hair with her. I lifted my head up with force, hitting her on the chin. She let go of my hair and fell back. Her mouth was bleeding. I felt bad, but it stopped the fight.

It was hard to fight back because there were two of them. When Jessica and Emily started a fight in the playground, the other students formed a circle around us and cheered, 'Fight! Fight! Fight!'

Jessica and Emily loved the attention they got.

I tried hard not to cry, but the beatings got more violent the older we got. The bullying had been going on for a couple of years. It only stopped when Jessica moved school. Emily didn't seem as tough on her own. I was grateful it all ended.

I had my first crush in Grade Four, Thomas. He said I was his girlfriend. He was cute and funny. We were girlfriend and boyfriend until Grade Six, and then for a short time in Year Two of high school, when we were 13. We never kissed, not once. Oh, we held hands. My little sister Wendy was his sister's best friend. We sat at the same desk.

I loved weekends. Sometimes Mum took us to the Baras. The Baras was an undercover area that had hundreds of stalls of clothes, toys, food, sweets, etc. Mum often bought a huge bag of broken biscuits for a pound. God, they were the days! We never got treats, so it was a great day when Mum came home with a bag of broken biscuits. In the bag were caramel wafers and caramel logs. It was like Christmas. She also bought whelks and mussels for Dad. I loved whelks and mussels, but we weren't allowed to eat them as they were too expensive. I was able to buy my own eventually when I got my first paper round.

Mum took me to the carnival one evening. It was just me and her. We went on the Waltzers (large seats that the man spun and spun) 3 or 4 times. We spun round and round that fast, I felt dizzy. I remember the song playing—'This Ole House' by Shakin' Stevens. We got candy floss, and I won a goldfish. I didn't get time with Mum often. I don't even remember where Wendy and Colin were, but I loved being with Mum that night and didn't want to go home.

Mum stole some yo-yos from a stall in the Baras one day. I loved those yo-yos. They lit up different colours. I learned all the tricks like walk the dog, rock the baby, forward toss and flips. I played with those yoyos for hours and hours.

We played elastics, joining hundreds of elastic bands together into a very large loop, singing 'London Bridge' and 'England, Ireland, Scotland, Wales'.

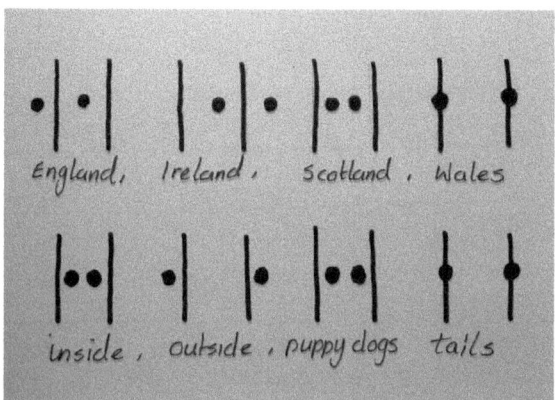

England, Ireland, Scotland, Wales, inside outside puppy dogs' tails.

The best present I ever got was a second-hand record player from my parents. It came with a single and an album. The single was a song called *Billy Don't Be a Hero* and the album was Billy Joel's greatest hits. I played them over and over again until they were all scratched and the needle broke.

I got a Walkman for Christmas one year, and Auntie Jane gave me tapes for it. The Nolans and Bucks Fizz were my favourite. I played them all the time. Music took me to another world, somewhere I could sing, dance and be free from the torment and intrusive thoughts for a bit. I would often sit by Rose's graveside and sing to her. Sometimes I swore she sang along with me. I felt free when I was with her, able to be me. She was my safe place, my best friend.

Chapter Four

1986 – 1988

Please note there are scenes in this chapter that may trigger some readers.

Pillar Street

In May 1986, a month shy of my 11th birthday, I went to the bathroom, wiped and saw blood and panicked. I went to Miss Wilkinson and told her I was bleeding. I was scared I was dying. She sat me down and told me I was having my first period, that it was nothing to worry about and it happens to all girls around my age. She told me it would happen every month, that it would go on for a few days then stop. She said I might get some cramps in my tummy sometimes, but not to worry about it. She sent me to the school nurse who gave me a sanatory towel to use and a few extra to put in my school bag. She also gave me a note to give Mum. I gave the note to Mum, and she said nothing, just that the lads were in the bathroom.

A lady came to our school one day to watch us sing. I was part of the choir and loved singing: it took me to another place. Me, my cousin Ronald and Thomas Beachum were chosen to go to a singing school called Music Matters in the city centre. Gosh, I was excited. Excited to be chosen for something. I couldn't wait to be part of it. Auntie Joan took me, and Ronald and I sat in the second row looking up at the stage. A beautiful lady stood there, and spoke about the importance of music, of how important it was to breathe properly. As she started, 'La, la, la, la, la, la, la', I got goosebumps. I was mesmerized and wanted to be her, to sing like her.

When we got home Auntie Joan told my Mum how boring it was, and that Ronald hated it. I said I loved it, and that I was going to be a singer one day. Dad just laughed and said, 'Yeah right.' I asked Mum if I could go back the following week, but she said they couldn't afford the bus fare every week. My dreams were shattered, and I went to my room and cried for what felt like hours. Just like that my dreams of being a singer were over.

Mum's Uncle Andrew lived on the same street and Mum visited him often. I think she borrowed money from him on occasions, and I sometimes went with her. One day Mum told me to look after Wendy while she spoke to Uncle Andrew. He kept pigeons in his bathroom and flew them. He asked Mum to go in and see them. Uncle Andrew said he was just going to show Mum the birds and didn't want them to fly away. They closed the door behind them. Then I heard strange noises coming from the bathroom. I wasn't sure at that time what they were doing in there, but I knew later on when I was a teenager. I told Dad about the noises I heard, and he dragged Mum into the bathroom and shut the door. He was screaming at her. I heard something smash. Dad had put his fist through the window. The whole thing was never brought up again.

I got really sick with mumps that Christmas. My face was swollen. I got a small guitar and there is a photo of me somewhere with the guitar in my hands and my swollen face.

Just as I was getting better from mumps, I got measles. I was home from school for a few weeks. I hated being at home because I would get in trouble and hit more often. I prayed every day to get well and go back to school. At that time, I actually preferred a beating from Emily and Jessica in comparison to Dad beating me.

We had a huge downfall of snow the year we moved into Pillar St. Wendy, Colin and I played in the backyard for hours, building snowmen and throwing snowballs. This is one of the only times I remember Dad smiling. He opened the window and started throwing snowballs at us from the window ledge. We were freezing cold and soaked by the time we finished. It was getting dark when we had to go into the house. We had a bowl of tomato soup for dinner. Not homemade but from a tin. We would break up slices of bread and put it in the bowl first, then the soup on top. This was delicious.

When I was well again from the measles, I went to Nannie's house as her garden was untouched and there was so much snow. I built myself an igloo. I dug out a big round circle in the snow and then cut blocks of snow and built them up. I was in the garden for hours while Nannie sat at the window watching me. Nannie's neighbour was Mrs. Fraser, who I came to call Granny Fraser. She watched me from the window, too, and called me over for a hot chocolate or hot milk to keep me warm. Playing in the snow felt like freedom. I built that igloo in a day and climbed inside. It was my safe space, and I was proud of myself and what I had done. I wanted to keep it forever but knew that one day it would melt and there would be nothing left. I went back every day, until it started caving in and melting, but it was fun while it lasted.

We lived much closer to family now, as they all lived on the same street. Mum's sister, Angela, and her family, Nannie and Grandad, Auntie Joan and her family.

Grandad was visiting us more now we lived closer. He was still touching me, my boobs and backside. That quickly escalated to him rubbing himself against me as he walked past. He encouraged me to sit on his knee while he stroked my hair and told me I was his favourite girl. I was still Grandad's special girl, and I loved the attention. He made me feel special, always telling me how pretty I was.

He was the only person in my life at that time to pay me any attention. The only person who showed me love.

I felt like a lucky girl.

My little brother, Colin, was christened on August 19th, 1986 in the local church. It was a Sunday morning and sunny outside. It would have been around August. Everyone went back to Nannie's house afterwards. She was making chips in the chip pan. Dad had had too much to drink, and he went to take a chip. Nannie got angry at him. But his sister, Joan, took one without Nannie saying anything. Dad got really angry, and a fight broke out. Uncle Robert had to hold him back.

When playing in the graveyard just a few days later, I was walking through the long grass and disturbed a fallen beehive. I was stung many times and ran as fast as I could to get away but I couldn't stop them stinging me. I had over 30 stings on my body and was sick for days. I had fevers and was swollen all over. To this day I'm terrified of bees.

We went to Nannie's house one afternoon and my cousins Ronald, Katy, Steven, Paul came too. My other cousin Nicole stayed next door to Nannie and joined us. We played Cowboys and Indians in the garden for hours. Auntie Joan gave us bows and arrows and guns. We had so much fun, and when we got hungry, Nannie threw pieces and jam out the window. (Pieces were slices of bread.) It was great. I wished my cousins visited more often.

I made a good friend named Jane. I used to cycle to her house and she to mine. I reckon we must have watched *Grease* more than 100 times. Between 1984 and 1985, we went to her house after school on our bikes, and the first thing we did was put the video of *Grease* on. I knew every word to that movie and every word to every song. I would run that movie over and over again in my head when I was struggling. It got me through some really tough days.

Jane and I went to Bill's Van one day. Bill's Van was a big ice-cream van that sold everything: milk, bread, tinned beans and spaghetti, ice cream and sweets. As I climbed the stairs to the back of the van, I found a rolled up paper and put it in my pocket. I bought the bread and, as we walked home, I took the piece of paper out of my pocket, unrolled it to find it was £50 in notes. Gosh, was I excited! I had never seen so much money before. I couldn't wait to tell Mum what I had found. Mum and Dad took the money and gave me and Jane £5 each. Not realising my mum and dad had kept £40 for themselves, we ran back to Bill's ice-cream van so excited to spend our money. We bought a cup of ice cream called a '99'. A 99 had a snowball, which was chocolate, cream and coconut at the bottom of a large cup, two scoops of ice cream and then raspberry ripple sauce. What a day!

Escape from Dad

I got home from school one Friday afternoon and Dad had been drinking. He told me to make him a cup of tea, so I went into the kitchen, boiled the kettle, put the teabag in the mug and some milk and poured the boiling water. I moved the teabag around for a bit then took it out. I took the tea into Dad, placed it in front of him and turned to leave the room. He then told me to make him some toast and he wanted the outsider of the bread. I went back into the kitchen, got the plain bread out and opened it to find the outsiders on both ends where gone. I panicked. 'He's going to kill me.' I went back into the living room and told him the outsiders were gone.

He flew up from the chair, and screamed, 'Come here ya bastard, who the fuck took my outsiders?' He grabbed me by the hair.

I shouted, 'I don't know, I didn't take them.'

He spat in my face. 'You fucking liar, you fucking took them.'

'I didn't, I knew never to touch them.'

He slapped me across the face and told me to get the fuck out of his sight. As I left the room he shouted, 'Your tea's pish.'

I went into my room and lay on my bed, thinking 'I don't know why I always mess up; I'm trying my best'.

Things just went from bad to worse that day. Dad was in a foul mood, and I tried staying out of his way. Dad was sleeping, so we sat in the living room for dinner. Wendy, Colin and I ate at the coffee table. We had pie and baked beans.

When Dad woke up, he had his dinner and started drinking again. He lay on the sofa with the coffee table pulled close, poured a beer and a vodka and orange—double vodka with a splash of orange juice is all he had. I stayed in my room with Wendy playing music. When Wendy was tucked up in bed, I lay on my bed colouring in.

I could hear screaming coming from the living room, so opened the door quietly and popped my head out. Dad was yelling at Mum about the curry being cold. You see, Mum would order a curry early in the evening and heat it in the oven later. This time it wasn't hot enough. I heard a bang, followed by a smash and then screaming from Mum. Dad had thrown the plate of curry across the room at Mum.

He screamed, 'Its fucking freezing. You trying to kill me?'

Mum screamed at him, 'It's been in the oven for nearly an hour on low. It should be really hot.'

I heard the table move, which meant Dad was getting up off the sofa. Mum came out into the hallway and he followed.

'Don't you fucking talk back to me.'

Mum said again, 'The curry should be hot.'

Dad moved towards her again, and I stepped out of my room. I don't know why I did as I should have known that by stepping out, he was going to turn his attention on me which he did.

'What the fuck are you doing up?

It was only 9:30 p.m. and I guess I should have been in bed, but it was a Friday night, and there was no school in the morning.

He pushed Mum out of the way and came towards me. I stepped back. He hit me hard in the face, and my head hit my doorframe. I cried out in pain. I pushed as hard as I could against his chest. He didn't move, but I could tell he was shocked. I had never stood up against him before. I don't know what came over me. I just didn't want him to hurt Mum. That was the first time I had ever hit him back.

But it only made matters worse.

He shouted, 'You fucking bastard,' as he grabbed me by the hair, slapped me across the face and pushed me to the floor.

Mum was screaming in the background for him to stop. She stepped forward, and he pushed her out of the way. He kicked me in the back, then the head. I curled into a ball on the floor, terrified to move, terrified to scream.

Mum screamed out again, so he went after her. He hit her hard across the face. She held her face, and he just walked back into the living room.

He shouted from the room, 'Clean this fucking mess up.'

Wendy and Colin were crying in their rooms. They had no idea what was going on. Mum told me to get Colin and put him in my room with Wendy. She said to get some clothes together, underwear, pyjamas a set of clothing, then get Wendy and Colin ready. She went into her room and got a suitcase and told me to put the clothes in, that we were going away for a bit. Mum then went back into the living room to clean up the curry.

I got Colin and took him into my room. I told Wendy and Colin to sit together on my bed while I got their clothes together. I ran into Colin's room and grabbed what clothes I needed and brought them back to my room. I helped him get ready and told Wendy to get ready while I grabbed clothes to put in the case. I was packed and we were waiting on Mum. She came in a short time later with some clothes, which she added to the case. She put the case in the wardrobe and told me to wait for her. Wendy, Colin and I sat huddled waiting for Mum. I sang songs to them both quietly. 'Love is like a butterfly, as soft and gentle as a sigh.'

Mum came back a short time later and told us to put on our coats because it was cold and raining outside. She grabbed the suitcase from the wardrobe, and we headed for the front door. I could hear music playing behind me. Dad must have been lying on the sofa listening to the music. Mum told us to be really quiet as she opened the door and we all stepped out into the cold, wet night.

She said, 'Be really quiet,' as we headed out the gate. We went the long way round to the main road, so that we didn't pass the living room window. She took us to the bus stop outside the graveyard gates and said, we're going to Auntie Cathy's house. It must have been really late because there was no traffic on the road. Everywhere was quiet, but it was lightly raining, the sort of rain that still got you soaked through.

After what seemed like a long time, Mum said she reckoned the buses must have stopped running. She started to worry, wondering where we were gonna go for the night. By now, Dad would have known we were gone and be angry as hell. We went in through the graveyard gate to an outbuilding just to the right of the caretaker's house to shelter from the rain. The building was open on two sides and closed on the other two. Mum put the suitcase down in the corner and sat on it with Colin on her lap. Wendy sat on the suitcase beside Mum, and I had a tiny piece of the back corner. My head was hurting bad from when Dad kicked me. I really wanted to go see Rose, tell her what had happened and to sleep in my tree. Mum told the kids to try to sleep. There was a cold breeze flowing through, but we were huddled together tightly to keep warm.

We lasted a few hours before Colin woke up crying and cold. It was still dark, cold, and raining outside, so Mum said we had to go to Grandad and Nannie's to get some sleep. We got up and walked out into the rain again and headed the long way around again until we got to Grandad's. Mum knocked and knocked on the door, shouting 'Jack' through the letterbox. He eventually opened the door. Mum said we needed somewhere to sleep for the night. She said, 'John has lost it. He hit me and Sharon. We just need a break from him'. .

He showed us through to the spare room where we got changed into our nightdresses and pyjamas. He gave us towels to dry our hair. We were still cold and wet when we climbed into bed. I was exhausted and went to sleep, waking when it was daylight outside. I could smell Grandad was making toast. Mum told me to get clothes out for Wendy and Colin and to help them get ready. She took her clothes and went to the bathroom to get changed. We went into the living room, and Grandad brought us some milk and toast with butter. When Mum joined us, she said she was going to see Dad later about us going home. I didn't want to go back home. I wanted to go to Auntie Cathy's.

After Mum saw Dad in the afternoon, she came to pick us up. It was like nothing had happened. Everything went back to normal. I hated it; Dad was never going to change. I feared one that day he would kill me.

Grandad Stevens and his wife Beth moved into the street. This was Mum's dad and step-mum. Grandad Stevens was a big drinker too. They moved just four block houses from us, and Mum would pop in and see them often.

Nannie was visiting Auntie Joan in Barleming, about 20 minutes away more and more after Joan had her sixth child, Julie, leaving Grandad home alone more often now. He would ask for me to visit and told Dad that I should pick up the debt money and drop it off. Grandad was now touching me in places I didn't feel comfortable with, my boobs and between my legs. I tried to tell him that I didn't feel comfortable, but he said that he loved me and that's what Grandads do—but it was our secret. He got me to stand behind the chair, and he stood behind me and rubbing himself against me. I hated how it made me feel—sick and scared. He said no one would understand our love or how he felt for me and that I should keep it between us because he was the only person that really loved me.

Granny Eve, who had lived next door to us in the flats we first lived in, moved closer to us. She moved into a small flat for pensioners. All the family helped pack up her house, and when they lifted the carpet in the living room, they found thousands of pounds underneath. Whenever Granny picked up her pension, she would put some under the carpet, and over the years, it was walked into the middle of the room. She had started to go senile.

In primary Grade Seven, I had Miss Wilkinson again as my teacher. She taught me for four years through the seven years of my primary school. She taught me so much and gave me a lot of her time. I loved drawing and painting and still do art today because of her. At the end of primary Seven, we were taken on a trip to the ice rink. It was our end of primary school event. I had never been before but was having a great time. One of the teachers, Miss Moody fell on the ice, and one of the students skated over her fingers, taking the tips off. Everyone was screaming, and the other teachers were trying to calm everyone down. Miss Moody was taken to hospital for treatment. I never saw her again because it was right at the end of primary school. I hope she was okay.

12 Years Old

In 1987, we moved into Hallwood St next door to Nannie and Grandad. My anxiety over him was getting worse, and I was scared to leave the house for fear he would see me. I had pains in my chest all the time and felt physically sick. Nannie was spending more and more time with her daughters and leaving him alone. He had more opportunities to ask me to go over and see him. I couldn't leave our house without him seeing me. I even passed his front door on the way to and from school each day. One day he came into our house, and I was standing behind the couch, behind Dad, when he stood behind me rubbing himself against me and making small noises. I'm sure Dad heard him and did nothing about it. I'm sure Dad knew.

Dad gave me a video and told me to go upstairs and watch it with Grandad at his house one night. I didn't want to, but he told me I had nothing better to do and to do it. I would have been happy to stay in my room and play my music, but I did as I was told. I took the video upstairs. Grandad put it on, and we sat down on single chairs that were side by side to watch it. The movie started. It must have been really boring because I remember feeling really sleepy. I wanted to go home, but Grandad told me just to stay and watch the film. I was so tired, I fell asleep, only to wake up with him touching my breast and rubbing himself down there, making noises. It was a horrible feeling. He jumped up quickly and zipped up his trousers. His shirt was hanging out. He sat down in his chair as if nothing had happened. Only I couldn't get it out of my head. I didn't know what was going on. What he was doing. I went home after the movie and didn't say anything to anyone.

I was visiting Rose one day when I came across a tree I could climb into easily. I often sat in the tree where I felt invisible to the world. I could see people on the main road, but they couldn't see me. This tree became my safe place over the years, my sanctuary. It saved me more times than I can count on one hand. I will speak of the tree throughout the book.

One winter, it was very icy outside. I was washing and drying the dishes when I looked out the window and saw our elderly neighbour, Elizabeth Fox, slip on her front doorsteps. I was drying a sharp knife at the time and holding the knife end towards myself. As I lunged forward to the window quickly, I stabbed myself in the stomach. It wasn't too bad but should have had stitches. Dad told Mum to put a plaster over it. Because I didn't get stitches, the scar is wide today. It took months to heal properly.

That year, I got chickenpox and was covered from head to toe. They were in my ears and all through my head. I was in agony and wanted to scratch all the time. Mum got calamine lotion from the chemist and covered me in the white chalky stuff. I looked awful, but it gave me a week of peace from Grandad and Dad. No one would come near me.

In August 1988, I started high school. I thought the building was really cool. It was blue and white, and the main building was shaped like a doughnut. I loved starting high school, making new friends and keeping old ones like Jane. My cousins Ronald and Nicole were also at the school in my year. I felt like I had more freedom as my hours at school were longer. I hated biology and science and was never any good at them. I loved music and woodwork. I wasn't any good at French although I liked the French teacher, who was funny, but also scary. One day Thomas, my first love in primary school, spoke back to the French teacher. The teacher took Thomas's head and pushed him against the wall hard, making a hole in the wall. Another day, one of the girls was talking over him, and he picked up the duster and threw it at her head. Martina stood up screaming and shouting at him with blood pouring down her face. 'My dad is going to kill you.'

He screamed back at her, 'You little shit.'

She screamed back, 'I'm going to tell my mum and dad.'

He said, 'Go ahead get them, and I will tell them that I called you a little shit.'

Another time he got so angry, he picked up a desk and threw it at the window, smashing the glass. We were on the third floor of the annex building.

He disappeared in my second year of high school. I don't know if he was fired or just left. A lot of the boys really missed him because they found him funny.

There was a prison next door to the school. Sometimes, when going to my friend's house, the prisoners would shout out their window, 'Take your blouse off, lift up your skirt. You're nothing but tarts.'

The bantering went on and on. You knew they couldn't get to you, but it was still scary.

Jane started going out with my cousin Ronald. I was happy for them both. My best friend and my cousin. I started hanging out more with Ellen, the girl I fought with in primary school. We became good friends. I also hung out with Nicole (my cousin), Izzy P and Lizzy C. We started hanging out in the evening. I was changing, feeling unhappy all the time. I played the goofball with my friends, but inside I was crumbling. I changed my appearance, became a real tomboy and got Mum's friend, Eileen, who was a hairdresser, to cut my hair short. My hair had been long, down past my waist, and curly. I asked her to cut it all off, but I cried afterwards.

I was now twelve when Mum and Dad sent me upstairs to Grandad's again with some videos. I protested, but it fell on deaf ears. I was to stay at Grandad's that night. I don't know why I had to stay considering we lived only downstairs. I packed my overnight bag and took the videos with me. We put the video on and sat down to watch it. I was tired by the end of the movie, and I asked if I could go to bed. I lay in the darkness, feeling scared and anxious.

I could hear his footsteps coming towards my bedroom. He came in. I couldn't breathe. My heart was pounding in my chest. I pretended I was asleep so that he would leave.

He climbed in beside me; I was too afraid to move, so I kept my eyes closed tight. He slid up close to me. He had no clothes on. I was really, really scared. What should I do? If I scream, he might hurt me. So, I told myself to stay real still. Maybe it was all just a really bad dream.

He was shaking as he lifted my nightdress. I didn't want him to hurt me. He was touching me with his fingers. His nails were sharp. I wanted to scream, to make him stop, but I was so scared. I could feel something digging into my bottom. Why was he doing this? I prayed for my mum to come and get me. I just wanted to go home to my own bed.

He turned me onto my back. I kept my eyes closed tight as he whispered in my ear. 'I know you are awake. I'm only doing this because Nannie doesn't let me anymore.' I still kept my eyes closed. I hated my Nannie so. Why wasn't she here?

He climbed on top of me. He stank of stale cigarette smoke. With his knees, he pushed my legs apart. I felt something hard pushing into me. It hurt. He started getting really annoyed. He was grunting. He stopped and spat on his fingers, started poking them into me, said I was too tight.

The pain was too much. I wanted to die. I cried out. He stopped and put his hand over my mouth. He pushed himself into me again and again and again, over and over. The pain was too much. I must have blacked out or something, because when I came around again, he was finishing. He stayed on top of me for what felt like forever. He was sweaty. I felt wet with his sweat. The smell of that and stale cigarette smoke made me feel physically sick. He climbed off me and left the room.

I was frozen. I heard the shower. I put my hand down where it hurt. It felt wet. I looked at my hand, and it was dark red with blood.

When he finished showering and I heard his bedroom door shut. I climbed from bed, but I couldn't stand up, so I crawled to the bathroom. I managed to reach up for the light. There was blood everywhere. My hands. My legs, my nightdress. I had never seen so much blood before. I thought I was dying.

I only had toilet paper to clean myself and the floor with. If I got it on the towel, he would kill me. I wet the toilet paper and cleaned as best I could. I put some toilet paper against myself down there so that I didn't get blood anywhere.

When I finally finished, I half crawled back to my room. Removed the bedding as it was covered in blood. I could smell it. SEX. I placed the bedding in the corner of the room near the window, put my clothes on and climbed onto the bed and cried myself to sleep.

I woke in the morning to the smell of toast. I was freezing cold. As I moved, I felt pain. I remembered the night before and cried. I couldn't sit up. I noticed the bedding from the corner was gone and started to panic. 'What do I do when he comes in?'

He came in a short time later with some toast and all he said was, 'Breakfast is ready, and did you have a good sleep?'

I couldn't look at him. I thought I would see the monster from last night, but it was him, it was Grandad. He said 'You're still my best girl. You know Grandad loves you and what we have is a special love. No one can know because no one will understand or believe our love.'

I couldn't eat the toast. I just wanted to go to the bathroom and go home. The toilet paper I placed against myself the night before was soaked with blood. I changed it, brushed my teeth and told Grandad I was going home. He gave me some cigarettes; I had started smoking a few months before, and he was feeding my habit. He said he loved me and that he would see me real soon. He gave me some chocolate M & Ms before I left.

When I walked into my house, Mum and Dad were still in bed. I wanted to wash and put a sanitary towel on my pants. I used a facecloth to clean myself, changed my clothes and went to my room. I put the Nolans in my Walkman, lay on my bed and listened to the music.

Mum and Dad noticed nothing, or if they did, they said nothing. I asked Mum if I could go out for a bit in the afternoon. It had been raining all morning, but I needed to see Rose. I found it hard climbing the wall to the graveyard because I was in pain. Now that we lived on the opposite end of the graveyard, there was no gate, and I had to climb the wall.

I went straight to see Rose, picking some wildflowers on the way. I knelt down in front of her and broke down.

'Rose, Grandad came into my bed last night. He really hurt me, but he said he loves me. What do I do? I can't tell anyone. He says no one will understand the love we share. I will get in trouble. Please help me, Rose.'

I sat with her for some time and started to feel cold, so I climbed my tree. While sitting there, I thought about packing a bag with clothes and a blanket and hiding them in the tree just in case I needed them in the future. I sat there for some time thinking about my life and how much I hated it. I decided to take some paracetamol that night and end my life. I knew where Mum kept them. I thought of being with Rose at last and how peaceful it would be.

I got home around dinnertime. Mum was making pie and baked beans. Dad was in the living room watching TV, so I crept into their bedroom and took the paracetamol from the wardrobe and put them under my mattress for later.

I sat on the kitchen counter and ate my dinner while listening to the Top 40 on the radio. Mum, Dad, Wendy and Colin were in the living room. Most Sundays I sat in the kitchen and recorded the Top 40. That day I didn't record it; I just listened.

After dinner I went into my bedroom, took a bottle of Irn Bru (fizzy drink) from under my bed. I bought it with the pocket money Grandad gave me. I took all the pills out of the packs and placed them on the bed. Poured a large glass of Irn Bru and started taking the tablets one by one until they were finished. I lay down on my bed with my music playing, Whitney Houston, *I Believe the Children are our fFture* and fell asleep only to wake up a number of hours later. I ran to the bathroom, vomiting constantly. In the end, all that came up was bile. I was ill for days. No one ever asked questions. No one knew about the overdose.

I met up with the girls a few days later. We used to sit in a close at night, sheltered from the weather. A close is what you would call a tenement block. Two houses on the bottom floor, two on the middle and two on the top. We would sit in a close when it was cold or wet.

Ellen introduced me to gas in an aerosol can, the one you fill your lighters with. She bought a few tins and showed me how to inhale it by putting my teeth around the tip and pushing down on it. I got an instant high. It was amazing! I was taken to another place, a place without pain, without abuse. The only problem was the high didn't last. I wanted more, but couldn't afford it.

I took a video up to Grandad's when Nannie was there one evening. I knew he wouldn't touch me with her around. I sat down by Nannie's legs watching her knit. I wasn't feeling well and asked if I could go to bed. I cried out shortly after 11:00 p.m. with severe pain in my side. I didn't know what was going on. Nannie said it was probably period pains. She made me some warm milk and sat with me for a time, until the pain had settled. Nannie was tough as nails but could be gentle sometimes. This was one of those times. Before I left for school, Grandad gave me toast in the morning and a pack of 10 Club king size cigarettes and a packet of chocolate M & Ms. He wanted me to visit after school. Nannie was going to Auntie Joan's for the night.

I didn't plan on going up to see him after school, but when I got home Mum said I had to take the videos back to the rental guy, and I had to collect a few from Grandad too. I went up to pick up the videos, telling him I had to take them back and pick up more. He told me to go in the room first. I told him I really needed to go, but he insisted I go into the bedroom. He touched my face, put his hands through my hair and told me how pretty I was. He kissed my neck, undid my tie and placed it on the bed. I still had my uniform on. He was gentler this time, loving. He undid my blouse with care and placed it beside the tie. He said how beautiful I was as he undid my skirt button and zip. My skirt fell to the floor, I stepped out of it, and he picked it up and placed it with the blouse and tie. He told me to sit on the bed while he took off my shoes. He said to 'lie back' and lay beside me, touching me between my legs. I hated his fingers; his nails were sharp and long. He undid his trousers. That's when

I got scared. I knew what was coming next. He pulled down my pants and took them off, pulled down his trousers and rolled on top of me. I hated him on me. I hated even more him inside me. He said he loved me, that I was his girl as he pushed into me over and over again. I turned and looked out the window, wishing it to be over soon. He finished and rolled off me. Stood up and pulled up his trousers. Told me to get cleaned up, and he went to get the videos. I put my blouse and pants on and took my clothes to the bathroom. I cleaned myself. There was a little blood, but not like the first time. I got ready, putting on my tie but not doing it up. When I came out of the bathroom, he was standing in the hallway with the videos in his hand. He put them on a shelf above the radiator and stepped towards me, took my tie in his hands and started to knot it.

'No one will understand our love, so we have to keep it between us, okay?'

I was seeing Grandad two or three times a week. Whenever Nannie was away, he would call me to go up, hug me from behind and whisper he loved me more than anyone else in the world. I could feel his love. No one had ever told me that before. I felt special.

I hated what we were doing—but I felt loved.

Mum went to the Baras and stole some rubber balls. They were slightly smaller than tennis balls but bigger than bouncy balls and very bouncy. She showed me how to play with them.

We hit the balls against the wall. Threw with the right hand and caught with the left. Opposite if left-handed. We had rhymes to the games.

'Over the garden wall, I let my baby fall,

My ma came oot and gave me a cloot

over the garden wall.'

I would play against the house for hours on end. I loved it.

Dad was drinking most days now, day and night. He was also getting more violent. I was trying to stay away from home as much as I could, but it was really tough. I would hang out with my friends, be with Rose or hide out in my tree. I would hang out with my friends, be with Rose or hide out in my tree.

It was coming up to Mother's Day, and a friend gave me the idea to pick rose petals and place them in water until they made perfume. I went into the front garden and picked a load of petals from the rose bushes and placed them in a plastic cup of water. I put the cup on my dressing table for a few days to allow it to ferment. Mum came into my room to put some clothes away and saw the cup on my dresser. She told Dad it was me that had taken the roses from the bush. He came into my room, picked up the cup and threw it at me. He pushed me onto the bed, pulled me towards him and started punching me anywhere he could reach. I curled up as tight as I could into a ball, but that didn't stop him. He wasn't stopping until he was tired.

I lay there not knowing what I had done wrong, but heartbroken because Mum's Mother's Day present was ruined.

I was in pain all over and hated my dad so much in that moment. Afterwards, Mum told me Dad had noticed the flowers missing from the garden. She didn't have to tell him it was me, though. I hated her at that point, too.

Mum bought Wendy and me a karaoke machine. We were in our room all the time, singing. We had to keep the volume low when Dad was watching TV, but I would turn it up loud when Dad had his music on. I would sing to Whitney Houston, Celine Dion, Toni Braxton, Barbra Streisand, Abba. Wendy and I would sing the Celine Dion and Barbra Streisand duet *Tell Him*. I loved singing, and I loved spending time with Wendy.

The Gala Queen, July 1988, 13 Years Old

In July every year, the local community ran a Gala Queen contest. I said to Mum and Dad I would like to enter the competition.

Dad said, 'You don't have a chance in hell winning something like that. Look at the state of you, you look and act like a boy. You're useless, stupid. They won't take a second look at you. There's no point in going'.

I went to my room, threw myself on the bed and cried. I felt small in that moment, worthless, a nobody. I was no good at anything. I cried myself to sleep.

The competition was in two days' time in the local community centre.

The next day I talked myself out of going. Told myself I wasn't good enough, so there was no point in going.

At school, a few girls in my year were talking about going to the Gala. It seemed everywhere I turned, people were talking about it. I felt sad, defeated, worthless. I remember walking home that day feeling alone.

My cousin Nicole came over on Saturday afternoon. She was going to the community centre to watch the Gala Queen and asked if I wanted to go too. I said no, but she insisted, saying she didn't want to go on her own. I thought, it will be fun to go and watch.

The community centre was full of people. There were around fifty, sixty seats, but I reckon there must have been another one hundred people standing around the room.

One of my friend's aunts came over and told Nicole that all the girls were through the doors to the left of the stage. She said that's where we needed to be. I told her we weren't part of the Gala. We were just there to watch. She told us not to be silly. 'You're here, might as well have fun with the other girls.'

I looked at Nicole, and we both nodded. We were shown through to a corridor where there had to be at least forty girls. They were all talking and laughing excitedly. A lady came over and took our names.

We joined the queue. Emily and Ellen were standing just in front of us, so we got to talking. They said their mum and dad told them to go and have fun. I wished I had parents like theirs. I wished them both luck, said I was there just to have fun. Secretly, I wanted more.

Sarah's aunt came through the doors to tell us they would be starting in five minutes. I must say, I had butterflies in my stomach, but they quickly disappeared when my dad's voice came into my head: 'You don't have a chance in hell.'

The excitement in the room was electric. Sarah's aunt told us to listen for our names being called. She said, 'When your name is called, you enter the stage, where you will be asked three questions by the judges. After you answer the questions, you leave the stage and enter a second corridor. You remain there until all the girls have entered and exited. You then wait for the judges to make their decisions. If you make it through, your names will be called. You will then enter the stage again, where you will be crowned.'

It all sounded exciting, but I didn't believe I would get through, so I chose to have fun with the other girls. Cheering them on as their names were called.

The names were called in alphabetical order. My name was close to the end, so I got to observe all the excitement, nerves and laughter. I did feel a little flutter of excitement in my chest as it got closer to my name being called. I felt nervous about what questions they would ask me and terrified I wouldn't be able to answer them.

To be honest, I cannot remember the three questions they asked. I remember my name being called; I even remember standing on the stage. I know I felt anxious when I looked out into the crowd of people and saw many faces. I tried hard to focus on the three people sitting behind the desk in front of me. The rest went by in a blur. I obviously answered the questions because I was then ushered off the stage and through another door. I was grateful it was over.

The girls were gathered together talking about their questions and the answers they gave. Nicole came in after me. We stood together. I didn't expect anything else to happen, so the nerves subsided. Sarah's aunt came in after all the girls had been on stage. She said it would be about thirty minutes before a decision was made and said we could all go see our families. I had no one there, so I stayed in the little room.

It felt like a long thirty minutes. All the girls were called back into the room, a decision had been made.

The two princesses were called first, followed by the queen. Susan's name was called first, everyone cheered. Susan was a year ahead of me in school. God, I was happy for her. She was such a lovely person. She had long curly blond hair and had the biggest brightest blue eyes. I could feel her excitement as she was ushered out and onto the stage.

Second name was Sarah O. I hadn't heard anyone with the same surname as me before. The lady called her again, and a girl called Sarah was ushered through the doors. We all cheered. Everything went quiet as Sarah came back through the doors. They had called the wrong girl. A lady called back up the line of girls, 'SHARON O!' I thought I was hearing things. Nicole started shaking me, saying, 'It's you! They are calling you! I couldn't believe it I was in shock as the lady ushered me through the doors and onto the stage. Everyone was clapping. I was a princess! I couldn't believe they chose me.

I stood proudly beside Susan. The Queen was called. Bernadette Fraser. She had long red hair that almost went down to her bottom. The three of us stood proudly together as pictures were taken.

Afterwards, all the girls from backstage gathered on stage, where they hugged and congratulated us. It didn't feel real.

The three of us were taken into a room to discuss what happens next. The ceremony would happen in three weeks. In that time, we had to meet at the Baras to be fitted for our dresses, but we had to pay for half of the dress. This had to be paid just before the parade. We would then meet at the chapel on the morning of the parade and get dressed there. They said congratulations again, and we went home.

Nicole was waiting outside for me. We were jumping up and down with excitement. I couldn't wait to tell Mum, so we ran all the way home. We got to the house, ran in and I blurted out, 'I'm one of the princesses in the Gala Queen. I won!' Mum looked at me, surprised, and Dad said, 'What the fuck are you talking about?'

Nicole said, 'Sharon is one of the princesses in the Gala Queen, Uncle John. She won out of 40 girls. It's exciting, Auntie Margaret.'

My mum said, 'Wow. Who else won?'

Nicole said, 'Susan is the other princess and Bernadette is the Queen.'

Mum said, 'I knew it. I knew Bernadette would win. Her family is on the panel.'

Dad said, 'I thought I told you, you weren't going.'

I said, 'I only went to watch, but Sarah's aunt told us to join in. I won.'

The following weekend, Susan, Bernadette and I were picked up from outside the community centre and taken to the Baras to be fitted for our dresses and choose our tiaras. We arrived at one of the market stalls, where we were taken into little cubicles and given a few dresses to try on. I felt like a princess. The dresses for the princesses were peach, and the Queen's dress would be white. They said the dresses would be ready for collection in 3 weeks. Perfect timing as the Gala Queen procession was in four weeks' time.

The only problem was we had to pay for half of the dress. Mum and Dad refused to pay, saying they couldn't afford their bills, let alone a dress for me. That's because Dad was drinking the money away. I was going to have to tell the organisers I couldn't be a princess. There was no way I would get £20 in time.

Jimmy upstairs' daughter, Clara, asked if I would be interested in delivering the local paper (The Glaswegian). She said I could make around £20 a week. The only problem was, it was four hundred and thirty papers. I asked Nicole if she would be interested in making some money, too, so we decided to split the block houses and the tenements. Nicole took the blocks, and I took the tenements. I took 300 papers and Nicole 130.

The papers were delivered to me on a Friday afternoon, and we had until Sunday evening to deliver them all. I can tell you, it was tough going. I was able to fit around 80 papers in my Nannie's shopping trolley, then head off. I would leave the trolley at the bottom of the closes, take out 6 papers at a time and run up and down the stairs, putting each paper in the post boxes. You see, in the UK the post boxes are in the front doors. I delivered to 50 closes. By Sunday night, I was exhausted. I delivered those papers for about 4 weeks. I just needed the £20 for the dress, which I had in two weeks.

Nicole got bored and didn't want to deliver in the rain. She dumped a load of the papers over the fence of the motorway. We got in trouble for that. The paperman came to my door screaming and shouting at me for what happened. I had no idea until that moment what Nicole had done. No one else could have done it as we were the only two delivering in that area. So, we didn't get the last payment, but I kept one of Nicole's payments.

I had the £20 for the dress, which I had to keep hidden from my parents. I had already loaned them money for a curry from my first pay packet.

We tried on the dresses the week before the parade, and they fit perfectly. The colour was beautiful and the lace around the neck was gorgeous. The flowers on the tiaras worked with the dresses. I was a princess, and I felt special.

The night before the parade, Dad was having one of his off nights. He argued with Mum over some food that was cold. I could hear him from my room. I remember sitting on the edge of my bed, praying for him to stop. It escalated; I could hear Mum screaming. He was hurting her. I knew that if I opened the door, he would start on me, but I couldn't let him keep hitting her. I opened the door and shouted at him to stop. He turned and started coming at me. I tried to turn and run, but he was in front of me before I knew it.

He punched me on the side of the head, and I fell to the floor. The pain in my ear was excruciating. I screamed out. He kicked me, kept me down. Mum was screaming, 'Stop!' He wouldn't. He kicked me in the head, the back, my legs, my arms, over and over. When he was tired, he fell back against the wall, sweating and exhausted. He walked into his bedroom.

Mum looked down at me. 'You should have stayed in your room, Sharon.'

I woke up on my bedroom floor, hurting from head to toe. I cried out, tried getting up off the floor, but I was in agony. I had to be at the chapel by 10:30 a.m. I still had a few hours, so I ran a bath, took my pyjamas off. I was red all over my back, side, and the top of my legs. I had a bump just above my ear, and it throbbed.

Mum came in to use the toilet. She saw the bruises and said, 'You can't go to the parade like that.'

I said, 'I have to.'

I was determined not to let Dad win. He was against me going all along. It was looking like he was going to get his way. I asked Mum for some painkillers.

When I got out of the bath, I put a vest over my bra and pulled my knickers on. I didn't want anyone to see the bruises while I was changing into the dress. I put on my earrings, watch, jeans and t-shirt. I took the painkillers and lay on my bed until it was time to go. I prayed the painkillers would work in time.

Dad would be passed out until at least one or two o'clock. Mum said I shouldn't go. She was scared someone would see the bruises.

It took me around 30 minutes to walk to the chapel when it usually only took 10 or 15 minutes. A lot of people had already gathered outside. I was ushered through to a side room, just to the right of the chapel. I had never been in the chapel before. It was very up to date, unlike the Church of Scotland.

I met Susan and Bernadette in a room. They were very excited, but I wasn't feeling the excitement yet.

I was helped out of my clothes. I struggled to lift my left arm when putting my arms above my head and it hurt. As I lifted my arms, my vest lifted showing bruises at the base of my spine. The lady asked what had happened, and I said I fell down the stairs.

She said, 'That looks nasty.'

I was in excruciating pain and trying not to show it. She placed a tiara of peach flowers on my head and stood back. 'Just beautiful,' she said. I was beaming. Now, I felt the excitement.

We were taken out the side door and into the courtyard, where a glass coach with two beautiful black horses were waiting. The coachman helped us into the coach. As he took my waist, I squirmed with pain. He apologised, and I said, 'I just have a sore back.' Once seated in the coach, I could relax back against the leather. Bernadette sat between Susan and me. I was a princess. I felt special. This moment, this day was mine, all mine.

The horses were guided out onto the road, and we made the journey around the scheme (area). We weaved in and out of the streets, around the shops and pubs. Thousands of people lined the streets, clapping their hands and cheering us on. We travelled around the area for about an hour, then headed back to the chapel, where we changed our clothes and headed to the local pub for a celebration. I struggled to walk the ten minutes to the pub. It hurt to do anything. There must have been around 80 people in the pub. I think most of them were Bernadette's family. My mum popped in for a few minutes, and I was happy to see her there. Bernadette's mum showed her some pictures that were taken on an instant camera. I had a Coke, and Mum had an Irn Bru.

She said she was heading to the shops and thought she would pop in and see me. I thanked everyone, picked up my dress and headed home with Mum. Dad was still sleeping. I went to my room, put my dress away and lay on my bed. I couldn't do anything for the next few days. I stayed out of Dad's way as much as I could.

The day after the parade, my grandad gave me a beautiful gold locket and 20 king-size cigarettes. He said he was proud of me for being the princess and that I looked like a real princess. He was part of the crowd in the street. I didn't see him. He told me to lie down on the bed. I knew what was coming next. I didn't like it; I never liked it. I was still in pain from all the bruises. He made me feel uncomfortable, unsure of myself. He lifted my skirt, undid himself and lay down on top of me, in me. He was gentle, making noises as he pushed.

Something happened to me; I felt something I had never felt before. A rush of feelings, intense feelings. I must have made noises because he whispered in my ear, 'You see, it's love you felt there. That's what happens between a man and woman in love.'

I was grown up, I was a woman. He said so. Afterwards, he put the locket around my neck and clasped it.

Going Back to High School

I started year two of high school in August 1988. A new year, a new me. I loved music with Mrs Clift and woodwork with Mr Deecko. It was great being back with my friends. We would meet at break and lunch to grab a quick ciggie behind the annex building. I loved being away from Dad. I was at peace in school. I was feeling tired all the time, though, unwell. I had put on a little weight; my skirts were feeling tight.

Around October, I went to visit Auntie Jane. She saw a huge change in me. I told her how I was feeling, and she took me to a place in the city, a medical place that was run by nuns. I gave a urine sample, which the nun took away.

When she came back, she spoke to Auntie Jane first. Auntie Jane sat down beside me and said I was having a baby.

She said, 'Sharon, you have a baby in your tummy. You are going to be a mother.'

I said, 'I can't be having a baby; I'm not married yet.'

She said, 'You don't have to be married to have a baby.'

She asked if I had a boyfriend, and I said, 'No.'

'What boy have you let touch your vagina?'

'No boys.'

'That's the only way to get pregnant, Sharon.'

'I promise no boy has touched me, Auntie Jane.'

'Someone has.'

I was terrified. Could what me and Grandad had been doing caused this to happen? I couldn't tell her my secret. Grandad said I couldn't tell anyone.

'Fuck, my dad is going to kill me.'

'The nun said you're around 6 months pregnant.'

'What am I going to do? I can't have a baby. I'm too young.'

I really wanted to tell Auntie Jane who the father was, but I was terrified she wouldn't believe me. He was her father.

After hours of crying and Auntie Jane holding me, she came up with a plan. She would have to convince my dad that I needed to stay with her for a bit. At least for the next four or five months. She came home with me, sat down in front of my dad and asked if I could live with her for a bit. Auntie Jane was a big lady with a bubbly personality. She could be funny, always cracking jokes. She told Dad she was pregnant and just needed some help with things. My dad didn't care. Mum on the other hand was concerned. I was leaving her alone with Dad, I always took the beatings for her. She would have no one now.

I must say I was worried for her too. But I had to hide this baby. Mum said I couldn't miss school. Jane said it wasn't such a big deal at this stage. She told me to pack my bags, so I had everything packed within 20 minutes. Dad didn't look at me before I left, but Mum came to the door. I stood in front of her and said, 'I'll see you in a few months.' Wanting her to wrap me in her arms, tell me she would miss me, that she loved me.

I got none of that, just, 'I'll see you in a few months.'

Auntie Jane went to visit Nannie and Grandad, so I said I would visit a friend. I went straight to tell Rose everything that had happened and was going to happen. I grabbed some wildflowers on the way; and replaced the flowers I'd put there a few days before. I sat down in front of her.

'Rose, I'm pregnant, I'm having a baby; Auntie Jane says you can only get pregnant if a boy touches you. I haven't let a boy touch me. The only man who ever touched me is Grandad. Am I pregnant because Grandad touched me, Rose? I'm so scared, I don't know what to do. I'm going away for a while. Auntie Jane says I have to stay with her until after I have the baby. She's gonna take the baby and look after it. I'm gonna miss you, Rose. I won't be able to visit you for a long time, but I'll talk to you every day, I promise. I love you.'

Poem

This tragedy of life, a child torn and hurt.
Her innocence taken away.
So violent was his rage, so angry, the pain.

What's going on?
What did I do?
Why is he hurting me, the pain?

I try to scream, and nothing is heard.
Why is he so angry with me?
What did I do to deserve this punishment?
He's gone now, I lie here bleeding and hurt.

I'm crying, but I don't know why?
Nothing's happened, not really.
I must have awakened from a bad dream,
I lie shivering, clutching my pillow.
Finally, crying myself to sleep.

It wasn't real,
Just an evil nightmare
The first of many I'm soon to know.
It couldn't have really happened,
So it doesn't matter how I feel...

Or does it?

Living with Auntie Jane

Auntie Jane lived on the 18th floor of a high-rise block of flats about 30 minutes away from Mum and Dad's. The view from her apartment was amazing. You could see for miles. The whole city. She had a two-bedroom apartment. It was decorated in beautiful colours; the living room was decorated with mint green wallpaper on the top half and mint and white stripes on the bottom with a mint and white border. My bedroom was decorated with light pink wallpaper and a big double bed. Oh my God, I never had a big bed; it was so nice.

We went food shopping that first day. She bought things I had never tasted before, peppers, broccoli, leeks, onions, lettuce. She made shepherd's pie that first night. I remember it well because of how good it tasted. She served it with broccoli and carrots. I was in heaven.

She said we had a hospital appointment the following week and then told me what to expect. She said they would put something on my tummy so that they could see the baby and make sure it was okay. I was really scared;

I didn't know what was happening to me. Auntie Jane said I would put on weight over the next few months. She told me my tummy would get big. We talked about baby names and wondered if it would be a boy or a girl. Secretly I wanted a little girl, but I didn't tell her that.

Auntie Jane had to go to work on the Monday. She worked as a care assistant in an old people's home. She was also the cook in a disabled centre. I would sometimes go there with her. One of the residents there, Deirdre, loved hugs. As soon as she saw me come through the door, she would run straight for me and give me a big hug. She squeezed really hard.

Another resident, Tommy, loved to play pool, so we would often play in the games room while Auntie Jane made the food. Going to work with her gave me something to do. I was lonely sitting in the house all by myself.

The months went by really quickly, too quickly. I was getting bigger each day; I was also getting more terrified of what was to come. Auntie Jane sat me down one night and told me that I would go into labour and what it would be like. I didn't like the sound of it and was terrified. The closer it got to having the baby, the more terrified I got.

We went to her work one day, and there was chaos. All the residents were on edge. Deirdre was rocking back and forth, and Tommy was pacing the floor. The prison was behind the centre and a group of the prisoners were up on the roof protesting. They were holding up bedsheets with writing on them and burning sheets. It went on for about 12 hours. It took the longest time to calm the residents down. We gave them dinner, played some games and got them into their rooms. It was a long night. The prisoners gave in around 4:00 a.m. It was scary listening to them. I was scared, too.

On the 14th of February 1989, I went into labour. I was 13 years old. I had no idea what was happening to me. All I knew was that I felt tremendous pain. I had no idea it was going to get worse. I have no idea how long I was in labour, but it was a long time to be in pain. With my Auntie Jane by my side, sometime after 9:00 a.m., I had a baby girl. Straightaway, I named her Caitlyn. She was beautiful. I got to hold her for what felt like two seconds before she was taken away. They rushed her from the room. Auntie Jane looked worried. Something was wrong, but I didn't know what was going on. The nurse said the baby wasn't feeling too good, so they took her away just to check on her.

We were in the room for a long time before the doctor came to speak to us. He said the baby had a bubble in her brain. He said it looked like she had a stroke. 'We will have to do some more tests.'

The nurses came and cleaned me up. They put a nice, clean hospital nightdress on me. Auntie Jane came back and asked if I'd heard anything, but I hadn't.

After a while, a doctor came to see me and told me the baby was mentally handicapped. He said, 'She would likely never walk or talk. She will be in the hospital for a while because she needs extra care.'

I was in hospital for three days. I got to visit the baby a few times and then I went home to Auntie Jane's house. I asked Auntie Jane if we could call her Caitlyn. She loved the name.

Caitlyn

Jane became Caitlyn's legal guardian. She adopted Caitlyn as her own. I knew she would be a great mum to her. I was too young, just a child myself.

We visited Caitlyn every day in the hospital, but only behind the glass for a few weeks, and then we were allowed to hold her. She was wrapped in a white shawl. She was tiny when I held her in my arms—all I felt was love. She was awake and looking up at me, so small and innocent. She had 10 tiny toes and fingers, beautiful brown hair, and dark eyes. I could never hate her or how she was born.

The day we got to take her home was exciting. We had everything ready for her, a Moses basket set up in the living room, her cot in the bedroom. Her pram was by the door. I loved bath time. Auntie Jane and I would both bathe her. We both fed her, put her to bed, sang and read to her.

She was loved by us both. Auntie Jane never asked who the father was, and I never told her it was her own father.

At three months old, we could see some issues. When looking at you, one eye seemed to be looking away. She cried a lot. Caitlyn went back for tests. We were told she was deaf in one ear and blind in one eye. All down the left side.

And Just Like that, My Bubble Burst

We moved back home in June 1989; Caitlyn was 4 months old.

Auntie Jane needed support from her family to bring Caitlyn up. She put in for a house in the same area as Mum and Dad and Nannie and Grandad. I didn't want to go home, and I began to have nightmares. I was really scared, but I couldn't tell Jane. She needed her mum.

She managed to get a council house near her mum. It was on the same street, just at the other end of a long street. Since I had been away, my mother's sister Angela had moved into the street as well as my Great Granny Stewart, whom I didn't know.

The first thing I did was visit Rose. I had missed her so much. I picked some wildflowers as I walked through the graveyard. The grave was overgrown and my old flowers still in the pot. I removed them and put the new flowers in. I then pulled some of the weeds out and sat with her and apologized for not being there for the last seven and a half months. I didn't mean to be away so long, and I promised I wouldn't leave her again. I then told her about everything that had happened while I was away.

I stayed with Jane the first month I was home. I visited Rose most days and Nannie and Grandad would visit most days. When I saw Grandad for the first time, I felt chills run through me. I now knew that what he was doing with me was wrong. He touched my face and said he missed me and was happy I was home. Nannie fell in love with Caitlyn and decided to move in with Jane full time to help her, which meant I had to move home to my parents.

Chapter Five
1989 – 1991

So, I moved home. Wendy and Colin were excited to have me back. Mum even looked happy. I think she'd missed me; I hope not just because I was her protective shield. I missed her too. Dad didn't show excitement for having me home. In fact, he asked why I had bothered at all. I wanted them both to love me, to say they were happy to have me home, that they had missed me.

We had a new addition to the family, Fluffy the cat. She was grey and white, and having her first litter of kittens. She was so affectionate and lay beside me in bed. She had five kittens a few weeks after I got home.

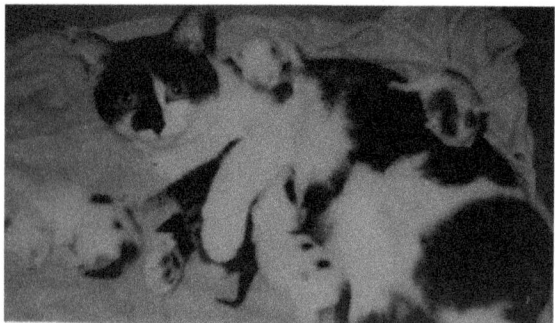

Fluffy became my constant companion. We were inseparable. We had the kittens for 6 weeks, then they went to their forever homes, leaving Fluffy lonely without them. I had her by me all the time. I think she missed her babies as much as I missed Caitlyn.

New neighbours had moved in across the road while I was away. The girl was the same age as me and we became good friends. Sarah lived with her mum and her grandparents, and we played together a lot.

I still visited Caitlyn and Jane every day and never missed a day. Nannie would get cranky at me, ask why I wasn't out playing with friends, why I was stuck in the house with a baby all the time. I would tell her my friends weren't out at that time. I think Nannie was jealous of the relationship I had with Caitlyn. Caitlyn loved being tickled, she would giggle so hard. I would sit and sing lullabies to her. You could see she was trying to sing along to the songs by making noises and staring up at you. She was adorable.

Poem

She's a beautiful girl of just 15 with sorrow in her eyes.
Masked by a smiling face and laughter while a part of her dies.
Her clothes are baggy, tattered and worn, to hide what can't be seen.
And while she pretends to all her friends, inside she feels unclean.

She imagines she is still a girl when she's all alone.
Trying to hide her new beauty and how much she has grown.
She wears no makeup or fancy clothes and doesn't style her hair.
But still, she shines from deep within. Though she doesn't seem to care.

She was just 12 years old as she started to grow,
Becoming so much more beautiful, than she will ever know.
Then in the silence of one night, when Granddad's little girl became a woman in her bed.
Trapped in a different world.

She was old enough to understand, but too young to disobey.
Confused by her morality, the shame of it would stay.
She did not want to disappoint the Granddad that she loved.

I got myself an evening paper round and went from door to door, getting customers. I would pick the papers up outside the chapel every afternoon, delivering around 85 papers at one point. It kept me busy for a few hours Monday to Friday, and I had 40 papers on a Saturday to deliver. I learned over time I had to hide my tips or Mum and Dad had their hands out on a Saturday afternoon. I already had to give them £10 a week. I was making about £40 but I didn't tell them that. I told them I was making £20.

When school started back, I got back with some of my old friends, which wasn't a good thing. I was 14 years old, and I was drinking, smoking, buzzing gas. I did this by putting the nib between my teeth and pushing down on it. Nothing had changed; Dad was still drinking every night, and I was still getting beatings. Grandad started abusing me again, although I would try hard not to visit him.

I started escaping into the graveyard again to be with Rose. I sat in my tree, slept prayed there. I packed a bag with spare clothes and a blanket in it and hid them in the tree, just in case I needed them.

One day, Dad caught me smoking out my bedroom window and decided to teach me a lesson. First, he beat me, then sent Mum to the ice-cream van for a pack of 10 cigarettes, the cheapest ones that were disgusting to taste. He sat me down and told me to light up. I refused at first, but he slapped me over the head. So, I lit up my first cigarette in front of my parents. He told me to keep puffing. I needed a break, but he wouldn't let me. When the first one was finished, he told me to light up the next one, and it went on and on. I thought I was going to throw up. I could feel the blood drain from my face. It didn't stop me from smoking again; probably made it worse. I craved cigarettes more.

I spent my free time when not at school or delivering papers with Caitlyn. She was growing too fast. Nannie was always around, though it made it hard to be myself with Caitlyn and Jane.

Grandad was calling on me for one thing or another, so he could relieve himself. He wasn't getting at me as much as he used to and that was getting to him. He told me how much he missed me. Missed his special girl.

Grandad would sometimes leave me at home alone after he had his way with me. He would go shopping for himself and some of the elderly around our area, for the paper and milk. I started snooping and came across a bag of newspaper clippings about Uncle Joshua's death. It was heartbreaking reading. There were also some birth certificates, at least five of them, three sets of twins. Uncle Joshua was one of them. It was rumoured Nannie had 16 kids. I only knew five that were living, my dad being one of them. I put everything back in the bag and put it back in the wardrobe.

I came across three giant piggy banks full of money. I got a knife from the kitchen and dragged some money through the slit to the surface and took £10 out. That would pay for my gas and cigarettes for a few days. I took more money every now and then.

I slipped up to Mum one day when she saw I had some money. I told her I had just done it the once, and I was sorry, but instead of telling me off, she told me next time Grandad left for the shops, I was to call on her. So, I shouted over the back garden, and she came up and used a knife to take £10 out. That paid for their curry for the next two nights. Mum realized that the piggy banks all took the same key, and she had one. Next time, she opened the banks up and helped herself to more. Each bank held different coins. 50-pence pieces, one pound and £2 coins. There must have been hundreds of pounds in the banks and Mum became a regular visitor after Grandad had his way with me and left for the shops or to see Nannie.

Grandad eventually figured out his money was disappearing. He asked if I had been in the wardrobe. I said no, but he didn't believe me. He started putting a piece of paper in the banks with the total amount on them. Mum had to stop at that point.

Five of the neighbours would gather on the corner of our street, all of them alcoholics. Dad never joined them; he was too good for them. He drank vodka, while they all drank the cheap stuff, Buckfast.

They gathered around the same time most days with their bottles in hand. Most of them flew doos (pigeons). They would hang around for an hour or two just talking about pigeons. One of the men, Alan, would call to me when I passed, 'Hey, there's Princess Diana.' He knew I was in the Gala, and I had short hair, so he said I looked like a young Princess Diana. I don't think he ever really knew my name. One by one, they died until there were only two of them left.

The nieces of one of the men, Charles, took a real disliking to me. I have no idea why; I hadn't even talked to them. They were two sisters, Elizabeth and Angela, and their friend Andrea. They were related to family. My mum's sister's partner was their cousin. That didn't stop them, though. They would be waiting for me on my way home from school, or on my paper round, or when I would take videos back. They beat me black and blue; I had a huge bald patch on the left side of my head from where they pulled my hair out.

One night I was walking with my cousin Nicole, wearing a new mint green jacket. We had just bought some chips and curry sauce and were on the way home. Angie and Elizabeth walked towards me. Elizabeth flipped the tray and covered my new jacket in curry sauce. All I could think about was what my dad was going to say. He'd beat the living daylights out of me, but he didn't.

Another night they caught me outside the video guy's house. I had just picked up two videos. It was drizzling outside, so I put the videos inside my jacket and zipped it up tight, so they didn't get wet. Angie, Elizabeth and Andrea were waiting outside, behind the hedge. They pulled my hair, dragged me around, threw me to the ground and trampled on me. I was more worried about the videos and hoping they didn't get broken.

The beatings happened most days for about a year.

One night Dad grabbed me by the hair, and told me that if I didn't fight back, he would give me something to fight back for.

I cried and said, 'But there's three of them.'

He said, 'I don't give a fuck if there's 3 or 10 of them, you fucking fight back.' So I did.

One day I saw Elizabeth on her own, coming out of her Uncle Charles' house, and I took my chance. She came at me, went to grab my hair. I don't know where I got the strength from, but I grabbed her by the hair and kept punching her face. I got her on the ground, kicking her. She cried for me to stop, but I didn't, I couldn't. I had rage built up inside me. I just wanted to get it all out. Her Uncle Charles came out the gate and peeled me off her.

I honestly thought Elizabeth, Angela and Andrea would come back for me. I thought they would kill me. After all, there were 3 of them, but they didn't touch me again. In fact, I never saw them around much after that night.

The summer of '88, before school started in August, was the best one. All the kids on the street would gather and play rounders and water fights—Sarah, Catherine, Star and Anne upstairs, John, Peter and Chris from across the road, Nicole, my sister Wendy, and myself. Sometimes the parents came out and play rounders too. Mum came out a few times to play. Dad never came out, though. He was always too drunk or passed out. We stayed outside until it was dark.

Auntie Jane came out one night, and the two of us played 'Kirby' for hours. Two people stood opposite each other on the pavements, one with a football. They threw the football to the opposite curb. And if it hit the curb and came back you, you then walked out into the middle of the road and threw the ball again, trying to hit in the hope it would bounce back. You then went back to the beginning, to stand on the pavement and throw the ball again. You kept doing this until you lost the ball. When you lost the ball, your opponent took it and threw the ball to your curb trying to hit it. The game went on for hours. It was simple, but so much fun.

I went to visit Rose one day and walked through the graveyard, picking wildflowers as I went. I changed the flowers over, cleaned the stone and sat down to talk to her about my day. As I was talking to her, a movement to my left caught my eye. I jumped a little at first, but as I looked closer, it was a baby hedgehog, small and beautiful. He approached me, not scared at all. I put out my hand, and he climbed onto it. He was tiny; I was in awe of him. I thought he would be sharp and spiky, but he wasn't. He was soft and gentle. I decided to name him Robert.

I took him home with me and put him in the back garden. I went inside and asked Mum if I could have an apple. I cut some of it up into tiny pieces for Robert. I didn't know if he liked apples or even if he was allowed apple, but I took it out to him. He loved it. He was going to be mine, and I would look after him always.

I visited Robert many times a day, a few minutes at a time. He grew fast. I didn't share him with anyone. Mum saw him a few times when she was hanging the washing out, but he didn't bother her, so she let him be.

Granny Stewart

My great-granny Stewart, Mum's gran, moved into the street. I supposedly met her when I was really small, but I don't remember that. She was an old lady who wore a pinny and had loose grey curls. She was tiny, about 4 foot 8 inches. I loved her instantly. She spent time with me. I visited her most days after school, sat by her feet and she played with my hair. I was growing it again. She gave the best hugs.

In the summer, we sat by the front door watching the world go by. I sketched the people passing. Granny always complimented me on my drawings. I loved doing art whenever I could. It was something I picked up on in primary school. Miss Whilkinson, my teacher, encouraged me to draw. Drawing helped me escape my problems.

When the ice-cream van came into the street, she told me to fetch her purse and sent me to the van for an ice-cream cone. She loved ice-cream, and she told me to get two 20p bags of mixed penny sweets. We went inside and put the TV on and I sat on the floor by her feet, eating our sweets.

Granny Stewart and I were close. When she got sick, I still visited her every day, and I helped her onto the commode, get dressed, and made her a slice of toast and butter and a cup of milky tea for breakfast.

I used to ask Mum why I'd never seen Granny Stewart before, why we had never visited her. Mum said she lived too far away, that we couldn't get a bus to Granny's.

She was my world. She was the only person who ever showed me affection, the only person who ever showed me true love. The only person that when she held me, she held me with her whole being. I believe she's my guardian angel to this day. I feel her around sometimes.

Granny Stewart started coming to our house every Sunday for dinner. When she came to visit, Dad wouldn't drink through the day. We would have homemade steak pie, mash potatoes, carrots and peas. Granny then sent one of us to the ice-cream van with the pie dish to get it filled with ice cream, wafers and raspberry sauce. Sundays were the best days; not only did we get to see Granny Stewart, but we got to have good food.

I was dogging (wagging) school one day due to another beating from Dad, so I went into the graveyard to see Rose. On the way, I decided to pop into the witch's circle to buzz some gas. I was still doing this on a regular basis, at least 4 or 5 times a week. I was high and watching a tiny mouse dodging in and out through the leaves on the ground.

I loved the way the gas made me feel, all warm and tingly inside. I have no idea how long I was in the circle. I caught the little mouse and put it in my cigarette box. I left the can of gas under the hedging for next time and headed towards Rose's grave, picking some flowers on the way. I showed Rose the mouse, told her what trouble I had got into this time, and why Dad had beaten me.

'He hates me, Rose. I'm always doing something wrong.'

After visiting Rose, I walked to Nannie's and asked her for a small box to put my baby mouse in. She gave me a teabag box.

Auntie Jane said, 'If your dad catches it, he'll kill it.' I got some plants and grass from Auntie Jane's garden and put them in the box with the mouse. I took him home with me and put the box under the bed.

A week or so later, Mum found the box under my bed, opened it up and screamed really loud. Dad came in to see what was going on. He grabbed the baby mouse and flushed him down the toilet. I screamed at Dad, and he turned around and slapped me across the face, grabbed me by the hair and dragged me into my room where he threw me on the bed. I started kicking my legs at him, which only made him madder, but I was so angry for what he'd done.

He screamed, 'You fucking bastard,' and grabbed the straps of my dungarees and pushed me hard into the bed over and over. My chest hurt. I scratched his hands, tried to pull his hands away.

That's the first time I really lost it with him. He won though; he punched me in the stomach, winding me, and I gave in.

To get my pent-up anger out, I started running around the local loch. I went there a few times a week and just ran. I would sometimes cry out when it was raining. The loch was deserted and so when I ran no one could hear me cry and scream. Visiting Rose and running were my only outlets.

Marbles

Mum came home from the Barra's one day with marbles. They were beautiful, all different colours and two different sizes. There were cat's eyes with two colours inside, there were marble effect ones and steelies. They were all great. The boys across the road played with them in the middle of the road on a stank (a drain cover). I was excited to learn how to play, so I watched them. Not many cars came up the street in those days, maybe three to five per day. I watched for a few days, worked out the strategy to win your opponent's marble. You had to get as close as you could, line them up and hit their marble with yours. I became very good at marbles by practicing everyday, and after a time I was beating every kid in the area. Playing marbles and being good at it helped with my self esteem. At one time I had four large ice cream tubs full of marbles. My favourites were the steelies (metal silver ones). I think this must be one of my favourite childhood memories. Finally, something I was really good at.

One day, I was in the graveyard with Nicole, Ronald, Katy, Ellen and John C, playing hide and seek. John wasn't one of the group, but he liked hanging around us. He had some mental health issues (autistic) but was a nice enough boy, a couple of years younger than us.

I can tell you, it is near impossible to find everyone in a graveyard when playing hide and seek. There are just so many hiding spots, and after a while we gave up on hide and seek. We walked towards the witch's circle when we saw a girl jump from a tree. There was a rope around her neck. I was frozen to the spot, numb with shock. John ran forward, lifted the girl by her legs and screamed for someone to undo the rope. I could see she had wet herself and her body was shaking. Ronald managed to undo the knot, and John and the girl fell to the ground.

When I was in my body again, tears were pouring down my face. John told Ellen to go to the caretaker's house and phone an ambulance. I knew the girl; her name was Michelle. She was a few years younger and lived with her grandfather just around the corner from us. I felt that she could be experiencing something like me with her grandfather. It felt like forever until the ambulance arrived. One of the paramedics asked us lots of questions, while the other looked after Michelle. They took her away, and we walked to the witch's circle in silence. I sat down on the ground and started to cry. I was terrified for Michelle. I hated that I couldn't help her because I froze. No one spoke about why she would want to take her life. All I wanted to do was tell Rose. I wanted to be with Rose. I didn't want to be sitting here. Michelle survived the incident. She was never the same, though.

Kevin, Mum's brother-in-law, turned up to the house drunk one night. He wanted to start a fight with Dad. Dad was lying in bed drinking, so wasn't in the mood for a fight, but Kevin kept pushing, so Dad jumped from the bed and pushed Kevin up against the wall, punching him in the face a few times.

I ran into the room to see if Mum was okay, because she was screaming. Dad just had his underpants on. He wouldn't stop punching Kevin, and Kevin was too drunk to hit back so, when he got the chance, he ran for the front door. Dad ran after him, but Kevin was gone.

As he came back to the room, you could see he was pissed. His hands were clenched, and he was pacing the room. He turned to me, asking what I was looking at. I said, 'Nothing,' and stayed in the corner of the room with Mum. I tried to pass him to head back to my own room, but he grabbed my arm.

'What the fuck are you doing and where the fuck are you going?'

I said, 'I'm going to my room.' I could see he wanted to keep fighting.

He slapped me and told me to hit him back. I said, 'No!!'

He sat down on the bed and poked his finger into my shoulder.

'Fucking hit me, do it.'

I said, 'No' again, but he pushed his finger at me harder and harder. I could feel the anger rise in me as my hand clenched into a tight fist. I lifted my arm above my head and brought it down hard on his face.

His nose exploded, and blood went everywhere.

I could feel myself trembling inside, terrified of what he was going to do next.

He just laughed and said, 'Is that all you've got? Come on.'

I raised my fist again and brought it down hard on his face. At this point, he punched me. I flew backwards, hitting my head on the wardrobe and cracking the mirror.

This enraged him more. He started punching, slapping and kicking me.

Mum was screaming, 'Stop!'

I begged him to stop, but he just spat on me, screaming, 'You are a worthless piece of shit.' He left and went to the bathroom,

Mum helped me to my feet and walked me to my bedroom. I crawled under the covers and curled into a ball. Wendy came over and lay behind me, gently putting her arm around me. She was only eleven, and she must have heard terrible things.

Ronald

Please note this section includes scenes that may trigger some readers.

I didn't see Ronald as often as I used to because his mum and dad moved house. He lived about 20 minutes away, half an hour on the bus. I visited as often as I could now that I had a paper round and was earning money. He was my best friend apart from Rose. Auntie Joan said, 'When you two grow up, I think you'll get married.' We laughed and said to each other, 'We can't get married, we're cousins.'

She said, 'That doesn't matter these days. You can marry your cousin.'

We hung out in school, and sometimes he came over to my house after school. We would go and see Nannie. We often went to the graveyard and played games. Sometimes his sister, Katy, and his brother, Joseph, would be with him. We climbed and built tarzies from the trees, played hide and seek and built fortresses with the old palettes we would get from B&Q.

When Auntie Joan was around, I think she noticed the way Grandad was with me. How he would always put his hand on my shoulder or on my back. I don't think she liked it very much, but she never said anything. She would tell me to go out and play or sit by her.

One day I was in the graveyard with Ronald on my own. We were sitting on the grass on the hill when Ronald put his hand around my shoulder. I thought he was just giving me a hug, so I hugged him back, but he said, 'We should be girlfriend and boyfriend.'

I said, 'Don't be silly. We can't be boyfriend and girlfriend; we're blood cousins.'

He said, 'Mum said that doesn't matter.'

He was making me feel very uneasy. I took his hand away from my shoulder, but he put it back. He pushed me back down onto the grass and started kissing me. I didn't kiss him back. I just wanted him to stop, but he didn't. He lifted my skirt, then pulled at my pants.

I kept saying, 'No' and pushing against him, but he wouldn't stop. He undid his trousers and pulled his penis out. He pulled down my pants and pushed into me over and over and over, until he was spent.

I felt violated, hurt. I didn't know what to do next. Ronald said, 'Let's go to Nannie's house.' But I just wanted to go home.

My house was on the way to Nannie's, so I made an excuse and told Ronald I was going home and that I would see him soon.

I couldn't look at him the same way after that. He was no longer my best friend, no longer someone I wanted to hang out with.

I felt like it was my fault I didn't say no, enough. I didn't push him away.

I went to see Rose and cried hard, asking her what I had done wrong. 'Why would Ronald want to do that to me?' I didn't believe Auntie Joan was right that cousins should marry. I didn't know how to fix it.

'Please tell me how to fix it, Rose. I wish I was with you. I wish I could be with you.'

I had no idea at that time that I had been raped. Not until I understood things better.

I never looked at Ronald the same way after that day. I didn't know how to. I became very distant. I changed my attitude. I changed the way I dressed. I became a completely different person that day. I became a tomboy. I started taking gas more and more. I smoked a lot, and sometimes, when I could get hold of some hash, I smoked that, too.

A number of weeks after Ronald had sex with me, I went to see the doctor. I told her I wasn't feeling well, and that I was feeling sick all the time. She asked if I'd been with a boy.

This time I knew what being with the boy meant, and I said, 'Yes.'

She took a urine sample, came back and told me I was pregnant.

I told her I couldn't have a baby because I was too young.

She gave me a tablet to take. I went to the hospital the next day and had a Dilatation and Curettage, a procedure to clear everything away.

I now knew what Grandad was doing was wrong. I didn't know at that point if the baby was my Grandad's or Ronald's. I still don't know.

I started delivering the newspaper for one of the gangsters in the area. He was a lovely old man and gave good tips. I wasn't scared of him as he never gave me cause to be scared of him. However, I was scared of the stories I was told about him. How he killed people, how he ran the underworld. But, to me, he was a nice old man.

I would often fantasize about asking him to kill my grandfather, Ronald and my dad, because I didn't want to be hurt anymore.

Ronald had sex with me more than once after that. In the graveyard, at his house, at my house. His mum had given him condoms to use, so he was safe. My childhood GP, Doctor Marian, gave me the pill to take. She told me to take this tiny pill every morning, and she said it would stop me falling pregnant again. I took that little pill every day without fail. I didn't want to get pregnant again.

A beautiful Golden Retriever turned up on my Nannie's driveway in the summer of '89. He had no collar and was filthy and limping. I think he had been dumped there. I sat with him and fed him some meat we had for dinner. He was placid. After the second day of him being there, I asked Mum if we could keep him. She said she would talk to Dad, and by some miracle he said yes, and we had a pet. I named him Benji. He was my dog, and I loved him. I walked and fed him, and he would sleep on my bed at night.

I came home from school one day to no Benji. He had been with us for 4 months. I went to Mum in a panic asking where he was, and she said, 'I took him and walked him.'

I said, 'Walked him where?'

She said, 'I took him somewhere far away and left him there.'

I screamed at her, 'You got rid of my dog. He will die out there. It's cold and wet.'

She said, 'He never listened to anyone but you. He would whine at the front door until you came home from school.'

She said, 'We couldn't keep him anymore. We couldn't afford to keep him, anyway.'

Poor Benji was gone, and I was devastated. I never forgave my parents.

It was Christmas time again, and Mum and Dad were having a party. Mum's brothers came and Dad's brother and his wife as well as Jim from upstairs. Everyone was in good spirits and drinking hard. The music was blaring, and Auntie Grace, Wendy and I were having fun dancing and singing to 70s and 80s music. Auntie Grace took Wendy and me into the bedroom, and we practiced the 'Shoop Shoop' song and danced in front of everyone. Dad was cheering Wendy on for her good dancing. Everyone cheered after we had finished, but the night ended in disaster when Dad and one of Mum's brothers started fighting. Dad punched him, and he fell on the Christmas tree, breaking it in half. Everyone was shouting and screaming. Jim ran from the house, and I rushed Wendy into the room with Colin and told her to stay there. As I walked back to check Mum was okay, Dad's fist came through the glass door. Blood ran down his arm, and he was angry. Mum told everyone to leave and wrapped a towel around Dad's arm. He left the house and went to see Nannie. She closed his cut with a needle and thread and then she bandaged it up. She was always looking after him, but they had a real love-hate relationship. I guess that's because they were alike. They both had short tempers and disliked everyone.

I visited Auntie Jane and Caitlyn. We played in the garden on the swing. Caitlyn loved the swing. She laughed when I pushed her. Nannie was watching from the window. She always had a stern look on her face and would tell me I should be out playing. I couldn't be myself when she was around. I went home, but Auntie Jane told me to go back at 7:00 p.m. She said to go into the front garden, and she would be in her bedroom. We would talk through the window. We did this often throughout the summer. Some nights she sent me to the ice-cream van for a 99p ice cream cup. We would laugh and talk for ages.

After visiting Jane one night, I went to meet Ellen outside the local pub. We hung out there at night, listening to music and smoking. Sometimes we would go behind the building to buzz some gas.

One night when meeting Ellen, I looked at my watch and noticed I was going to be late for my curfew. I ran fast to get home. Nannie and Grandad were in the house. Nannie told Dad to take his fucking belt off and beat me with it.

'She has to be taught a lesson, John.'

He took his belt off and pushed me onto the bed.

I was screaming, 'No,' as the belt came down on top of me over and over again. Not just in one place, all over.

Mum was screaming for him to stop. I didn't think he would. He didn't know his own strength, and he was a big man. I lay there hanging on the edge of the bed, skin raw, unable to move. When they left, I slowly crawled onto my tummy and stayed there, tears silently falling until my pillow was soaked. When Mum put the light off, Wendy came in and laid a blanket over me. I lay on my bed for a few days because I couldn't move, due to the pain. I made sure I wasn't late again.

I started seeing a boy named Alex. Well, I wouldn't actually call it 'seeing', he was 18 and I was 15. He had a car and would pick me up after school and take me places, usually the park. He gave me his ring. He wanted more but I couldn't, wouldn't give it to him. He rented an apartment in a high-rise block of flats and decided to have a housewarming. He invited my friends and me because he didn't know anyone in the area. I asked some of my friends to come. We were all drinking Mad Dog 20/20, cider and smoking hash. Some of them took speed, too.

My friend Jessica was being flirty with Alex all night. While we were all dancing and having fun, the two of them disappeared from the room. I caught them in bed together. I felt heartbroken. I walked out and slammed the door, but I didn't cause a scene. I left, telling my friends I was going home.

At that time, it felt like I was always going to be stamped on physically, mentally and emotionally. He turned up at my Auntie Jane's house asking for his ring back. I threw it at him and slammed the door in his face. I found out later on that Alex had HIV.

I caught up with a few of my friends one afternoon. We had bought a two-litre bottle of cider, three cans of gas and twenty king-size cigarettes between us. We decided to go in one of the closes. We sat on the middle floor, as no one was in the houses on either side, so we could make more noise. A girl I went to school with lived on the top floor. Her name was Geraldine. We were all smitten with her older brother, Paul. Geraldine's family were Jehovah Witnesses. Paul played the keyboard and sang. He had a beautiful voice. We were 15 and Paul was 22. He was gorgeous, such a gentle soul.

We were sitting in the close that night, listening to Paul sing when Nicole took her turn buzzing the gas, Emily lit a cigarette behind her and Nicole's hair went up in flames. I took my jumper off, threw it over her head and pulled her to me, falling to the ground. I put the fire out, but Nicole's hair was ruined. Back in those days, we all had perms, and we put too much hairspray on. Nicole's mum was fuming. She was so mad at us. We said nothing about the gas. We said Ellen was doing Nicole's hair and put hairspray on when Emily lit a cigarette. Nicole was told to stay away from us after that night. She had to have her hair cut short as most of her long hair went up in flames.

Ellen started seeing a friend of ours, Anthony. He was really kind. I went with her to his place. He had an older brother, Christopher. One night I ended up stuck in a cupboard with Christopher for a good 20 minutes so that Ellen and Anthony could make out. We just talked the whole time. It was bloody dark in the cupboard though. I told Ellen she owed me one.

Nicole got me into huge trouble one night. I was visiting Granny Eve, great-gran on Mum's dad's side, and she asked me to go to the shops as she was eating jars of baby food at that stage, I don't know why really, she still had her teeth. Nicole said she would stay with Granny. I had no idea she'd been visiting Granny often, but I knew she always had cigarettes and money as she was always flashing it around. I didn't piece it all together until a lot later. Granny Eve put her pension under her mattress, and Nicole was helping herself to it. One night we walked into our street, and I could hear Nicole's mum, Angela, screaming our names. Nicole took money out of her pocket and stuffed it into my Nannie's hedges. She looked terrified. Grandad Sam came around the corner He was fuming, throwing his hands in the air. He had rage in his eyes. He hit me hard on the face, and I fell backwards. I had no idea why. He grabbed Nicole by the hair and slapped her. Angela then grabbed Nicole by the arm and dragged her home. Grandad grabbed me and dragged me into my mum's. He told my mum and dad I had been stealing money from Granny Eve. I begged him, told him 'I didn't. It wasn't me'. He didn't believe me, and Nicole didn't say otherwise. I was never cleared of the accusation.

That night I ran away. I was terrified of what I was going to get from my dad later when he was drunk. I grabbed my Walkman and ran to the first place I thought of: the graveyard. I climbed the wall and headed straight for my tree, got my blanket out of the bag that I had left there and wrapped myself up in it. I put my headphones on and listened to my Walkman. Bucks' Fizz *Making Your Mind Up* was playing. I wasn't scared in the tree; it was the safest I'd felt in a long time.

In the morning, I knocked on my bedroom window, and Wendy let me in. She said Mum made excuses to Dad about where I was. She said they weren't angry with me. I didn't see Mum until after 11:00 a.m. and she just asked what I had done with all the money I had stolen. I told her again I didn't do it; I had no idea about the money. I told her Nicole had thrown money into Nannie's hedge. She went outside and rummaged through the hedge and found £37, which she kept. This infuriated me. That was money I was accused of stealing, money I didn't take, and she took it and spent it on alcohol and curry. I never trusted Nicole after that.

I took the blame for it and was blamed for something I didn't do. Dad sent me upstairs to Grandad with the change from his loan money. He hurt me that day, more than he had done in a long time. He was aggressive, and his nails were long. He scratched me down there. It stung. I wanted this to end; I needed this to end. He couldn't be doing this anymore.

That afternoon, I took 3 strips of Codriamol, (the main ingredients are codine and paracetamol). I went to sleep, not wanting to wake up. But again, I woke up hours later throwing up bile.

I was drinking more, and I had moved up a level to inhaling lighter fuel. I poured it in a bag, put it to my mouth and inhaled deeply. It gave me the most amazing feeling. I was in another world, my world, a world without pain. I was really messed up. I had to tell someone what was happening to me. I had to trust someone with my secret. I got high with Izzy E one night and told her what my grandad had been doing with me. I was terrified but felt relief. Finally, I had told someone, and a weight had lifted.

God, Izzy, why did you tell Ellen? I got scared. Ellen came to me and said she knew what my grandad had done to me. I denied it, telling her it wasn't true. I got really pissed, lost it, I was so angry and had to face her. I went looking for Izzy. She was at Izzy G's house, and I screamed for her to come out. I told her I wanted her behind the church and that I was going to kill her. I beat Izzy badly that night. She had had her appendix out five days before, and as I sat on her, her stitches opened up. I couldn't stop punching her face. Ellen and Izzy G peeled me off her, but I pulled back and went for her again. They pulled me off her, and there was blood everywhere. I sat on the grass in a trance. Ellen ran to her house to phone an ambulance. I got up and walked away almost in a daze. I could hear my name being called in the background, but I didn't look back. I could hear the siren, but I kept walking. As I reached my gate, my legs gave way, and I collapsed to the ground. Next thing I knew, Jim was helping me up and walking me to my door, asking if I was okay. He opened the door for me and walked me in. He then left because he and my dad didn't get on—in fact, they hated each other. I went into the bathroom and put the light on. My hands and clothes had blood on them. I stared into the mirror, my eyes dead. I was shaking, but I wasn't cold.

I didn't feel rage or anger anymore, just confused, guilty, afraid, and scared.

I went to my room and changed my bloodied, dirtied clothes, put on my pyjamas and crawled into bed. I couldn't close my eyes; I was scared to sleep. All that went through my mind was, 'What have I done? Was Izzy dead? Did I kill her?'

There was a lot of blood.

'When are the police going to come and take me? Am I going to go to jail? Will her mum come for me? Would Ellen and Izzy ever talk to me again?'

I felt dead inside. I didn't want to live anymore.

Izzy didn't come to school for a few weeks. Ellen told me she had been in the hospital for a few days. When she did come back to school, she never looked at me or spoke to me again.

I was taking lighter fuel most days. I was high most of the time, and I loved it. I loved the warm feeling—it took me away from my thoughts and feelings. At school, I would go to the bathroom as often as I could. I wasted so much time. The only classes I loved were music with Miss Davidson and woodwork with Mr. Deecko. I started making a desk for Caitlyn for her 3rd birthday. It was designed specifically for her. I shaped the desk so that it would surround her so that she wouldn't fall off the chair. I worked hard on that desk, and it was my last year of school. Caitlyn loved the table. She sat at it every day, drawing.

I went home for lunch most days so that I could see Caitlyn. My dad was there one day and asked me to make him a cup of tea. Auntie Jane said the kettle had just boiled, so I used that water to make him his tea. I gave it to him, and he screamed in my face, it's fucking freezing. He jumped up, so I ran from the room into the kitchen. I shouted at him that Auntie

Jane said it had just boiled. He punched my head, and it swung and hit the window frame. I screamed out, so he hit me again and again. No one came to see what was happening or if I was okay. I couldn't go back to school that afternoon because I was scared someone would see I had a black eye. I sat on the stairs across the road from the school all afternoon, next to the motorway. No one was around, I stared at a little bird as it splashed in a puddle. When I did go back to school, teachers and friends asked what had happened. I couldn't say, but I was scared people would know and, if it got back to Dad, he would kill me.

I was running track one day in PE, (Physical Education) when I fainted. As I ran towards the finish line, I became very dizzy, and just as I reached the end, I fainted. This happened every time I had PE, every time I exercised or played hockey. I fainted when playing rounders, and when I ran after hitting the ball, I fainted. This went on for a few months. My mum was called to the school to take me home. One afternoon, as I ran to the finish line during PE, I collapsed into the arms of the PE teacher, Mrs. Adams. She phoned for an ambulance. Mrs. Adams came with me in the ambulance, and Mum headed to the hospital on the bus.

They ran a lot of tests, then told me I was anaemic and had low blood pressure. I was told to take Dextro energy tablets before physical exercise. Dextro energy tablets dissolve in your mouth like a sugar tablet. Mum got to the hospital shortly after I arrived and stayed with me while they did tests.

When I was free to go, Mum took me to the oldest house in Glasgow, a National Trust property. It was a big tourist attraction directly across from the hospital and built in 1947. It had 17th century historic furniture. I couldn't believe how old the house was, and inside, it was like nothing had been disturbed. The furniture and the crockery were just as they were back in the day. In the bedroom, you could see the outline of where a body would have lain in the bed. Mum had never done anything like this with me before, and it felt special just to spend an hour with her. I was sad when we had to catch the bus and head home.

At music one day, Miss Davidson asked what happened to my eye, and told me to stay back after class. It was the end of the day, and she asked me again what had happened. I broke down and told her. I told her everything. What Dad was like, what he had done, what Grandad was doing. Everything. I bared my soul to her, and afterwards I was terrified of what would happen next. I couldn't sleep that night, and I was scared to go to school.

The next day I was called to the deputy head's office and told some social workers would be coming to see me about what I had told Miss Davidson. I was angry that she told people what I had told her. Miss Wilson, the deputy head, took me into a room. Two social workers were sitting on a couch. One of them was Liz Thompson, my local social worker, who worked in the area where I lived. I was terrified. Liz started asking me questions about what I said to Miss Davidson. I said I didn't say anything.

I thought my dad was going to kill me. And what would Nannie do? God, she would kill me too.

I denied everything. I denied saying anything to Miss Davidson. I said I didn't say anything. I said the things that she said didn't happen, not to me. I was terrified.

Miss Davidson said nothing more about it in class. Two days later, I went home for lunch, and Mum was hanging out the washing. Dad wasn't home. He was at Auntie Jane's. Mum said I was in 'deep shit'. They had received a letter saying that the family had to go to the social work department. Mum said the whole family were marching down to argue with them: Nannie, Dad, Jane. Grandad stayed at home with Caitlyn.

I got the beating of my life from Dad. No one spoke to me for months., I was shunned. Nannie was angry with me, called me a liar. Said I'd been sleeping with other boys, and I had to stop lying. I believe she knew I wasn't lying then because she stopped leaving Caitlyn alone with Grandad.

When I went back to school I tried to go in and see Miss Davidson, but Miss Wilson said I couldn't see her on my own. I was mad, so after school I waited until I saw her car leave the school grounds. I stood in the middle of the road on the island and, as she passed me, I swore at her, 'I fucking hate you so much.'

Deep down I was relieved I told someone. Especially someone I trusted, and I trusted Miss Davidson. I was just terrified of what would happen to me when it got out.

With the money I had saved from my paper round, I went on a school trip. The girls were in half the building and the boys in the other half. We had bunk beds, and I was sharing with Ellen. Nicole and Izzy were in another and Jane and Tracey in another.

We went canoeing, abseiling, orienteering, and had some money to spend at the tuck shop at night. I bought a postcard and some chocolate for my first night. I had never been on holiday, so I wanted to send Mum and Dad a postcard.

We did everything in groups of six with a teacher. Mr. Dorwood was with us 6 girls. On the day we went out in the canoes, it was freezing so I had a big Aran cardigan on to keep warm. We were in the water for about forty minutes when Mr. Dorwood told us to join together, holding each other's canoe. He told half of us to stand up, so every second person stood up. I had Ellen on one side of me and Mr. Dorwood on the other. I was really unsteady in my canoe, and I leaned too much to the side and fell into the water. Because I had the Aran cardigan on, I was being pulled down. I panicked because I wasn't a strong swimmer and thought I was going to drown. As I went under again, I felt someone behind me. Mr. Dorwood had jumped in, pulling me to the surface. He swam with me to the jetty where other teachers helped pull me out. I was very grateful to them. Despite that, I had such a good time, and I didn't want to go home.

A few weeks later, Dad had been drinking all day and wasn't in a good mood. I tried to stay in my room and out of his way. I sat in the kitchen on the breakfast bar after dinner to record the Top 40 charts. It was a Sunday afternoon, and I hadn't recorded them in a while. Dad shouted me into the living room, and I reluctantly went. His eyes were red with anger.

He said, 'You have fucked up my family, you worthless piece of shit. You fucked everything up.'

He looked really scary. I told him, 'I didn't do anything.' He stood up and punched me in the stomach.

He screamed, 'Don't talk back to me, you fucking bastard.'

I screamed, 'I'm not a bastard.'

He went to hit me again, and I ran down the hallway and into my bedroom. I jumped on my single bed, trying to get as far into the corner as possible. He came through the door right behind me. He tried to grab at me. I knew he would get me and kill me. The only thing I could see was a glass bottle of Irn Bru (juice) on my bedside table. I grabbed it, lifted it high above my head and brought it down with as much force as I had on his head. I could hear Mum scream, 'Nooooo,' in the background. Too late, I had done it. It gave me time to grab my jacket and run out the front door into the night rain. I went straight to my tree, took out a can of lighter fuel and the plastic bag I had put in my bag a few days before and started inhaling. I got warm really quickly and the shivering and shaking stopped.

I got down out of the tree and went to see Rose.

'Rose, I have fucked up. They are going to kill me. I can't be here anymore. I want to be with you. I have to be with you.'

I suddenly felt warm. Not in pain anymore. Everything became clear, and I now knew what I had to do. I had to fight back, and fight back I did.

After the letter from the social workers, Grandad stopped calling on me. He stopped coming by to pay Mum and Dad the loan money. I didn't see him much. I was grateful for the peace.

I thought long and hard about Miss Davidson and what she had done. She may have saved my life the day she listened to me. I decided to buy her a gift to say sorry and thank you. I had been hiding some money away from my paper tips, so I bought her a gold treble clef pendant. I waited for her after school and handed it to her with a letter of thanks. I saw her two days later, and she took my hand and said, 'I'm so sorry for what you have gone through. I only wish I could do more.'

My friend Robert came by one afternoon after school. He was visiting his aunt and asked if I wanted to hang out. We rode our bikes through the graveyard for what seemed like hours, then stopped to sit on the grass for a bit. The grass had not long been cut, so we took our jackets off and put them on the ground and sat on them. We talked for about an hour and decided to call it a night. We rode out of the graveyard gates, Robert going one way and me going the other, heading home. As I got to my gate, I could see Wendy's head at Nannie's window, and I panicked. I parked my bike at the back of the house and ran around the corner. I tried to open the door, but it was locked. I started banging on it until Grandad opened it. I ran past him upstairs into the living room. There was a movie paused on the TV, and it took me right back to that first night with Grandad. All those memories came back; the first time he touched me. I couldn't let that happen to Wendy. I had to protect her. I said, 'Why don't we go downstairs and sing karaoke? We can go now.'

Wendy was happy to come with me, and I was grateful. As we walked into the hallway, Grandad grabbed my arm and twisted it. He said, 'Who have you been lying with?'

'No one.'

'You fucking liar. You have been lying with someone. There's grass all over your back.'

I said I had been sitting on the grass with my friend.

He said, 'Yes, your friend from earlier?'

I said, 'Yes.'

'You fucking lay with him?'

As I turned to pull my arm away, he pushed me, and I fell down all the stairs, hitting my head off the door. I lay there for what felt like ages. Wendy knelt beside me, holding my hand. I think it scared her too. I got up when I could and walked home with Wendy. At least I had stopped him from hurting her. I told Wendy to never to go up there on her own again, never to be around him on her own. I am grateful she never was. I asked her, and she was adamant nothing ever happened to her.

Friday nights were disco nights. I got together with the girls and headed for the Community Centre. We inhaled gas or smoked hash and headed into the disco and danced the night away to the *Locomotion*, *Thriller*, *The Only Way is Up*, *Push It*, *I Owe You Nothing*. The 80s music was amazing. The disco started at 6:00 p.m. and ended at 9:00 p.m. Music saved me and kept me alive. My Walkman was my life. I took it everywhere with me. Especially when I was sitting in my tree. I could stay there for hours listening to my music. It would take me out of my body and into another life. On disco nights, all the kids from the area gathered at the disco. We all went there to dance. That's all you saw, kids dancing. I felt alive and free at the disco and hated missing any when grounded.

One Friday, the centre was cordoned off with police tape. All the local kids were hanging around because the disco was cancelled. The body of a glue sniffer was found behind the centre. Joey was in his twenties and had been sniffing glue behind the centre for years. But he was dead, and it made me think about the lighter fuel and gas. Was I going to be another Joey? Was someone going to find me somewhere one day?

Chapter Six
1991 – 1994

Please note this section includes scenes that may trigger some readers.

I finished school in 1991 aged sixteen (10th grade), not getting the best marks. I did well in Music and Woodwork, but I failed everything else. I didn't have the best time in school. I wasn't there for some of the four years, and the friends that I had, I got high with. I still met up with the girls but not as much as I used to. I started my first job at a small newsagent working for £29 a week. Not much in those days and I had to give my parents £15 dig (rent) money a week.

I liked the job. The couple that I worked for were really nice, but I wasn't making much money. I was offered a job in the local grocery store only 5 minutes from my house, so I took it. They paid me £45 a week, a lot more than I was getting at the other shop, but I then had to pay my parents £20 a week dig money. The people I worked for weren't the nicest people. It was a Pakistani family. The wives were at home with the children and the husbands worked. I heard one of them say one day that white women were easy. This angered me but I said nothing as I needed the work. I worked there for four months during that time, one of the men asked me if I would go in the back room with him. He offered me cigarettes and a quarter bottle of vodka. I said no.

I had to look for another job. A girl I went to school with, Jennifer, said they were looking for people at a bakery in the city. I decided to go for it and got the job. I got on well with everyone. It seemed like a nice place to work. The Deputy Manager didn't seem to like me very much, though.

I don't know what I did to her to make her dislike me. She got on to me for everything: not cutting the bread properly, not putting the cream on the cakes properly, not washing the floor properly. It was one thing after another.

I made good friends with a girl called Leslie and we often met up. She lived not far from me in a caravan on a car lot. I took a taxi down to her place one night and we had a few drinks. Her boyfriend got home from work with his mate Harry. Harry took a liking to me, but he seemed old. He tried hard to talk to me that night, but I was unsure.

Leslie said, 'He's a nice guy. He'll treat you good.'

I decided to give Harry a go. We had some speed one night and went to the local pub. I might have been 16, but I looked older. We had a few drinks and Harry got up and sang, 'Hey Jude,' to me. He was nice, but I couldn't sleep with him. I wasn't ready.

One night I got off the bus heading to Leslie's house when three girls approached me and asked me for some money. I told them I didn't have any, but they didn't believe me. One of them punched me in the stomach and they walked off, crossing the road. I kept walking but had a nagging pain in my stomach. I put my hand down to hold my tummy only to realize I was bleeding. The girl had stabbed me. I managed to make it to Leslie's, and she took me to the hospital. I got eight stitches. I was terrified to go back to Leslie's, and she couldn't come to my house because of Dad, so after a while we drifted apart. I didn't last in the job either. The Deputy Manager accused me of stealing 20p from the till. She said my initials were on the receipt. When I looked at the initials, I knew they weren't mine, but she was determined to get rid of me, so I left.

On Christmas Eve, we went to the carnival in the Exhibition Centre. My cousin's dad had tickets for the rides. I went on the Waltzers many times. Wendy and my cousin Nicole loved the Big Wheel and Dodgems. I also loved the machine you put money in and watch it drop, hoping to knock the coins off. I never won money though and ended up losing more than I got out.

After the carnival, we jumped on the bus and headed into the city centre to the Baras. We bought warm mussels or whelks and, while we ate them, we listened to the man bargaining off the toys, cosmetics and bags. Christmas Eve was when you got a real bargain so that's when I bought all my Christmas presents. I never wanted the night to end. Christmas Day was never much fun because Mum and Dad were never there to open the presents with us, to enjoy breakfast or see us get excited about our presents.

Dad was getting sick, complaining of pain in his legs all the time. He was severely overweight. He went to the doctor and found out he had gout in his knees. So, when he was drinking, he would lie on the floor or on the sofa. One night he lay on the floor saying he couldn't walk to the bathroom and asked for a jug. Everyone had to leave the room while he peed in the jug. Mum had heated up a curry and placed it in front of him. He tasted it and threw it up in the air saying it was fucking freezing. That's the first time I saw Mum get mad. She picked up the jug and poured it over his head. He was spitting piss all over the place. She ran from the room while he screamed. He was going to kill her. We hid out in my room, praying he wouldn't come in. I hadn't seen Mum that scared in a long time. He went to the bathroom a short time later and washed and then passed out on his bed.

In April 1991, Dad's grandfather (my great grandfather) died. I was in a bad way with the drinking and buzzing the lighter fuel. I didn't really know my great grandad, so didn't feel any emotion at the funeral.

Afterwards everyone went back to Auntie Jane's for drinks. I went to the local grocery store and bought a half bottle of vodka. The guys in there knew I was underage but still served me, anyway. They also offered me my job back, which I accepted. I went back to Jane's and drank the vodka in her room. My head was spinning. I couldn't focus. I got all emotional, not for my dead grandfather but for myself. For all I had been through, for all I was going through physically and emotionally. I walked out of the house that day, barely able to stand straight. I walked out onto the main road in front of traffic in the hope that someone would hit me and kill me. One of the neighbours pulled me off the road and asked what the hell was going on. All I could say was my grandad's dead. How could

I tell her my grandad and my cousin have sex with me, and my dad beats the crap out of me. No one would believe me. My family had lived in the area all their lives. Grandad was a well-dressed man who did the shopping for the elderly. No one ever saw my dad to judge, and Ronald was never around. I would be called crazy. I staggered home and lay on the sofa. Uncle Robert came in a short time later, saying he had been looking for me everywhere. He said the neighbour said I was walking in the middle of the road.

'What the hell is going on, Sharon? I'm really worried about you.'

I said I was just sad Grandad died.

He said, 'Bullshit. You didn't even know the old bastard.'

I couldn't tell him. I couldn't open up. He told me to sort myself out.

I was spiralling out of control, and I couldn't find a way back.

I was invited to Izzy G's 16th birthday party. It was held at her aunt's place. I had no idea what I was walking into. The house was full of teenagers. It was a hash party. There were bodies everywhere. People were doing handstands against the wall while someone blew smoke into their mouth. They were smoking from pipes, smoking joints, eating hash cookies. I felt high as soon as I walked into the living room. I gave Izzy her present and sat beside Ellen for a while. She was high; all she did was giggle. I didn't need to touch any of the stuff as I was already high by just inhaling it from the air. I got up and went to the bathroom. I shut the door behind me but could hear noises from the bathtub. I pulled back the curtain screen to see Nicole and Anthony having sex. I felt sick and had to get out of there, so I started walking home. I don't think I was walking in a straight line as I felt out of it.

When I got home, I sat on the doorstep for a long time, trying to sober up. I shouldn't have bothered. As soon as I walked in, Mum shouted from the bedroom, 'Is that you, Sharon?'

I said, 'Yes.'

She didn't bother coming out of the room, didn't see that I was high. I went to the bathroom and washed, then went to my bedroom, put on my pyjamas and went to bed.

Granny Eve died in 1991, the year I turned 16. I hadn't seen most of the family since being accused of stealing her money, but I knew I had to go to the viewing and say goodbye. I went with Mum and Wendy and as we sat in the living room, a lady walked past and into the bedroom to see Granny lying in the coffin. I had never seen her before, so I asked Mum who she was. She said it was her sister, Jessie. I'd never met Jessie. Supposedly, I'd seen her when I was a child, but I didn't remember. According to mum she was a wild child, a hippie. She wore strange bright clothes and had colourful tattoos and grew cannabis plants in her house and had bean bags as chairs. She sounded cool to me. She and Mum's brother, Anthony, and Grandad all came back to our house for drinks. Jessie was telling us about her life, and it all sounded like a fantasy. I was intrigued by her, but she was leaving the next day to go home, and I never saw her again.

One day after work, it was pretty dark out, and when I got to the corner of our road, I heard a loud bang followed by another then another. As I turned the corner, a car sped off. I didn't see the colour, make or license number. I was in shock. I could see someone lying on the ground. I was scared. People started appearing from everywhere. I ran home fast, terrified.

Dad was in the hallway and said, 'What the hell is wrong with you?' I said I think someone was just shot in the street.

Mum put her coat on and told me to show her where. When we got there, police were everywhere, and an ambulance. People were saying he's dead. I was terrified.

In the news the next day, it said a man had been shot three times and died at the scene. I delivered his parents' paper. I didn't know what to say or do. I delivered the paper as usual, and on Friday, when I collected the money, I said I was sorry for their loss. I never told them I had heard the gunshots.

The funeral was a big affair. Men lined the graveyard wall wearing Crombie coats (long coats) and you could see they had guns underneath. It was all quite scary. The news reporters were there too.

Sunday was payday. I loved it. I would buy my cigarettes for the week, a few cans of gas and a few bottles of Irn Bru. Then I would give Mum my dig money, which left me with about £10 to last the week.

Mum and Dad played cards sometimes for coins. 10p, 20p, and 50p at a time. So, Sunday became payday and card night, playing for money. But Dad got competitive and wanted the stakes to go higher. In the beginning he was winning, but I started getting better at playing Rummy after a few weeks of watching. It really pissed him off when he lost money. One time, he flipped the table up in the air, throwing the money everywhere. He couldn't cope with not winning. He was a bad loser. But he wanted to keep going and going and going to win his money back. When he didn't, well, all hell broke loose. Once he even asked for the money back, saying he didn't have any money for the curry that night.

Mum bought a litre bottle of vodka every day and poured some of that vodka into a quarter bottle. She would have the quarter bottle, and he would have what was left of the litre bottle every day. At least five times a week, they ordered a curry. So, when he played me at cards and lost that money, he was bitter and wanted the money back so that he could get a curry. He never played with his vodka money, ever. That was something he could never do without. After a few months we stopped playing cards because I had gotten too good, and he hated losing.

One night, Mum and Dad were arguing over something. I've no idea what it was. All I remember is Mum running past my bedroom door to the front door trying to get out. Dad managed to get to her, turned her around and had his hands around her neck, squeezing tightly. Her face was red, and it was turning purply-blue. She was struggling to breathe.

I came out of my room and screamed at him, 'Stop! You're killing her.'

He just said, 'What are you gonna do about it?' and as he said it, he smirked at me.

I asked him again to let her go, and he told me to piss off. I was crying, but the anger was bubbling inside me. I knew I had to stop him. I ran to the kitchen and grabbed a knife, went back out into the hallway and told him again to let her go.

He just laughed at me, so I lunged forward, sticking the knife in his shoulder. I jumped back, couldn't believe what I'd done. 'He's going to kill me' kept going through my mind. His hands dropped, and he let Mum go. She fell to the ground, and he turned and lunged at me, punching me in the face. He cut my lip.

He pulled the knife out. It wasn't that big, but big enough. He pushed Mum out of the way and went out the front door. I was terrified. I helped Mum to her feet and took her into the living room. She sat on the couch, and I sat beside her.

She said, 'Sharon, you're going to get it now. He's gonna kill you.'

I had nowhere to go and didn't know what to do. I put some things in a bag and left. I could see Dad up at Nannie's house. She was looking at his back. I silently opened the gate and closed it again, and headed for Rose and the tree, straight for the graveyard.

I stayed in the graveyard for three nights, terrified to go home, terrified that he would kill me. I still went to work, and I spent so much time with Rose.

I asked her, 'Why me? Why does it always have to be me? Why does he hate me so much? Why doesn't he love me like he loves Wendy and Colin? Why doesn't he love me like he loves his mum? Why can't I be good? Why am I always bad? I wish I could be good. I wish I could make them happy, make them love me.'

I was lucky it didn't rain for those three days. I had a few days of good weather. I imagined Rose there with me as I slept, protecting me. She was my guardian angel.

Granny Stewart was getting older and struggling to get around. We hired a commode and put it in her bedroom so that she didn't have to walk to the bathroom. I was still popping in every morning to give her tea and toast, and to help her get ready for the day. She loved a fresh new pinny every day, and she liked her hair brushed back. She had soft, grey, beautiful natural curls.

One Thursday morning, I popped in to make her tea and toast, but she didn't seem herself. She was pale and still lying down on her bed, not sitting up waiting for me. She was always full of life, always had a smile on her face as soon as I walked in the room. I could tell something was wrong. She was hot to touch, but she asked me to make her toast and tea. I did, but she wasn't eating. I helped lift her out of the bed and onto the commode, then helped get her ready. I decided to call Mum.

Mum and her sister, Angela, turned up and decided to phone an ambulance. I told them I was going to the hospital with her, but Angela said that her son and daughter would take me. So, Angela and Mum went in the ambulance with Granny. I went in the car with Andrew and Nicole.

We were taken to a little room. The doctor came in and spoke to us all. He said that Granny was deteriorating fast, and that she was not in a good way. I wanted to stay with her, to hold her hand. I loved her more than I loved anyone. She was my Granny; I was the only one that ever went to see her.

Angela said I should go home with Nicole and Andrew, that there was nothing I could do at the hospital. I didn't want to go, but Mum said I should. I went back to my Auntie Jane's. Dad was there. I burst into tears and said, 'I think my Granny's dying, I think she's going to die.'

A couple of hours later, Mum got home. Dad was already drinking by the time she got there. She came into the living room. Her eyes were red. I could see she was going to give us bad news. She just said, 'Granny died an hour ago.' I screamed at her, 'Why didn't you let me stay with her? Why didn't you let me hold her hand?'

I didn't get to see her; I didn't get to tell her I loved her. I just told Mum, 'I fucking hate your sister.'

My Granny was dead, and there was no one else in my life who loved me. I was alone. I hated Angela from that day. I hated her.

I went to Auntie Cathy's house one Friday night for a few drinks with my cousin. Auntie Cathy gave me a video of one of her daughters getting married, so I decided to take it home and watch it. Mum and Dad were up in Nannie's house, so I took the video upstairs to watch. My dad put the video on and started watching. Tracy was a beautiful bride, her dress trailing behind her as she walked down the aisle. Her sisters looked beautiful too in teal-coloured dresses. To me, it was the perfect wedding, but Nannie said all the girls were sluts because their mum and dad went to swinger parties when they were young. She said they probably didn't even know who the fathers of the girls were, they could all have different fathers. I was so angry with her. I loved my cousins. They were all nice. They never treated me badly. I took the video back to Auntie Cathy's the week after, and I told her what Nannie had said. When I got home, Mum and Dad were in Nannie's house, so I went up. The phone rang, and it was Auntie Cathy. She wanted to talk to Nannie about what she's said. Nannie denied everything. She said, 'I would never say anything like that about your daughters, Cathy.'

She lied—she lied to the point of putting my dad on the phone and getting him to lie for her. Dad said, 'Auntie Cathy, Mum would never say anything like that about your daughters.'

They both lied. When they came off the phone dad, came for me, but Mum walked past and said, 'I'll take her downstairs.'

She took me into the house and said, 'What the hell have you done, Sharon? He's going to kill you now.'

She left me, locking the door behind her. I was pissed. I took a can of gas from under my bed and inhaled it giving me Dutch courage. I went into the bathroom, lifted the window, it only opened about four inches and screamed out.

'I fucking hate you, Nannie, I fucking hate you, do you hear me? I fucking hate you. I wish you were dead.'

Dad came home and grabbed me by the hair, slapping my face over and over. He said, 'My ma's gonna kill you, you piece of shit.'

He threw me in my room and shut the door. I must say, for the first time, I didn't feel the pain; I was too high.

Eileen

I was in the city centre one afternoon doing some shopping when I ran into an old teacher from high school. We got talking—I must say it was nice to connect with someone outside my circle. We met up more and more over the next few weeks and connected in a way I hadn't with anyone before. She listened; she cared. I told her a lot about my past, even the scary parts. She was easy to talk to, and I felt comfortable around her. We went for walks in the botanical gardens. It was calm, and she treated me like a normal human being, like someone that meant something in the world.

We would walk in the park every week; it became our thing. We met up every weekend and just walked and talked. She was caring, loving and, after about three months of meeting every week, I told her I'd fallen for her. She told me she loved me too, so we started seeing each other properly. For the first time in my life, I felt whole. I felt like a real person. She made me feel special. The first time we made love was gentle, caring, loving, soft. She taught me what it was to love someone, truly love someone. With no boundaries, no hidden agendas, no pain. We would lie in each other's arms for hours. I didn't want the bubble to burst. I didn't want it to end. I wanted to stay like that forever.

But I was having nightmares about my past, and I wasn't coping well. She could see this. I loved her so much I had to let her go because I had to deal with my past; to fully open up and let my heart feel whole. Life was unfair; I was haunted by my grandfather. He had haunted my sleep since I was 12 years old. I had just never dealt with it before. And she was witnessing this as we slept together. I knew it wasn't fair on her, so I had to say goodbye. I had to let her live her life, a happy life. I will be forever grateful to her for what she showed me, what she gave me. She allowed me to believe that there was love, real love and happiness out there. I will always have love for her for how she made me feel.

I went back to inhaling lighter fuel again. I was at Jane's one night seeing Caitlyn, and after I'd put her to bed, I took the lighter fuel out of the cupboard and went to the bathroom. I put some into a bag and inhaled it. It was such a good feeling. I don't know how long I was in there, but Jane smelt the lighter fuel on me and put two and two together. She said I had to stop what I was doing, or it would kill me. She said I was on a slippery slope.

I didn't care. I had been through so much shit, and I'd lost the love of my life. I didn't care anymore.

I got offered a job working at the Exhibition Centre, and I took it. The money was amazing: £120 a week plus tips, depending on the jobs I was doing.

My first job was selling merchandise for Disney on Ice; The Little Mermaid. I loved every minute of it. I got to see the show twice a day while I sold the merchandise. It was out of this world. I had never seen anything like it before. I made an absolute fortune in tips, sometimes coming away with between £50 and £100 a night.

I never told my parents how much I really made. I gave them £30 a week, and they were happy with that. One of the managers asked me if I would like to travel with them, to work for them. They were heading to Paris next. I said I couldn't go; I don't know why I did that. I guess I didn't feel worthy. I was stupid, really stupid. God knows where I would have been now. I guess I was scared of what lay beyond Glasgow. I didn't know if I could survive on my own.

My second job was working with the group Erasure. I was there the night the singer Andy Bell approached his keyboardist Vince Clark and said he was in love with him, that he was the love of his life. The crowd erupted, everyone was happy and cheering.

I then got to work with Cliff Richard. I took Mum to the concert. He came out on stage in a pink Cadillac. My mum was so excited. I had the best job in the world. I went on to work with the Pet Shop Boys, Simply Red, and Wet Wet Wet, but my favorite had to be Whitney Houston. I was at the door taking the tickets and, when the room was full, I got to stand down by the stage. At times she never wore shoes on the stage. When she came over towards me, I touched her foot. I was in heaven. I had touched the foot of the best singer in the world. I loved her so much.

With all the money I made, I took Wendy to the wallpaper shop to buy paper for our bedroom. We chose black and white stripes for the bottom half and white for the top half with a black border around the middle. We decorated the room with the help of Mum and Dad. I had two giant posters of Patrick Swayze and small posters of Kylie Minogue and Whitney Houston that I put on my side of the room. Wendy was into Take That at the time. She covered her wall and ceiling with posters. I used to say, 'Take That to the bin'. I wasn't a fan of them. It was our sanctuary. We both loved 80's music and would play all the tapes I had recorded on a Sunday. We would get our mics out and sing when Dad was in a good mood.

The work ended because the centre was struggling financially and had to let people go. Unfortunately, I was one of those people, so I went back to the grocery store. Mum was working there part time, too. It was nice working with her, but I think she liked people thinking we were sisters.

Habib

Please note there are scenes that may be triggering in this section.

I had built up quite a bit of money working at the Exhibition Centre, but if I wanted to escape home, and escape Dad, I had to keep working. I went back to the grocery store full time, getting £65 a week. I fought for that money because I told them what I was paid at the other job. Habib, the boss, chose to have me back. But he came to the shop more and more, and I didn't like the way he looked at me. He wasn't looking me in the eyes but more at my breasts. He was scruffy and acted strange around me. But he was my boss, and I got on with my job. They made curries in the back shop, and the whole place stank. He would come down and talk to me while I was working. One day I asked him why he came to our shop, because I knew he had a shop in another location. He said he only came in to see me, and then laughed. I laughed too, thinking he was joking.

One of the other workers there, Malik, was a nice guy. He must have been about 6 foot 5 and was really big-boned with kind eyes. He used to tell me about his wife and kids, and I could see he loved them very much.

He said one day, 'You'll be happy too, Sharon.'

I said, 'I hope so.'

One day, Habib came into the shop when I was pricing items and packing the shelves. He asked to see me in the storeroom. He said he had a proposition for me. When I reached the storeroom, he asked if I would marry his cousin, who was in Pakistan and coming to Glasgow in a few weeks.

I gasped. 'What?'

He said I would only need to stay married for 6 months, then divorce him.

I said, 'I couldn't do that.'

Habib wanted his cousin to stay in the United Kingdom, but he needed to get married or otherwise apply for a visa and wait years. He offered me £3000 to do it.

I refused again. There was no way I could marry a stranger, even for money. He wasn't happy with me for refusing him, and he must have spoken to Mum about it because she came to me the next day and said I should do it.

She said, 'You could ask for more money. After all, you only have to stay with him for six months. You don't even have to have sex with him.'

I couldn't believe she was asking me this. I felt betrayed, hurt. How could she? I couldn't believe this was coming from my mother of all people.

Habib came into the shop a few weeks later and said I had to go to the Cash and Carry with him, because he couldn't spare any of the guys in the shop. I'd never been to the Cash and Carry before, and it was all very new to me. I put my jacket on and climbed in the van and went with him.

We stacked the van and headed to his other shop, which was about an hour out of Glasgow. He kept trying to talk to me, asking me questions about my family, my home life, what I wanted to do when I was older. It seemed like polite conversation. There was no radio in the van, so it was hard to ignore him.

We unpacked everything onto the trolley and wheeled it into the shop and into the storeroom. It was Sunday afternoon, so the shop was closed. We stacked everything in the storeroom, put on the alarm, locked up and got back in the van. About 20 minutes into driving, Habib pulled off the road and into a wooded area. He said there was something wrong with the van. I stayed where I was, and he got out. He went to the back of the van and opened the doors. I didn't bother looking back as I thought we'd be back on the road soon. Habib told me to get out of the van—that there was a problem. I climbed out and went to the back of the van when he grabbed my arm and pushed me in, shutting the door behind us. A filthy mattress was on the floor. I had no idea how it got there. It must have been up against the side, and I didn't see it when we loaded and unloaded the van. He was grabbing at my clothes, and his eyes were dark and angry. He pulled my shirt open, releasing my breast from my bra and kissing my chest. He bit me hard, then started kissing my neck, and while doing that, he pulled at my trousers. I was screaming. I couldn't move. I couldn't push him off. He was heavy. I was terrified. I could smell curry all over him; his beard was rough. He undid himself and pushed into me roughly.

I couldn't breathe because he had his hand over my mouth and nose. I tried to scream, but he pushed harder. I was suffocating. He pushed a rag in my mouth. It made me feel sick. He bit my chest, and the pain was excruciating. I focused on a dark spot on the roof of the van for as long as I could.

He grabbed something to the side of me and started pushing into me with it over and over again. The pain between my legs was severe. I prayed he would kill me. I begged for him to. I fucking hated him.

'Just kill me,' I said in my head over and over. I was screaming through the rag in my mouth. I wanted it to end. I needed it to end. I wanted to die. I prayed for death to come and take me.

His eyes were bulging, black. He had hate and anger in his eyes. The frustration in him was intense. He was rough, aggressive.

I must have blacked out because when I came to, I was on my side, and he was rolling me over and onto my knees. He pushed me forward onto all fours, wrapped his fingers through my hair and pulled back hard. I thought he was going to snap my neck. As he pulled my hair back, he pushed into my back end with force. I screamed out in pain, but my screams were muffled. When he had finished, he picked up what he had before and pushed it into me hard. He was killing me, I was dying. I wished him to kill me.

'Kill me and get it over with you fucking monster.' I must have blacked out again. When I came to, he was climbing out of the van and fixed himself. He closed the doors, leaving me alone on the filthy mattress.

I must have blacked out once more, and when I came round, I was lying in the fetal position. I had wet myself. The smell of blood, urine, sweat and curry encircled me, and I threw up.

I didn't want to live any longer. I was in so much pain inside and out, it felt like I was dying. I didn't want to feel the pain anymore, but there was nothing in the van I could use to kill myself, only a disgusting mattress and a bloody pipe.

The van came to a stop. He opened the doors and pulled me out, leading me down a path to an apartment. I couldn't walk properly; my legs were like jelly.

In the apartment, he pushed me down on a filthy bed. There was dust and dirt everywhere, and there was a prayer mat in the corner of the room. I wondered how he could pray to his God after what he did to me.

He stood in front of me and started to undo his trousers. I couldn't stop shaking. His eyes were dark, and I had never felt so alone and so scared in all my life.

He pulled his penis out and told me to open my mouth.

I wouldn't stop crying and shaking my head, 'PLEASE DON'T.'

He hit me across the face and screamed at me to open my mouth. He had blood on his penis. He told me if I bit him, he would kill me. He pushed his penis into my mouth, grabbed my hair as he pushed himself deeper and deeper. While he pushed, he pulled my head towards him. I was choking.

I wanted to scream. 'YOU FUCKING BASTARD'

He came in my mouth, his body shaking as he came. He peeled himself from my mouth, and as he did, I threw up all over myself, all over the mattress, the floor. He didn't give a fuck.

He put his food in the microwave and sat on the bed opposite me. He gave me a half-bottle of vodka and told me to drink it straight from the bottle.

He said, 'This is the drink you like, is it not?'

I didn't answer. My throat was burning, but I drank it down as fast as I could. I wanted the memories of what had just happened to go away, and the quicker the better.

I was dizzy and in pain all over. I looked over at him, and he was using his hands to scoop up his food. It was disgusting. He hadn't washed his hands when he offered me some food, but I refused.

He still wasn't finished with me, and I begged him to take me home. I wanted Mum to hold me, to comfort me. I was lightheaded and dizzy from the vodka. He slapped my face and told me to take off my trousers. I begged him again to take me home.

'Please take me home. Please don't hurt me anymore.'

He slapped my face again and again and shouted at me to take my trousers off. I undid them, but he was impatient and pulled me to a standing position. He pulled my trousers down and pushed me back down onto the filthy mattress. He used his knees to push my legs apart and pushed himself into me again. The smell of sweat, curry, urine, blood and vodka were all around me.

His eyes were bulging. FUCK, it hurt.

I wanted to scream, 'KILL ME, YOU FUCKING BASTARD, FUCKING KILL ME.'

He didn't kill me, though; he took me home.

I wanted Mum; I needed Mum. I needed her to tell me it was all a bad dream. I wanted her to hold me and tell me I was a good girl, that I had done nothing wrong. He dropped me outside my gate. I couldn't walk. I had no control over my body.

When I entered the house, it was all in darkness. Mum and Dad were in their bedroom drinking.

Mum shouted, 'Is that you Sharon?' and I quietly said, 'Yes.'

She didn't come out of her room and see me; she didn't come to me. I put the light on in the bathroom and ran a bath. I saw myself for the first time, covered in blood, my clothes ripped, in so much pain.

I took my clothes off. I had bruises on my inner thighs, chest, neck and arms. There was blood where he bit my chest.

The smell of blood, urine, vodka, and stale sweat was everywhere. It stung as I climbed into the bath; the water turning red immediately. My hair was matted with blood and vomit. I washed myself as best I could in the bloody water. I climbed out of the bath and had to dab myself dry with a towel. I couldn't rub myself it was too painful. I was still bleeding heavily down below.

Mum still hadn't come to see me.

I put my bloody, ripped clothes in a bin bag, snuck out to the bin and threw my clothes away. I went into my bedroom, took my sheets off the bed, put my pillow on the floor and lay down, covering myself with the sheet. Put my face in my pillow, screamed and screamed and screamed. I cried myself to sleep.

I woke in the morning in severe pain. It was late morning, and Mum had already gone to work. I couldn't move because of the pain. I cried into my pillow, which was still wet from the night before. I curled into the fetal position and held myself. I was soaked with blood, and I crawled to the bathroom, watching out for Dad, but he was still in bed. I had to clean myself and change my pad. It hurt to go to the toilet; it stung. I doubled up the pad so that it covered the front and back end.

I crawled back to my bedroom. There was blood on the floor that I had to clean before Dad woke up. I managed to get into the kitchen, grab a cloth and soap. I ran some water in a bowl, took it back and cleaned the floor as best I could. Then, curled up on the floor in the fetal position, holding myself, wishing the pain away. I cried myself to sleep again.

When I woke, Mum was home. She asked why I was sleeping on the floor. I didn't know how to tell her I had been raped by Habib. Her boss, our boss. I told her I wasn't feeling good. She made me some beans on toast to eat. I stayed lying on the floor until the next day.

I was in pain. I struggled to walk, but I had to see Rose. I had to tell her what happened, what I'd been through. I couldn't climb over the wall, so I walked the long way around, through the main gates. I got to the grave and dropped myself down on the grass in front of her and cried a million tears.

'I don't understand, Rose. I don't know what I did. I don't know why he would want to hurt me. What did I do?'

'I fucking hate him, Rose, I hate them all. I want to die. I can't do this anymore. I can't handle the pain. I want to be with you.'

I lay there with Rose for what felt like hours. It was getting dark by the time I left the cemetery.

I went to see Caitlyn next. Jane noticed something was wrong with me, but I tried to hide it. It was obvious, though. I couldn't walk properly, I couldn't stand straight, and I was in tremendous pain. She took me into her bedroom away from Caitlyn and Nannie, and I told her what had happened, excluding most of the details. She said I should tell Mum. But how was I going to do that? She worked for him, too.

I went home and stayed in my room waiting until Mum came home. When she arrived and did her jobs, I asked her to come into my room where we could talk.

She said, 'Habib was in the shop today. He asked how you were.'

I told her, 'He raped me. He took me to the Cash and Carry and then he raped me.'

She looked at me blankly for a few minutes and asked, 'Will you keep it quiet? We need the money to pay for Dad's drink.'

I couldn't believe what I was hearing. This was coming from my mum—the person that's supposed to love and protect me.

My heart and soul were crushed. She didn't hold me, didn't tell me it would be okay, didn't tell me to go to the police. Nothing. Mum didn't care that I was in tremendous pain, that I was broken.

I didn't go back to work after that. I also lost a lot of love for my mum. I needed her more than ever. I needed her arms around me. I needed her love and support. I got none of it, and it broke me. I was ready to end it all. In that moment, I had never felt more alone.

That night I took enough tablets to knock me out and put me to sleep permanently. I woke up really groggy to Mum shaking me. She stuck her fingers down my throat to make me vomit. I was ill for days after. She saved my life, but I don't know why because she stayed working for Habib. Nothing changed except me. I was damaged, a shadow of my former self. I isolated myself. Only going between my bedroom and the graveyard to see Rose.

I started smoking hash often, inhaling gas and lighter fuel, and when I had the money, I was drinking Mad Dog 20/20, cider and vodka.

I was an absolute wreck on the verge of an explosion. I could no longer keep my food down. Every time I ate something, it reminded me of him in my mouth. I had to bring the food up by putting my fingers down my throat. It became a habit, and I couldn't stop. It was beginning to become a problem. I would binge, then purge multiple times a day. Just another thing to be ashamed of, but one I was in control of, and I needed to be in control of something.

Malik called me one day to ask if I wanted to go to the movies with him and some friends around my age. I went along and was introduced to Shona and Angela. They seemed really nice girls; in fact, Shona would become a lifelong friend.

One Saturday night I was babysitting my younger cousin while his parents went out. I was close to Auntie Grace and Uncle Robert, but I didn't get to see them often. When they came home, I sat up with Auntie Grace, drinking. We sang along to 'A Star is Born' by Barbra Streisand. Auntie Grace had a beautiful voice, and I could listen to her sing for hours. I got drunk that night and told her about Habib and what Mum said afterwards. She was angry with Mum and told me I should have gone to the police and reported the rape. I couldn't now because it was too late. I just needed someone to talk to, someone to listen. I was still angry at Mum for not supporting me, but I still loved her.

Then Auntie Jane hit me with a bombshell. She said she was moving, and that Nannie and Grandad were moving in with her to help look after Caitlyn. She said there was no point in having two houses to look after.

I froze on the spot. How was I meant to protect Caitlyn now? How could I make sure she was safe? How did I make sure he didn't touch her like he touched me? I didn't want this to happen. I didn't want her leaving me. Caitlyn meant everything to me. I saw her most days, but all I could do was sit back and watch it happen. I promised I would do everything I could to see Caitlyn. So, they moved into a 4-bedroom house together in October 1992. It took about 30 minutes to ride there on my bike, but I cycled up there every other day.

Caitlyn was now four years old and able to walk. She would stand on a stool by the window and watch for me coming, then she'd run to the front door and open it for me. She would open her arms really wide for me to run into them and pick her up, swinging her around.

She was such a beautiful little girl, so funny. We would sit in Jane's room, playing songs and singing along to them. Caitlyn's favourite song was *Love is Like a Butterfly* by Dolly Parton. She would get me to sing it to her over and over again. She had long brown hair and loved me brushing it. She was walking and had started talking a little. She was bumping her head off the floor and off the walls and hitting it with her fists when she got frustrated. It was scary to watch. We took her to be fitted for a helmet to protect her head when she hit it on the floor. She was changing. She had her own personality. It still really worried me that Granddad was around her all the time, day and night. I wasn't coping well with that. It was keeping me awake at night worrying about Caitlyn.

One night, I went out with Jane and Joan to the local pub. I ordered a Blue Lagoon, and Jane and Joan ordered Sex on the Beach cocktails. We must have been there for at least three hours. We listened to music and danced and had a great night. We decided to do it once a week. I would stay at Jane's house, sleeping beside her. I needed to be close to Caitlyn, and that was the closest I could get. I was almost 18 years old.

But I felt like I was in a living nightmare with all that had been done to me. I had no one to talk to. I couldn't tell Jane and Joan that their father had raped and abused me for years. They both knew what their brother was like and how abusive he could be; they had seen it many times, but I think they were scared to stand up to him, so they said nothing.

I was still getting high most days, losing my mind with worry thinking of Caitlyn being in the clutches of Grandad all the time. I needed an out, but I didn't know what to do. When I was high on hash, I got sentimental, really depressed and would think too deeply. I couldn't do anything to fix the situation, so I decided to take "the easy way out" and take my life. I got the sharpest knife from the kitchen, sat in my bedroom and swallowed a whole box of co-codamol painkillers. I sliced my wrists, but the blade wasn't sharp enough and didn't cut deep enough. I went to sleep and woke up in the hospital with a tube down my throat. Mum had called an ambulance. I woke in a panic, not sure what was happening, flailing my arms around. I was so scared. All that went through my mind was I shouldn't be there. I should be dead.

My stomach was pumped, washed out with saline, then everything was sucked out. I was then given charcoal to make me vomit. I had to stay in hospital for a few days. It's not nice having your stomach pumped; it feels horrible. I couldn't leave the hospital until I had seen the resident psychologist.

She was a lady and didn't look like a doctor, but she was just a normal human being. She sat by my bedside and asked me what was happening in my life that would warrant me taking my life. At that moment, all I wanted to do was see Rose, talk to Rose, to be with Rose. I told the psychologist everything was fine, and I told her I was just depressed, that I didn't mean to kill myself. I don't think she believed me, but she couldn't force me to say anything else, and so it was left at that. After 4 days, Mum picked me up, and we went home on the bus.

Dad got angry with me that afternoon, that they had wasted money on Mum's bus fare coming up to visit me. He wouldn't have cared if I'd died. He didn't care about me. All he cared about was his drink.

My 18th

In June 1993, Auntie Jane organized an 18th birthday party for me at Mum and Dad's house. I got money and 4 bottles of vodka as presents. Hilarious gift? It was a fun night, though. I dressed in a pink suit with a white polo neck. Most of my family attended: cousins, aunts, uncles.

It was strange seeing Ronald and his friend there. I hadn't seen him in a while. Dad was happy to have a party. I loved all of the music of the 60s through to the 90s, and I was up dancing half the night. I could be the life and soul of the party when I was drinking. Everyone thought I was fun, but inside I was a mess. Auntie Jane had organized a gorillagram. He came in, picked me up and carried me outside into the middle of the street. I was embarrassed, but I couldn't fault Auntie Jane for what she'd done as she was trying to make me happy.

After a few more drinks and dancing to a few more songs, I decided I was going to do something bold. A guy who used to come into the shop when I worked kept asking me out, and I kept saying no. He lived just around the corner from us and, because I had been drinking, I had the confidence to go to his door. I knocked and he welcomed me in.

Mark lived with his grandfather in a two-bedroom house. I really liked him, but I was always scared to tell him that. We were standing in the hallway when he turned around and looked at me. I kissed him, and he kissed me back. I was really doing this; I was going to have sex with this man. We went to his room and slowly took off each other's clothes, lay on the bed in our underwear and kissed. But I could feel myself getting more and more anxious, more scared. I allowed him to take my pants off, and he took his own off. He climbed on top of me and inside me, and that's when I started to panic. I could see and feel Habib all over again. It hurt too much. The pain inside was just too intense, and I didn't see Mark on top of me—he had turned into Habib. I pushed him off, jumped off the bed, got dressed and ran out the door as fast as I could. I didn't stop running until I was home.

The party was still going on, and everyone was dancing and in good spirits, but I was crumbling inside. I was a mess; I didn't know if I would ever get past what happened to me. I eventually joined the party again. It was in full swing. Everyone was happy and enjoying themselves. I stayed up talking and singing with Auntie Grace. We walked to one of the local grocery stores at 6:00 a.m. to get cigarettes. We then walked home again and went to bed, waking up later with huge hangovers.

Chapter Seven
1993 – 1996

Wendy got her first proper boyfriend, Brian, at 15. He was 17. He seemed a nice boy, but he sold hash and acid. I started buying my hash from him, but I wouldn't go deeper into the drug taking. I had speed, but that's as hard as I would go.

Wendy and Brian seemed good together. Brian didn't take drugs, he only sold them, so Wendy was safe, and I was grateful for this. Dad liked Brian because he would drink with him. But when he was drunk, he didn't like Brian and Wendy together in that way. She was his baby girl. One night he walked in on them in bed together, so he went to the hall cupboard and took out the hedge trimmer, starting it up. He went back into the room threatening to cut Brian balls off. Brian jumped out of the bed, grabbed what clothes he could and ran out the door. It was all forgotten and forgiven a few days later.

Brian was a smoker, too, and brought out some hash in front of Dad one night. Dad asked what all the fuss was about, so Brian made up a joint, lit it up and took a few puffs. He got down on the floor where Dad was and told him to open his mouth, blowing the smoke into his mouth a few times. Dad felt the effects immediately—he was high—and, a short time later, he hit the giggles. He wouldn't stop laughing and got the munchies. Mum had to make a pile of sandwiches to satisfy his hunger. I had never seen him like that before and it was good. Not that he was high, but that he had lightened up for once.

Aunty Joan invited me on a night out in the city centre at one of the nightclubs. I was happy to be invited, and it was just the two of us. I went to her house, and we went out around 9:00 p.m. She took me to a pub just around the corner from the nightclub while we waited on the club opening at 11:00 p.m. We had a few vodkas and danced a little. I was having a great time. We were at the front of the queue when the club opened and went straight to the bar for drinks, then onto the dance floor where we stayed for most of the night. I went back to the bar to order a drink, when a guy started talking to me. I wasn't interested but was being polite to him. Joan joined us, trying to chat the guy up, but he wasn't interested in her. I introduced her as my aunt. That didn't go down well with her, either. I guess she didn't want to be seen as being that much older than me. The guy bought us a drink. Joan picked up her bag and said she was leaving. I said goodbye to the guy, but she said, 'No, you stay and have fun,' but I didn't want to. She pushed it, so the guy said, 'I'll take her home,' and just like that Joan left me there. I realized a short time later; Joan had my purse, so I had to rely on this guy getting me home in one piece. I must admit I was scared. We got in a taxi together and the guy gave his address, not asking me where I needed to go. I quickly gave the taxi driver our address and asked if he could take me there first.

He said sure, but the guy said, 'You should come to my place.'

I started to panic a little more. He said, 'Come back for a few drinks.'

I said, 'No. I'd had enough and really should go home.'

After a bit, the guy pushed again, telling the driver to head to the other address first. But I said to the driver, 'Please take me home first. PLEASE.'

He took me home and I got out of the taxi as quick as I could. I was trembling inside, feeling sick. I couldn't believe Joan just left me there, that she was okay with that sort of thing. She spoke about the many affairs she'd had over the years, and yet she was married with six kids and had anorexia. She even claimed she had an affair with her husband's boss, who lavished her with expensive gifts. She was never truly happy in her marriage. I think inside she disliked her husband very much. She wasn't a happy person.

John

Mum and Dad decided to have an anniversary party, family members mostly. They were married just after Christmas in 1974 aged just 19 and 17 because they were three months pregnant with me. Around 20 people came. We were spread between the living room, hallway and kitchen.

The party was all a go, everyone was having a great time. We were up dancing all night. Around 9:00 p.m. the doorbell went and John, a boy I knew from my time working in the shop was standing there. He looked smart in black trousers and a crisp blue shirt. He was quite tall, around 6 feet. I had invited him to the party a few weeks before but didn't think he would show up. But there he was, standing in front of me. I didn't know what to do. Auntie Grace came from behind and asked who it was, and I introduced them. She invited John in, and I introduced him to everyone. He handed a bottle of whiskey to my dad—worst drink to give him but John didn't know that. Mum took the bottle and put it into the kitchen, giving John a drink from it. We danced the night away to the 70s and 80s. Mum put on a disco mix, *I Will Survive, Dancing Queen, Oh, What a Night*.

My cousin, Ronald, was a little standoffish with John. Almost seemed jealous. We had a great night singing and dancing. Poor John was put through the ringer with my Uncle Robert telling him he had to do right by me or he would go after him. I only had that one date. I reckoned that would have been the last one. At the end of the night, I walked John to the corner, and he asked to kiss me. He was gentle and asked if he could see me again. I said yes.

We saw each other often over the next few weeks. I met his mum, who was very protective of her boy. She would walk into his room without knocking every hour or so. We were never doing anything, just talking. He loved his car magazines and talked about cars nonstop.

One night he said, 'Maybe it's time to go all the way.'

I got really anxious and said, 'I'm not sure if I'm ready.'

Not after what happened with Mark. I knew I didn't like it then, so why would it be any different now?

He said, 'Maybe we should go to the loch in the car.' He said, 'I have flavoured condoms.'

This terrified me more after what Habib made me do.

I walked home that night, playing the evening over in my head. I needed to talk to someone. Mum was in the kitchen when I got home and I asked her if we could talk, and would she keep it to herself. She said she would.

I told her, 'John has proposed we have sex, he said he has flavoured condoms.'

She laughed and said, 'What are you going to do?'

I said, 'I am scared and don't know how to tell him no.'

She didn't give me advice, just thought the whole thing funny. I went to my room and cried into my pillow.

The next evening, I answered the door to John's mother and brother. She started screaming at me.

She said, 'My son would never talk about flavoured condoms or taking you to the loch to have sex. He's a good boy and would never dream of such a thing.'

I said, 'What are you talking about?'

She said, 'Your mum is telling people in the shop all kinds of things about my son.'

No wonder she was mad, I would have been mad, too. I called on my

mum and she came to the door. John's mum shouted at her.

My mum said, 'I didn't say anything to anyone in the shop.'

John's mum said, 'You told his aunt and his aunt told me.'

Mum couldn't get out of that one, she had done it and there was no getting away from it. I apologized to John's mum and she said don't you ever come near my son again.

I must say a huge part of me was relieved I didn't have to see him again. I didn't know how I was going to let him down.

The Last Time

I went to visit Jane and Caitlyn and decided to stay over. I stayed up longer to catch the end of a program I was watching. Grandad came into the living room and sat beside me. My body tensed. He put his arm around my neck and whispered in my ear, 'You were awake all those years, weren't you? You pretended you were asleep.'

My eyes filled, and a tear escaped. I wanted the floor to open and swallow me whole. He pushed me back against the arm of the sofa and started kissing me and rubbing himself against me. I pushed against his chest, not wanting this to happen. Caitlyn, Nannie and Jane were in the house. I turned my head away from him just as the door was shutting. Someone had seen what was happening and just walked back out. It wouldn't have been Caitlyn—she would have burst in—and I'm sure Jane would have said something. It must have been Nannie, and she must have seen what was happening and walked right back out.

He didn't have sex with me that night. In fact, he didn't have sex with me ever again.

A few weeks later, I was having drinks with my Auntie Maria and cousin Carol. I told them outright about Grandad and what he had done all those years. Auntie Maria held me, told me to tell Mum and the police. I was terrified when she said this. Auntie Maria was my Nannie's sister, but she believed me. She told me the only way forward was to speak up about it.

I went home that night hoping to talk to Mum, but she and Dad were drinking in their room. I wouldn't be seeing her until after work the next day.

It was Sunday, and I went in to help out at the handicap centre. I loved helping out there. I sat and talked with the residents or worked with Auntie Jane. When I finished work around 3:00 p.m., I took a strip of Co-codamol and, as I walked, I could feel it kick in. I was starting to feel the effects. I did anything to get a high at that time, and pills were cheap.

That day I went to the phone box outside the pub and phoned Auntie Grace. I don't know what came over me, but I just blurted it out.

'Grandad has been sexually abusing me and has been since I was eight years old.'

Auntie Grace screamed down the phone, 'What the fuck are you talking about, Sharon? What the hell is wrong with you? Do you know what you're saying? Do you really know what you're saying?'

She gave the phone to Uncle Robert. He said, 'What the fuck is going on, Sharon?'

I told him, 'It's true. Please believe me.'

I hung up the phone and slowly walked home to await my fate. I took a detour on the way and went to see Rose, to say goodbye to her. I sat in front of her, tears rolling down my face, and told her I would be seeing her real soon. I then walked home knowing what I had to do next. I knew that now I had told someone in the family, all hell would break loose. I knew I had to end it, and it had to work this time. All I wanted was to save Caitlyn. I had to save Caitlyn, and I prayed that by speaking out I had done that. When I got home, Wendy told me Mum and Dad were up seeing Nannie and Grandad. I knew it was just a matter of time before everyone knew. I went into my room, sat on my sofa and took a whole box of Co-codamol and waited.

The phone rang, and Wendy came to my room to tell me Nannie was on the phone for me. I held the phone to my ear and Nannie screamed, 'You fucking little whore. How dare you fucking do this again. What the fuck are you playing at? I will fucking kill you when I get my hands on you, do you fucking hear me?'

I just said it was true. I didn't have the strength to fight back. Dad came on the phone and said, 'What the fuck are you playing at? You trying to ruin this fucking family? Just you wait until I get home.'

That's when I started to panic. I had to be dead by the time he got home, otherwise death by his hands would have been worse. It didn't bear thinking about. I went into the kitchen and took one of the knives, went back to my room and slit my wrists. I knew my parents would be home soon, so I phoned my friend, Shona, to come and get me. Twenty minutes later, the door went. Wendy came to my bedroom door and said it was Shona. I wrapped my wrists, grabbed a few things, gave Wendy a hug, told her I loved her and left.

When I was leaving, Mum and Dad were getting out of a taxi.

He said, 'You're not going anywhere. We need to sort out this shit that you've caused.'

I said, 'I'm sorry but I have to go.'

He grabbed me, pulling the towel off my wrist. My mum and Shona gasped. Shona said, 'I need to take her to the hospital.'

He grabbed my arm tighter but then let go. Shona picked up the towel wrapping my arm again and got me into the car.

She took me to the hospital where they stitched and dressed my cuts and pumped my stomach. Shona said I was going back to stay with her when I got out of hospital. I was in hospital for 5 days. I had to see a psychologist every day I was there. She referred me to see someone outside the hospital when I went home. Mum called the hospital every day, but I refused to see her. On the day I left the hospital, I phoned Mum and asked her to pack a bag for me and that I would come by to pick it up. Shona went to the door to get the bag, but Mum came out and got in the car with me.

She said, 'We need to talk about this. We need to sort this out.'

I told her I needed some time, that I was just out of hospital.

She asked if I would come back in a few days, and I agreed.

I saw a psychologist for a short while. We spoke a bit about my past, about what I had been through. I told her how I was struggling with coming out and speaking about what happened. I said I missed my family, that I had lost everyone that night. That none of my family would speak to me again. I told her how guilty I felt that my father had lost his family, and I had lost my family. I was torn in two. Part of me wanted to go back and change everything, pretend it never happened, so I could still have my family. The other part of me knew that I had to save Caitlyn, that I had done the right thing even though it didn't feel like it. I was the bad guy because I spoke out. I told the truth, and that hurt people, but I couldn't change what had happened.

The psychologist told me that sometimes the abused becomes the abuser. This terrified me, so that day I decided I didn't want children. I couldn't be a mother because I didn't want to hurt another child.

Auntie Maria contacted me and asked if I would see her. I caught two buses to her place from Shona's. When I arrived, Mum and Dad were there, along with my Uncle Michael. Dad's first words were, 'What the fuck have you done?'

But as he walked towards me, Auntie Maria stood in front of me. She said, 'This is not why I asked you all here. Sharon told me about this weeks ago, and we support her fully. What do you want to do, Sharon? Do you want to contact the police?'

Uncle Michael said, 'Let me take you to see a lawyer.'

Dad looked at me in disbelief. Mum turned round at that point and said, 'She's telling the truth, he raped me too.'

We all looked at her in disbelief.

Dad said, 'What the fuck are you talking about?'

She said, 'Nine months before Colin was born, I was raped by him and don't know if Colin was your grandfather's or your dad's.'

This information blew everyone away. I stood there in shock, not knowing what to do or say. All I could think was, 'Why the hell would you send me up to him over and over again if he raped you? Why would you do that to me?'

We all looked at each other, not knowing what to say. Dad had to sit on a chair. He looked like he might collapse. I just looked at Mum, but she couldn't keep my gaze. I guess she knew what I was thinking.

Auntie Maria and Uncle Michael sat on the sofa, but I was rooted to the spot still looking at Mum. I turned to Auntie Maria and said, 'I want the police involved. I have to protect Caitlyn.'

I could see the look on Dad's face; he was in shock.

So, the police were called, and two female police officers from the Female and Child Unit came to the house. I was taken into one room and Mum into another. I told the officer everything except one thing—that Caitlyn was my daughter; I had to keep that to myself. I had to protect both Jane and Caitlyn. To the family and everyone, Caitlyn was Jane's daughter, and I wasn't going to change that. But I told the police everything they needed to know. I was told after the interview that Grandad would be questioned, and they would be in touch when that was done. I picked up what was left of my things and headed back to Shona's to stay.

Living with Shona was an experience. She was my age, single and full of fun. She enjoyed going clubbing at the weekends with her friend Angela. I went along with them and had way too much to drink, danced and partied hard. I made out with a girl in the elevator in the nightclub one night. One weekend we went from the nightclub to an afterparty at someone's house. It was around the corner from Jane and Caitlyn. I got all emotional and wanted to knock on the door. Shona had to stop me; I was torn.

I got news from the police that my grandad had been charged with child sexual abuse. They told me that all the questioning of other family members and other people would now take place and that it would take time to put a case together.

I put in for a flat next to Shona and hoped I would get it. In the meantime, Shona wanted to introduce me to her neighbour, Violet. Violet was a psychic medium and performed at local spiritual churches. On the night I met her, as soon as she opened her front door, I smelled strong incense. She invited us in, and as I entered the flat, there was a male figure on his knees in the spare bedroom fixing a bike. He was scruffy and had huge glasses.

Shona called out, 'That's Norman, Violet's friend.'

I said, 'Hi' as we passed into the living room. The room felt very spiritual and calm. Violet made us some tea and chatted about church and what she did and when she had another evening booked. She invited us along to watch her work. Norman came into the living room and said we could go together to see Violet perform on the stage. I found her very interesting. She spoke of receiving messages from spirit for people.

Violet was amazing on stage, and many people praised her for being on point with the readings she was giving. She gave a message to one family—a child had spoken to her. Violet described the child to the family and left a message for her mum to stop blaming herself; it wasn't her fault, she had done nothing wrong. The mother broke down and cried. She came up to Violet at the end of the evening and thanked her for the message. She had been hoping to hear from her daughter who died of pneumonia.

We spent a lot of time with Violet and Norman over the next few weeks. Norman was a spiritual healer, and so were his parents. I found him fascinating when he spoke about his life and being a spiritual healer. It was a different world. Very calm and peaceful, no raised voices, no tension.

Norman

I grew close to Norman as a friend. He took me to Mum's to pick up some of my things. I found him easy to be around, someone I could talk to. We spoke about everyday life and a little about my family and past.

One afternoon I got a call from Jane. I was shocked, to say the least. Jane said Mum had given her my number. I asked if Caitlyn was okay. She said she had missed me, but she was great. She said Nannie wanted to see me.

I said, 'No way, I couldn't see her. Not after the phone call I got after I came out about Grandad.'

She said he wouldn't be there, that Nannie just wanted to see me. I agreed to go see her and asked Norman if he would come with me, if he would stay with me the whole time. We got in the car, but I was terrified because I didn't know what was waiting for me. We pulled up, and Jane and Caitlyn were outside waiting on us. I looked over at Norman, my eyes begging him to come with me. He did.

Caitlyn ran to me, and I hugged her tightly. She was beautiful. Jane hugged me and beckoned me to the gate. We walked up the stairs and into the house. I felt sick and thought I would throw up any moment. Jane said, 'Grandad is in the back garden and not in the house.'

She opened the living room door, and we all stepped through. I didn't expect to see everyone in the room. Nannie was sitting by the window as usual, Auntie Joan was on the sofa with her daughters, Katy and Julie, and Ronald was also in the room. I was praying Norman was still behind me.

Nannie called me over, and I knelt down in front of her, and she took my hand. She started crying and told me, 'I miss you and want my granddaughter back.' She told me how much she loved me. She had never told me she loved me; she never cried over me or held my hand. This wasn't the Nannie I knew; it was like she was a totally different person. But I loved hearing every word she said. I craved those words. I craved her hugging me, loving me.

I cried and said, 'I love you too, I miss you, I miss all of you.'

Auntie Joan stood up and came towards me. She put out her hands, and I stood up. She hugged me tight and said she loved me. My cousins, Katy and Julie, hugged me too.

Ronald stepped forward and said, 'I miss you too, Cuz. I love you.'

He opened his arms, and I hugged him, but as I hugged him, I looked at Norman. I could barely see him with the tears in my eyes. My Nannie asked, 'Is he your boyfriend?'

I said, 'No, he's just a good friend.' I said I had to go, and that I was going to Mum and Dad's to pick up my bike. Jane said, 'Can me and Caitlyn come with you?'

I said, 'Yes.' I said goodbye to everyone, left and got in the car. I cried all the way to Mum and Dad's.

I hadn't seen them for about six weeks and had no idea what I was walking into. I didn't know how my dad would be, sober or drunk.

Jane and Caitlyn walked in first, followed by Norman and me. I introduced Norman as my friend and said we were there to pick up my bike. Dad was sober for a change, and there was no confrontation. Everything was calm. We sat and had a cup of tea, and while we were drinking, the door rang. It was my Uncle John, Nannie's brother. I knew something wasn't right when he came to the door as we never saw him. He would never visit Mum and Dad. But he wasn't there to see them. He was there to see me. He said Nannie had sent him to ask me to drop the charges against Grandad.

Then I knew it was all just a show; the whole visit was put on to soften me up. I felt hurt and heartbroken. I felt betrayed, lost and alone, and bloody angry. I said, 'No way am I dropping the charges and, even if I wanted to, which I didn't, I couldn't; it's too late.'

I hugged Caitlyn tightly and said, 'I love you. Please never forget that.' I told Norman we were leaving and got my bike. I didn't look back. It was all a show—Nannie didn't love me. She'd never loved me. Norman took me home to Shona's. I reckon I cried for days if not weeks.

One night before church, Violet asked if I would ask Norman if he was interested in her, so I went out for a cigarette during the intermission and Norman came with me. I stood on a little wall so that I could be level with his eyes. I asked him if he was interested in Violet, and he said no; he liked her as a friend. I took the opportunity to ask him out on a date, and he said yes. I was shocked at myself; I had never been that straightforward before.

Our first date was at Pizza Hut. In the UK, Pizza Hut had a great salad bar and pizza slices. We sat by the window and chatted for hours about his work, his family, his spiritual side, and life. I told him the basics about me, not too deep. We got on well, and it was lovely. I didn't feel threatened at all. In fact, I felt safe with him. We had a gentle kiss at the end of the evening when he took me home. We saw each other most days after that.

I got my apartment in the fourth block of flats, first floor. I was getting the keys in 2 weeks' time, and I was excited—for the first time ever, I had something that was all mine. I couldn't wait to move in.

Norman won two large bottles of wine at work, one white and one rose and brought them to Shona's. Shona had gone clubbing with Angela, so I invited him over to watch a movie and have dinner. We had bolognese and sat back with a glass of rose and watched *Ghost* with Patrick Swayze and Demi Moore. It remains one of my favourite movies to this day. By my third glass of wine, I felt confident and in control. I took Norman's hand and placed it on my chest. He was nervous, so was I, but it felt right. We made love on the floor. He was gentle, and his touch was soft. I had never felt safer in someone's arms before. I was falling for this man. Because we had a few drinks, he slept on the couch and went to work from there.

I was given the keys to my new place, and with help from the government, I furnished the flat. Mum and Dad bought me a double bed, and I bought a new sofa from Mum's catalogue. The concierge gave me a small fridge-freezer someone had left behind in one of the flats. Norman helped me wallpaper the apartment. We laughed a lot while playing music as we worked.

Everything was falling into place. Norman stayed over most nights, except my flashbacks of Habib on top of me were out of control. Whenever we made love, I would get a flashback and scream out, pushing against Norman's chest. I would see Habib's face instead of Norman's. I hated it, and I felt for him. I would end up crying in his arms.

Liz

I got a call from Liz, the social worker I had seen back in high school. She had come to the school when I told Miss Davidson what my grandfather and dad had been doing to me. She said that she wanted to meet with me, that she'd heard that I was going to court. The police had been in touch with her, and they questioned her about our time together when I was at school. They wanted to know what we had spoken about. Liz said she was proud of me for speaking out. We met once a week on the run-up to the court case. She came to my house and picked me up, we would go to the botanical gardens or a coffee shop. I would have been lost without her. She kept me sane when I felt confused and lost. There was no news of the court case, when or if it would even happen. I started opening up to Liz more and more as the weeks went on. She made it easy for me to talk to her. We must have seen each other once a week for a good eight to ten months.

I made friends with a girl named Mandy; she lived in the third block of flats on the first floor, too, and her window faced mine. She lived with her partner and son. We got on well, but Mandy was different to me. She loved talking about sex and throwing wild parties. She would instigate sex with her partner when she saw me on my balcony or standing at my window. This made me very uncomfortable. I loved her, but she was intense. She claimed she was a psychic medium and would read tarot cards for people. I would go along with her and take notes as she did readings. It all sounded the same to me—your son loves playing sports and/or football, your daughter loves dancing and so on. It felt false to me, and she was making a fortune. I stopped going with her to the readings as I didn't like deceiving people.

Shona often popped by. She told me I should get a cat and that a man in my block of flats had a black cat he was looking to re-home, so I went to see him. Blackie came home with me. That cat drove me insane. He would come alive at nighttime, running all over the place. Jumping on the bed when we were trying to sleep. He was wild. I grabbed him one night and stepped out onto the balcony with him. I was going to leave him out there so that I could get some sleep. He scratched at me, jumping from my arms and over the balcony. I looked over, seeing him land on all four paws and run off into the bushes.

I heard nothing of him until weeks later. Shona was shouting up at my window, 'Sharon, I found Blackie.' She was holding him in her arms. I was sleep-deprived again. I found out the guy had been picking up wild cats. I had to find another place for Blackie, and so we found someone who could train him properly. I'm sure he lived a long, happy life; I only pray he calmed down for the next person.

I asked Norman to move in permanently, though he kept his apartment for a while. I was the happiest I'd ever been. I loved having him around. He made me feel safe with the way he spoke to me. He never raised his voice, and he was always gentle with his touch.

The only problem was I was still drinking often. I asked Norman to take me for my half-bottle of vodka one afternoon. I went into the shop and bought the bottle. Norman had parked behind the shop. We both got back in the car, and as he started the car up, it rolled back into a ditch. I panicked but all I could do was sit there and hold the bottle in my arms. A few taxi drivers from across the road came and helped us. They picked up the back end of the car and pushed it forward, back onto the path again. I was embarrassed because I was still sitting in the car holding onto my bottle.

I thought long and hard that day about what I was doing to myself and to him. I had to stop drinking all the time. It was one of the hardest things I've had to do as it had been my crutch for so long. I didn't know how I was going to give it up. But I knew if I kept going, I was going to lose myself and lose Norman, too. That day I stopped drinking as much. I still drank when I went out, but that wasn't often. I stopped taking pills. I stopped taking hash. I was sober for the first time in my life.

It was hard. I could feel myself getting agitated a lot. I was having withdrawals. I didn't know what to do with my hands, so I started smoking more. But it was better than being drunk all the time.

We were still waiting to hear about the court case. All I knew at that point was we were going to court and that my grandfather was no longer allowed in the house where Caitlyn lived. He was no longer allowed to be around children. At least I knew that Caitlyn was safe.

I was speaking to my parents again. I didn't go and see them much but called sometimes from the pay phone outside the flat to see if Mum was okay. I prayed things would calm down a bit at home. Dad was being more emotional than physical. He was crying all the time that he had lost his Mum, that he missed his mother. The whole family had stopped talking to him because of the court case. He would sometimes call me late at night and ask if I was sure it had happened. Was I sure his father touched me, sexually abused me? I was livid. A few times, he wanted me to drop the charges, but I ignored him.

On my 20th birthday, Norman and I went out with Violet and Shona to a nightclub called the Cat House. Violet said I should get myself a catsuit, so I bought myself a leather all-in-one catsuit, and we went out clubbing. Violet was wearing a leopard all-in-one catsuit, Shona was wearing trousers and a top, and Norman was in jeans and a shirt. I thought I looked amazing with my makeup on and my hair down.

Norman took me to the 'car park in the sky', which was at the top of a very large hill where he used to go sometimes. We stopped off at Zico's and got pizza and some chicken pakora, then headed up to the car park. There were only a few cars, and Norman opened the sunroof just as a plane flew overhead. The noise was overwhelming. It was a special thing to do, and we decided to do it once a week. We would grab some pizza and pakora, head straight up to the car park in the sky and just watch the planes fly overhead. It became our thing.

A few weeks before Norman's birthday, I was having really bad cramps. I didn't feel good at all, and Mandy said I should go to the hospital. When Norman came home from work, he took me along with Mandy. I was taken into a room where a doctor came in and checked my tummy. He did an internal examination and there was clotting. I was having a miscarriage. The doctor said that all the major clots were gone, so I didn't need a full D and C (dilatation and curettage).

I got into the car beside Norman, and I stared out of the window as we drove home. We dropped Mandy off, and as we drove on, I said to

Norman, 'We've lost a baby. I've lost a baby.' I didn't know how to feel. Part of me felt relieved; the other part of me felt heartbroken.

We had been together just over a year, and when watching a movie one night, I turned to Norman and asked him to marry me. I don't know what came over me, but it felt right. I don't know how I managed to form the words. But there they were. 'Norman, will you marry me?'

I loved this man so much. I knew he'd never hurt me. I knew I wanted to be with him for the rest of my life. I think he was a bit shocked that I had asked, but he looked me in the eyes and said yes. The next day we went into the city to get a ring. Norman came out of the shop with a single red rose that opened up and held an engagement ring. He then asked, 'Will you marry me?'

I said yes.

I phoned my parents. Mum was surprised, but I think she was happy for me. In fact, I think she really liked Norman. We then told Shona, Mandy, and Violet. They were all really happy for us, shocked but happy. I guess it was sudden, but it felt right. We had been together for over a year by then.

Meeting Norman's Family

We went down south on holiday to meet Norman's sister Chrissie. She lived on her own with two beautiful dogs, Snoopy and Muttley. After meeting her, I thought it wouldn't be as scary to meet his parents. Chrissie took us out to the pub one night for a few drinks. We played some pool with the locals and had a few laughs. We got on really well—she was likable. But, as usual, I got too drunk. When we went home, I fell in the garden and couldn't get up. I was laughing so hard. We were sleeping on a sofabed, so as I climbed over Norman, I stepped on his ankle, twisting it. He cried out in pain. I was still screwing up by getting drunk. I was a mess, but I was still the life and soul of the party because I was drunk. We spent a few days with Chrissie and the dogs, went out to dinner, spent our nights talking and getting to know each other. Norman's parents lived in Dubai at the time, so I didn't get to meet them for a while yet.

We held our engagement party in August 1995. Norman's parents were arriving two days before. I was terrified of meeting them and what might they think of me. Would I be good enough for their son? Was I worthy?

Chrissie was driving Norman's mum and dad from England to Scotland to meet me. Norman was at work, so I had to meet them on my own. They were coming straight to the apartment. I begged Wendy to be with me when they arrived. We kept looking out the window all morning because we didn't know what time they were arriving. A car pulled up across the road, and three people stepped out. I recognized Chrissie. Norman's mother was holding flowers. The butterflies in my tummy were going crazy, and I felt sick. Wendy grabbed my hand, held it tight, and told me I would be fine. 'They'll love you,' she said. The door went, and I opened it slowly to see three people smiling back at me.

Chrissie gave me a hug and said, 'This is Mum and Dad.'

They both gave me a hug and Norman's mum gave me flowers. I invited them in, and Chrissie asked where the kitchen was and if she could she make some tea. She loved her tea, just like Norman. Their parents were the same. I was praying that Norman would get home soon, but they seemed easy to talk to and we got on really well.

It was agreed that Chrissie would stay with me, and Norman's parents would stay with him in his apartment. Norman came home early that afternoon. They hadn't seen each other in quite some time as they had lived in Dubai for five years. Norman spent the next two days with his parents and sister before the engagement party. I spent time with them, too. We went to one of the big parks for a picnic and enjoyed the scenery. The day of the engagement party arrived very quickly.

Engagement Party

We had organized the engagement party for the 20th of August 1995, the date we would officially be engaged. I wanted to see my Auntie Cathy and invite her and her family. But first I had to tell her about her stepbrother, my grandad. She was estranged from the family so didn't know what had happened. Norman came with me. I took Auntie Cathy into a room, sat her down on the bed and told her that her brother had sexually abused me for eight years. She cried, said she was sorry and that he had abused her as a child too.

I was in shock, and I didn't know how to react to that. First Mum, now my aunt. What could I say? She said she would love to come to the party with Uncle Joe and my cousins, Kim, Sharon, Tracy and Joe. Dad hadn't seen his aunt in many years, and I knew he would be surprised.

The party was a huge success. Dad was happy to see his family. A few of the neighbours from my childhood came. Mandy and her family came.

We hired a DJ and had a great night drinking, dancing, singing and hugging family and friends. It was nearly Mum's birthday, so I got up on the mic, thanked everyone for coming and I asked them all to sing Happy Birthday to her. Mum was happy with this. I think she was pretty tipsy by then. I hadn't seen her that happy in a long time. She then took the mic and thanked everyone for coming, especially the family that my dad hadn't seen in a long, long time. She said it was a lovely surprise. She also congratulated Norman and me and wished us happiness. She then started singing, so the night ended in everyone singing karaoke.

Norman's dad videoed the whole night, so we had lots to look back on. It was great because there were no arguments, no fights, it was just a really good night.

Norman's parents and sister stayed a few more days, then returned to England and Dubai. Norman gave up his apartment after that and moved in with me permanently. I loved having him around. We spent our nights curled up on the sofa watching TV or listening to music.

Dad was calling night after night, telling me he had lost his family, asking if what happened was real and if I would just drop the charges. I was losing my mind, felt like I was going insane. He called me one day, going on and on as usual, and I got really angry at him, and at Mum for not doing anything to stop him. I found I could be really brave on the phone. He couldn't hit me.

I said, 'I know you're hurting, but you can't keep doing this.'

I told him to stop phoning. I said if he phoned me bringing it all up again, I would hang up on him.

I phoned Mum later when she was home from work and told her it had to stop and if it didn't, I would change my phone number.

He phoned again a few days later, and I asked where Mum was. He said she was at work. I got angry and just let it out. In a way, I wanted to take his mind away from his father and his family.

I was in a really bad place with all the calls. I went into a deep depression, wanting to drink all the time. Norman was worried about me. He would try talking to me, and sometimes I found myself getting angry and agitated with him. On the phone, I told Dad that Habib raped me two years before. I needed to change the topic from his family and him talking about missing them all the time. I also wanted to get all the frustration I was keeping inside about Habib and the fact Mum was still working for him.

He went quiet, and I thought he had hung up. He said he had to go and hung up on me.

This infuriated me. I lost it at the only person in front of me—Norman. Norman phoned Mandy, and she came over and tried calming me down. She and Norman decided to drive through to Glasgow and pick up my parents. They said we needed to get everything out in the open.

While they were gone, I went into a rage, taking a knife to my walls and doors. It was the only thing I could do not to cut myself and end it all. I had had enough. I was exhausted with not sleeping and the nightmares I was having each night, all Habib raping me and Dad phoning all the time. I was a timebomb waiting to go off, and I felt for the people on the other end of it. I really wanted a drink but had nothing in the house. I needed some Dutch courage to get me through this talk with Mum and Dad.

When they arrived, Dad looked hot, flustered and agitated. They both sat on the sofa facing me. Norman put his hand on my shoulder and said he and Mandy would be in the kitchen if I needed him.

Mum was the first to talk and asked what was going on. She said Dad had just beat the shit out of Habib. I must say, I did at that point think, 'God, he stood up for me for once,' but I think he was more interested whether Habib had touched Mum, too, which she said he never had.

I could feel my blood boil. He raped me. He physically hurt me inside and out.

I was angry at Mum and said, 'You still work for that monster.'

She said, 'We need the money, Sharon. We need to pay for your dad's drink and the bills.'

I said, 'Is everything about money? You drink the vodka too, not just him.'

I looked at him and told him he needed to stop calling, asking me to drop the charges. I said the charges would not be dropped, and I would not be taking anything back. It was all true, and I was protecting Caitlyn.

'If you call me again complaining, I will change my number.'

I don't know where I got the strength that day. I don't know what came over me. Norman took them home, and I fell in a heap on the floor and cried all afternoon.

Norman came home, lay on the floor with me and held me tight. I cried in his arms.

Wendy and her friend Nikki stayed over one night, but we only had one room for our bedroom and the living room, so they slept on the sofas. I woke in the night to Norman, Wendy and Nikki surrounding me. They looked panicked. Norman said I had stopped breathing during a nightmare. Nikki and Wendy were going to phone an ambulance, but I started breathing again. My nights consisted of nightmares about Habib and my grandad. I don't know why I stopped breathing sometimes, but

I know when I was in the van with Habib, I held my breath hoping the pain would ease, but it didn't.

I went to a party at Mandy's. Norman wasn't feeling too good and decided to stay home. I didn't know many of Mandy's friends, but some of them seemed nice. I was drinking vodka and Coke, and I'd had quite a few. People were coming and going from the kitchen, snorting cocaine and speed. I didn't touch that stuff. I hadn't had speed in years and would never touch cocaine.

I stayed in the living room most of the night talking to people and dancing. A few people filled my drink throughout the night. I was having a great time, but around 10:30 p.m., I started to feel a bit off, so I told Mandy I was going home. I only had to walk to the next block of flats. I left and went to the stairwell to go down the stairs, when Mandy's friend's boyfriend came after me and asked if I was okay. I said I was fine, just feeling a little unwell and wanted to go home. He said he would walk me home, but I told him I was fine. Then he pushed me up against the wall and started kissing me and touching me. I pushed him back and called out. I felt really dizzy, not at all feeling myself. I tried to shove him away, but he put his hand over my mouth and kept kissing down my neck. I managed to push him off and screamed as loud as I could. He ran off back towards the party, and I ran as quickly as I could down those stairs.

I ran all the way home and sat on the edge of the bed. I was all over the place. Norman woke up and asked if I was okay. I told him I wasn't feeling very well and felt dizzy. He put on the light and looked at me. I told him what had happened because he could see I wasn't myself. I think that was the first time I had ever seen Norman angry. He wanted to go to the party and find out who had hurt me. I begged him not to go, just to stay there and hold me. I was paranoid and scared. I needed Norman to be close by, to hold me and tell me it was okay. I needed to feel safe in his arms. He held me until I fell asleep.

I called Mandy in the morning and told her to come to my apartment, because I needed to talk to her. I told her what had happened, and she didn't believe me. She said her friend's boyfriend would never do something like that because he was too much in love with his girlfriend.

Norman told her I was high, not just drunk, and that I'd come home in a state. He told her it took ages to calm me down, that I wasn't myself. She didn't seem to care. She believed that he wouldn't do something like that. This caused a strain on our friendship. It was never the same again.

My older cousin, Sharon, invited me to her place for a few drinks one night. Her partner, Steven, was there, and my cousin, Joseph. Norman wasn't drinking much, but I was on a roll. We were smoking some hash, and I was on another planet. Norman wanted to go home around 10:00 p.m., but I was in party mode, so I told him I would stay on. He said goodbye and walked home.

Joseph and I were up dancing and singing. Sharon was singing on the fake mic and jumping up and down. I was drunk, and when Joseph flirted with me, I flirted back. We ended up in bed together, kissing and taking each other's clothes off, but when he rolled on top of me, I froze and said, 'No.' I couldn't. I got dressed again and lay on the bed. I couldn't walk home in the state I was in. Joseph lay behind me, and we both fell asleep.

When I woke the next day, he was still sleeping behind me. I slipped out of bed. The house was quiet. I walked home in a daze. I had fucked up big time. How could I do that to Norman? Norman, who had done nothing but love me. How was I going to explain this to him? I couldn't keep it from him because I held too much guilt inside. When I went into the house, Norman was sitting on the sofa with a cup of tea in his hand. I sat down beside him, looked at him and was about to tell him, but he actually said it before me.

'You slept with Joseph?'

I said, 'Yes.' He said he saw the way we were with each other. He saw the flirting. I took off my engagement ring and handed it to him, saying, 'I'm sorry, Norman, I never meant to hurt you.' But I had hurt him, and I couldn't take it back. I couldn't change it. I told him he could stay as long as he needed to until he found somewhere to live. We lived each day as friends. He didn't hate me. He was such a gentle, kind man, and I didn't deserve him in my life.

Maybe that's why I messed up bad. Either that, or I was meant to live a life of self-destruction.

A number of weeks later, my parents, sister and brother came up to stay the night. Mum and Dad had our bed, Wendy and Colin had the couches, and Norman and I slept on the floor. I hadn't told my parents we had split up. I didn't want that to be another reason Dad phoned when drunk.

Norman asked them if they minded us popping out for a bit. He took me to a nice pub where we ordered some drinks and sat in a booth. We spoke about everyday things, then he took me to the car park in the sky and opened the sunroof as a plane flew overhead. He handed me a little white bag. In it was a little toy hedgehog with an S on its tummy. On its nose was my engagement ring. Norman said, 'Will you marry me?' I cried and said, 'Yes.' It was one of the most special nights I've ever had.

I hadn't been feeling good for a few weeks. I was having stomach cramps and sickness. Norman decided when we were at Mum's one night to take me to the emergency room. They took me into a cubicle and asked for a urine sample. The doctor felt my tummy and asked how long I had been sick.

He came back and said, 'Miss Langford, you're pregnant.' I was in shock and didn't know what to say or do.

He said, 'Congratulations!'

I left the cubicle in a daze. Norman was in the waiting area and walked towards me.

The doctor and nurses were behind the desk, all waiting for me to tell him our news. I took his hand and walked out the doors and stood just to the right of the doorway. I looked at Norman and said, 'I'm pregnant.'

He held me and said, 'It's all okay. It's going to be okay.'

We drove back to Mum's in a daze. Norman held my hand between changing gears.

We stood in front of the fireplace. Mum looked at me and asked what was wrong. I said, 'I'm pregnant.'

All I remember is Wendy screaming in the background, all excited. She hugged me tightly. Mum stood and hugged me, then Norman. Dad stood and shook Norman's hand and hugged me. I think I was more in shock at the affection from my parents. I never remember Mum hugging me, ever. At that point, I thought maybe a baby could change many things, but I was terrified. The words of the psychologist came back to me. 'Often the abused becomes the abuser.'

Things needed to change, I needed to change, and to do that I needed to do something drastic. I needed to move away from the apartment I was in, and I needed to get a house. But I needed to move closer to my parents again to do that. You see, to get a house closer to your family, you have to live in the catchment area, so I decided to move back with my parents for a short time until I got my own house.

Was I mad? Was I going insane? Was I doing the right thing? All these thoughts were going through my mind, but if I was going to make this work, if I was going to do right by this baby, I had to do something. I had to stop drinking. I had to stop being around certain people, especially Mandy. So I asked my mum if we could move back home for a few months until I got my own place. They agreed. They were happy I was giving them their first grandchild. I had no idea what was in store for me and Norman, though.

We moved in with my parents over the winter. There was slush on the ground, and Norman hired a van to take all our belongings through to Mum's house. Everything else went into storage until we found our own place.

Things were calm in the beginning. Dad was still drinking, Mum, too. We settled in as best we could. I still felt like I was walking on eggshells most of the time. I didn't know when the volcano was going to erupt. I prayed it wouldn't. Wendy was still with Brian, and he was still selling hash, acid and speed. I wasn't buying now because I was pregnant, and I was being good for the baby. It didn't stop the cravings, though.

While Norman was at work, I went to see Rose again. It had been a long time since I'd seen her. There was no opportunity to go at any other time, so while I was staying with my parents, I went back as often as I could. I told them I was going for a walk, and I walked through the graveyard, picking wildflowers as I went, placing them on her grave as I used to do when I was a child. I missed her desperately, but I could feel her with me all the time. She was still my best friend. No one knew my secret, that I actually came to visit Rose every few days. No one would have understood; I had to keep it a secret.

Wendy and Brian broke up, and she started seeing a new guy. I remembered her saying she would never date a guy with red hair. Well, Josh had red hair. They seemed happy together. We went to see Celine Dion in concert. The Corrs came on first. Absolutely amazing. It was a great night, great singers.

Norman had a work Christmas night out, and I played music with Mum and Dad. I'd grown up listening to the 60s, 70s, 80s and 90s; the best music ever. I loved all the music from back then. I think I got that from all the parties Mum and Dad had over the years.

Dad seemed calmer around us, not as angry. Norman came home from his night out and stood by the living room doorway. We all just looked at him, and he burst out laughing. I had never seen Norman drunk before. He would usually have one or two, but I think he'd had three or four or five. He was grinning from ear to ear, and it was nice to see him relaxed. Mum and Dad burst out laughing, and in the end, we were all laughing until we had no idea why we were laughing so hard.

Mum's cat Tibby slept with us every night. Poor Norman was highly allergic to cats. One night, Tibby was really sick. He was shaking, and his nose was warm to touch. We didn't know what was wrong with him. He got on the bottom of the bed and was wriggling all over the place. I tried to put my hand on him, but he kept wriggling away from me. Dad came into the room, picked him up and held him tight against his chest. Tibby went limp and died in his arms. We were all heartbroken. Norman buried Tibby in the front garden. We found out later that our neighbour had put poison around her veggie garden to keep the birds away. Unfortunately, she killed our cat.

Dad was going through another period of missing his mother and started hating the English. He was drinking heavily, day and night. We stayed out of his way as much as we could in a three-bedroom house.

One night while we were sleeping, he barged into our bedroom shouting at Norman. 'Get the fuck out of my house, you English bastard.'

Norman had done nothing to aggravate him. I screamed at him, 'If Norman has to leave, I am leaving too.'

He said, 'You can't leave, you're pregnant.'

I said, 'I don't care. I will sleep in the car with Norman. He's my partner, and I love him.'

Dad walked out of the room, closing the door behind him. I regretted going back to that house. What the hell was I thinking? He hadn't changed one bit. He was still the same drunk.

Granny Fraser said Norman could park in her driveway while we stayed at Mum and Dad's. My cousin, Andrew, had been wanting that spot for a long time to work on his cars, but Granny Fraser said no. This pissed Andrew off. He decided to take a knife and slash Norman's tyres one night, which caused a big rift between the two families. Dad and Kevin started fighting again, and Mum's sister Angela became bitter and twisted towards us.

We had done nothing wrong. We were just close to Granny Fraser.

The police were called, but we couldn't prove it was Andrew. There were no cameras around in those days. Norman had to buy four new tyres. I was grateful that after only six weeks of living with Mum and Dad, we got word of a house.

Mum organized a 40th birthday party for Dad. It was just immediate family because we had no other family members left as they'd all abandoned us. Wendy invited her new boyfriend, Josh, Norman, Colin, Mum and Dad and me. We played great music and danced the night away to all the old music. Mum had ordered a birthday cake with a 4 and 0 she put 40 candles around it, and we sang Happy Birthday as she brought the cake in. We danced all night.

I think it was the first time we actually relaxed in Dad's company. I was still a little unsure and on alert, but I needn't have worried. I made some food with Mum, just sandwiches and little cocktail sticks of cheese, ham and pickles. She seemed to be changing a little too.

The night went well—no arguments, no fights. Maybe Dad was realizing what he had and what he could lose.

We got the keys to our new place. It was on the bottom floor of a tenement building. I was excited and couldn't wait to move in. Norman hired a van, and everyone helped us move our things into our new home. We decorated room by room, putting up wallpaper, laying new carpets and new linoleum in the kitchen. It looked amazing by the time we had finished. There was only a little electric fire in the living room which didn't keep the rest of the house warm. We bought a heater for the bedroom, to heat it up before we went to bed. We would cuddle up on the sofa together and watch TV. It was ours, and we were no longer walking on eggshells. I loved my new home, and I looked forward to Norman coming home from work, having dinner and snuggling up on the sofa. I was getting bigger and bigger each day. I was going to be 21 soon.

My 21st

I was heavily pregnant by my 21st, but Mum wanted to organize a get-together, so we held it at my house. Grandad E came although he was struggling with Parkinson's. Mum and Dad, Wendy and Colin were there. We got the karaoke machine out. Wendy loved to sing. She held the mic most of the night. She had a beautiful voice, still does.

I made some nibbles, and while in the kitchen, the song, *The Bump* came on. Dad was running the video camera and wanted me to point to my bump. He was in a good mood. I only had two months left of my pregnancy. Grandad E sang along to some of the songs as best he could while chomping down on a sandwich. Mum got up and sang with me, and Wendy helped at the chorus. Dad sang, but he always sang at parties. All in all, it was a great night. Even Colin got up and danced, and he wasn't a fan. He found the whole thing embarrassing. Everyone went home in taxis at the end of the night. Another successful evening.

Conor

On the 20th of August 1996, exactly one year after Norman and I got engaged, our son was born. Norman went to work, and I got on with my chores. I felt little niggles all morning, but I wasn't sure what was going on.

I had a doctor's appointment, so I got a taxi there around 9:00 a.m. I went in to see the doctor, and when he felt my tummy, he said, 'Sharon, you're in labour, but you've probably got hours before anything happens, so just go home and relax and wait.'

I was excited but scared also. I left the surgery and walked towards the shop Mum worked in, Habib's shop. When I was about 20 yards from the shop, I got a sharp pain and couldn't walk. I didn't know what to do. A neighbour from across the road came running over and asked if I was okay. I told her I was in labour and asked her to get Mum from the shop. She ran into the shop and came back with her.

I said I was in labour, and we had to get home.

Mum said, 'I just have to go make up some meat packs and some rolls for customers. I won't be long.'

I screamed out and said, 'But Mum, I'm in labour. I need to go to the hospital now.'

She said, 'You'll be in labour for hours, Sharon. Don't worry about it, you'll be fine.'

She turned and walked back into the shop. The neighbour said, 'Sharon, I'll get my car and take you to your Mum's. Is your dad home?'

I said, 'Yes.'

She went to get her car, put a towel on the seat and drove me to Mum's. I told Dad I was in labour, and that Mum was making up some meat in the shop. He got angry at her and asked why she didn't just drop everything. I told him she said I would be in labour for hours and it would be fine, but I said it didn't feel like it was going to be hours. The contractions were close together.

After 30 minutes, Mum came through the door. I was crying as the contractions were 3 or 4 minutes apart.

I asked Mum to phone Norman and tell him to come home, but she said again, 'You'll be in labour for hours, Sharon. Let's just tell Norman you're in labour, and I'll phone him back when it's time to come home.'

She handed me the phone, and I told Norman that I was in labour. I said I'd call him when it was time.

The pain was getting more and more intense. Within 20 minutes, I wanted to push. I was lying on Mum's bed, and when I pushed, my waters broke.

I screamed at Mum to call an ambulance, phone Norman back and tell him to come home. Mum put a blanket over my legs and took my shoes, socks, trousers and underwear off.

It was really happening. I was going to have a baby. The ambulance arrived about 10 minutes later, and Norman arrived just behind them. The ambulance guy's name was Colin. I remember that because he said to me, 'You'd better not have that baby in my ambulance. You've got to keep it in until we get to the hospital.'

He put a mask over my face and told me to breathe. They took me out to the ambulance and told Norman to follow. They had the sirens going, and I was praying Norman was okay behind us. He had to be there when the baby came. We got to the hospital, and I was wheeled into a room. Norman arrived about 5 minutes after we entered the room. He held my hand as the midwife looked at me.

She said, 'You can push when you're ready.'

The pain was intense. I grabbed Norman by the hair and pulled him towards me. Poor man had no idea what was happening to him. At 11:10 a.m., my beautiful baby boy was placed in my arms. As I held him and looked into his beautiful little face, I swore to him that no one would ever harm a hair on his head, that he was precious, and he was mine and no one would ever hurt him.

Conor was perfect in every way. He only cried when he was hungry or needed his nappy changed. He was a happy little thing, never any problems. We stayed in the hospital for two nights and then Norman picked us up and took us home. It was all set up and ready for Conor. We had the perfect little family, and we were happy.

I put Conor in the pram every other day and walked the 40 minutes to Mum's. That first day, I walked by the graveyard and decided to go see Rose. I took Conor out of the pram, sat on the grass and introduced Rose to him. At that moment, I felt surrounded by warm light and love. I believe she was there to welcome Conor into the world. I had to share him with her; she was my best friend. I told her I would come by as often as I could, so I went by to see her at least once, sometimes twice, a week.

The local Community Centre was holding a clothes show for local artists. I decided to take Wendy along with me as we hadn't been out together in a long time. We were sitting close to the runway, watching all the models as they strutted their stuff. I fell in love with a black minidress and white polo neck and decided to buy them. I bought Wendy a beautiful top. When we went home, we tried the clothes on. I remember looking in the mirror and loving the way I looked for the first time ever.

Norman and I had a night out while Wendy and Josh watched Conor. I got all dressed up, and we went by the lake and sat in the car for a while after dinner. Norman said I looked beautiful, and for the first time ever I felt beautiful.

The Court Case

I got a letter saying the court case was starting in October 1996. Conor was just two months old. I suddenly felt scared and anxious. I hadn't faced any of my family in three years—that's how long it took to go to court. We went to Mum's in the morning. Granny Fraser and her daughter, Mary, were going to look after Conor while we went to court.

Just as we left Mum's, sister Angela shouted over the back fence, 'I hope he gets away with it.'

I was enraged and wanted to know why she would be cruel, but I had to focus on what was ahead of me that day. Norman, my parents and I got in the car and headed for court. We were ushered into a little room and told to wait there until we were called into court one by one.

I went to the bathroom and saw my music teacher from high school, the one that I told about my grandfather and Dad after Dad had given me a black eye. She was called to give evidence. We said hello, and we gave each other a hug.

As I walked with her back to the little room, I saw Liz Thompson, the social worker. Liz and Eileen (my music teacher) the one I had a relationship with, were sharing the same little room, and my room was next door to theirs.

Liz took my hand and said, 'I hope everything goes well.'

I thanked her and went back to my room.

A guard standing by the door came into my room and called my name, then ushered me into a courtroom. As I stood on the stand, my legs went to jelly. Ahead of me were a lot of tables. People sat at the tables with laptops and paper in front of them. Beyond them was the jury. To my left was the judge, and to my right was my grandfather. Behind him were a lot of seats where the public could sit, but it was a closed court while I gave evidence. My lawyer stood to the back right of the room.

I was asked to raise my hand and repeat, 'I swear to tell the truth, the whole truth and nothing but the truth, so help me, God.'

I was asked to confirm my name and address.

My lawyer said she would ask me a series of questions and all I had to do was answer them truthfully. I was shaking. My lawyer asked the judge if I could sit down, so the judge asked the guard to get me a seat, and they would try it. I sat, but the judge wasn't happy with it as he said the jury couldn't see me properly, so I had to stand. They gave me a glass of water and, as I tried to take a sip, I was shaking that much, it was going everywhere, so I had to put that back down too. The whole thing was terrifying. I thought I was going to throw up. I hadn't seen Grandad in years, and facing him, I was that child again, not an adult with her own child.

My lawyer asked, 'Is the accused in the courtroom?'

I said, 'Yes.'

She asked, 'Can you point him out?'

Without looking at him, I pointed him out.

His lawyer interrupted by asking, 'Can you look at the accused and point him out?'

So, I looked at him and pointed. He had his head bowed.

My lawyer then asked, 'When did the abuse start?'

I said, 'When I was 8 years old.'

She asked, 'How old were you when he first got into bed with you?'

I said, '12.'

She asked me to describe what happened, and that was the hardest thing I'd ever done. To go through every detail of what happened, down to the fact that he had sharp nails, and his nails were brown and stained with cigarette smoke, that his hands shook as he touched my breasts. I was shaking the whole time. It was terrifying having to tell a room full of strangers about my traumatic past.

I was allowed a break partway through. The security guard led me from the room. I could see my mum with Liz and my Eileen, so I walked into the room and collapsed on the floor in front of them. Mum and Eileen held me while I sobbed, 'I fucking hate it, I hate it. It's horrible.' I had a break for 30 minutes before having to go back in and start all over again, only this time his lawyer was questioning me.

His lawyer stood by him, so I had to look at my grandfather to answer his question. Every question he asked started with, 'I put to you…' 'I put to you your grandfather never touched you. He only scratched your arm and back when you asked him to. He never actually touched you sexually. He was only ever a grandfather to you. Is this so?'

'NO.'

The whole experience was like being raped all over again.

'I put it to you, your grandfather was only ever loving towards you, never abusive.'

I was shaking with anger and frustration. I could feel myself getting angry at his lawyer. I screamed, 'He did those things I said. He abused me'.

He said, 'You have had multiple boyfriends, and you have had abortions.'

I said I had had one proper boyfriend, Norman, and I had only slept with one other person before him once. I said I had an abortion. I told them to check my medical records because what they were saying were lies.

Because of how intense the whole thing was and how upset I got, the first day was cut short. I had to stand up in court for two more days and give evidence. All in all, I must have spent three hours in the witness stand over three days. I commend my lawyer; she was amazing, and she was very caring towards me.

My grandfather's lawyer, although doing his job, was horrible and only ever stood by him when asking me questions. When I answered each question, I had to look at my grandfather to answer because the one time I looked away he told me to look his way.

I gave my evidence as best I could and was grateful when it was over. On the third day, after I had given my evidence, the court was allowed to open, and the public were allowed to sit and listen. My lawyer said I could go in and sit and listen if I wanted, but that I might find it hard. I decided to try it and see if I could cope.

I sat in the courtroom with Norman. My Auntie Joan was first on the stand. She said I had been with many boyfriends since a young age, and that I had made lots of things up. She said I had multiple abortions.

I stood up, took Norman's hand, and we left the room. I couldn't remain in the courtroom listening to all the lies that were being told about me. It actually hurt to hear the things that she was saying.

Norman said we were going home, and we were going to pack and go away for a few days. So, while the court case was going on Norman took me to his sister's place in England for four days. Chrissie hadn't met Conor yet, so it was nice to go and visit her while everything was chaotic. It was Conor's first long journey in the car, and he did really well. We stopped every few hours to give him a feed, and off we went. I phoned Mum when we got there and asked how the court case was going. She said that my dad had gone on the stand, then the teacher, then Liz. She said that Auntie Grace and Uncle Robert weren't there. They didn't see them at all. The case went on for five days altogether. We stayed at Chrissie's for four days, then headed home.

When we got home, Norman had to go back to work, leaving me at home with Conor. I saw my cousins passing my house and looking in a few times. I think they were hoping to get confirmation that I was there before they did anything. I phoned the police and told them what was happening. I had to be moved into a safe house. I was told to pack up as many of my belongings as I could take, and the rest of my house would be boarded up. We packed all Conor's belongings and what we could of our own stuff, packed the car and waited on the guys coming to board the house up. They put a big metal door on our front door and wooden shutters on our windows with all my furniture still inside. I was heartbroken. I loved that house.

The first safe house we moved into was really small, but it was enough for the three of us. After four weeks of living there, I saw my uncle cutting the grass outside, which terrified me. He looked up at the window, and

I pulled away, hoping he didn't see me. He was Dad's brother Robert. I let the police know he was there, so they moved us into another safe house. We had Christmas there. It was a much bigger apartment with four bedrooms—too much for what we needed, but it was okay. We were happy there.

We got news a few days later that the verdict had come in, and we had to go back to court the next morning. Mum and Dad came with us and Conor in the car. We were taken into a room to wait. A security guard came to take us into the courtroom. I decided to stay in the small room with Conor as he was sleeping in his car seat, and I didn't want to disturb him. I was anxious as I had no idea what the outcome was going to be. About twenty minutes later, Norman came back into the room. He knelt down in front of me, took my hands and said he was found guilty and sentenced to two years in prison, likely to serve one year getting out early on good behaviour. Two years, Two years. How was I supposed to react to that? Happy that he was found guilty? Yes, but how was I meant to feel about two years. He had taken eight years of my life, and I was still struggling with the aftermath of it all. I went through days of hell in court, just for him to get two years.

Would I go through it all again? Hell yes.

I saved Caitlyn and God knows who else from that monster. I saved myself too. I might not have believed that for a long time, but now I see I did save myself. I am grateful I am here today to tell my story. I no longer have to hide in fear of being touched, groped and looked at in a sexual way. I saved my own life. His name will forever be on the sex offenders register, making it hard for him to go anywhere after his release.

I would go through it all again to save anyone of YOU.

Conor's Christening

Mum told me our local minister wanted to see me. I had known Russell since I was a young girl in Bible Class, Brownies and Girl Guides. But I was at a loss as to why he would want to see me. I went to met with him a few days later.

He said he was sorry for what I had been through with my grandfather and said he would love to baptise Conor in the church on Christmas Day. I was speechless. We weren't churchgoers, so I was shocked he asked. I told him we didn't live in the area and that we weren't churchgoers. He said he didn't mind; he wanted to do this for me.

It was a few weeks until Christmas, so I said I would speak to Norman and let him know. Norman agreed to the christening, and so it was planned for Christmas Day when Conor would be 4 months old. We asked Wendy and Chrissie to be the godmothers, and they both agreed. I told my Great-Granny L, (my dad's mum's mum). She came and sat at the front of the hall. She hugged me and apologized for her daughter and the way she had behaved. I loved having her there. Russel christened Conor in a beautiful ceremony, and then we took pictures. It was pretty special on Christmas Day. We went back to Mum's and Norman popped some champagne. As he popped it, the cork went through the Christmas tree and landed beside Conor in his car seat. Everyone laughed. It was such a special thing for Russell to do, and on Christmas Day, that made it all the more special.

Conor had his first birthday in the safe house apartment. and then Princess Diana died on the 31st of August 1997. I remember Norman coming into the bedroom and waking me to tell me she was dead. I was absolutely devastated by the news. She was too young; it was a tragedy. I sat there all morning watching the news, crying my eyes out. I phoned my Mum to let her know; she was in shock. Such a beautiful soul taken too soon. Heartbreaking.

My Wedding Day

September 12th 1997

We planned our wedding while in the apartment. We wanted something small, just family. I stayed at Mum's the night before. In the morning, Wendy and I went to get our hair done. I got beautiful flowers from a flower shop to put in our hair. I had bought a white dress with a white jacket, and I got Wendy a white pantsuit with a blue blouse. She looked beautiful.

We were married in a registry office. Conor was our little pageboy, and my sister was my maid of honour, and Norman's father was his best man. There were about ten of us in the room as we said, 'I do'. It was the happiest day of my life. Norman's father took our photos. It had been raining, and with people throwing rice and confetti, the stairs were slippery, and Mum fell down, hurting her ankle. It swelled up like a balloon. We all headed back to the apartment. Mum elevated her foot and iced it. We popped some champagne, and everyone had a glass. Conor looked adorable in his little waistcoat. He was such a good boy all day, and I was proud of him.

Some of the neighbours from my childhood, my cousins Sharon and Joseph came, and Wendy's boyfriend's parents came, and that was it. Everyone was having a good time. My dad saw his brother outside and started crying about how much he missed him. I think he cried for over an hour. My cousin Sharon looked after him while the party went on.

Our first dance as husband and wife was *The Colour of My Love* by Celine Dion. I sang to Norman as we danced. I was the happiest I had ever been. Norman's mother and sister made the buffet, and Mum and Dad ordered the wedding cake. However, the cake shop went bust, and we found out the day before the wedding. We had to run around everywhere looking for a wedding cake and ended up buying a huge cake that said 'Congratulations' for £20. Not everything went smoothly that day, but everything was perfect for us; we were happy.

The next morning, I woke with the flowers still in my hair and a little hungover. We had to go and view a house that could potentially be ours. I was running late, so I had no time to shower, just brush my teeth and run out the door. The lady who answered the door just looked at us, mouth wide open. I had to explain that we had just got married the day before and I apologized for how I looked.

She put her hands up and said, 'Listen, as long as you had a great day and that you have a wonderful life together, that's all that matters.'

She showed us around the house. We were happy with it and couldn't wait to move in. We were finally moving back into a place of our own.

Chapter Eight
1997 – 1999

Moving into Our New Home

The day came for us to move into our new home. The lady before us had cats, and they obviously used the living room carpet as their litter tray. We had to lift it as the smell was disgusting, and it was stuck to the floor. I found myself getting agitated and angry as we pulled it up. Norman was calm, as always, whereas I was a loose cannon, screaming and shouting and taking it out on Norman. I kept telling him to argue back with me, but he would just say, 'Why would I do that when I know I wouldn't win, anyway?' He was right there.

We finally got our own furniture back after it had been boarded up in our old house for a year. Everything was musty and damp, as it had been lying in a cold, damp house. We had to buy a new sofa and beds, but we were compensated by the council. They helped us buy anything new that we needed.

We spent Christmas that year with both families. I'd bought a CD of The Smurfs singing Christmas carols, which I played every Christmas morning for Conor—in fact, we still do. He loved dancing to it, and we would sing along. Norman's dad videoed everything, and Conor loved the attention from everyone. He was spoiled with gifts—so many; he didn't know what to play with first. It was the year the 'Barbie Girl' song came out. Conor loved the beat and would stand and dance, not a care in the world. I loved watching him.

Norman's parents had just moved back from Dubai after 5 years away, so it was nice spending time with them both.

I got a call one evening to tell me Dad was in hospital after my cousin Andrew had beaten him up with a baseball bat. Dad was walking his mother-in-law home, and as Andrew was walking towards them, Dad asked him if he was going to visit his granddad in hospital.

Andrew said, 'It's none of your fucking business.'

Dad and his mother-in-law kept walking, but Andrew came up from behind and struck Dad over and over and over again. Dad ended up on the ground and couldn't get back up. His mother-in-law was screaming for help. One of the neighbours ran to get Mum, telling her Dad was lying in the street. They called an ambulance and got him to hospital. Mum phoned to ask if I would go to the hospital and pick him up, so Norman and I drove to get him

As soon as we walked into the room, we could see he was badly beaten: his face was all bruised and swollen. He had bruises all over his body. We took pictures so that we had proof. But Mum's sister stood by her son, believing what he had said, and this caused a huge rift between the sisters and the two families.

I was that angry about what had happened, and I called Crimestoppers and gave a detailed account of Andrew, his drug-dealing and his counterfeit CD racket. A few months later, Andrew was arrested and his assets frozen. He was sentenced to three years behind bars. I like to believe I played a part in putting him there for all he had done.

A few months later, in early 1997, Mum called, saying there was something wrong with Dad. She said he'd slept with his eyes open all night, staring at the ceiling, and he wasn't talking or moving. I dressed Conor and booked a taxi.

When I got to the house, the place felt strange. Mum said Dad was in his room, lying on his bed. She took Conor and stayed in the living room while I went to check on Dad. He was lying on the bed in just his pants and a t-shirt, staring ahead. It was hard to see my father like that. I went back out to Mum and asked her what had happened. She said she had no idea, that she'd just woken up through the night and he was just staring at her. She was terrified and didn't know what to do.

I headed into the kitchen for a cigarette, when Dad grabbed my arm and pulled me towards the bedroom. I didn't hear him behind me. He was standing in the doorway to his bedroom. I shouted at him to get inside and put his trousers on.

He kept saying, 'They're coming. They're coming for you. Can you see them? Can you see them? They're looking through the door.'

He was meaning through the slot of the letterbox in the front door. He said he could see Norman and Josh putting pizza through the letterbox. He was hallucinating.

I told Mum, 'I think we need to get the doctor. I think he's having a mental breakdown, and we can't help him.'

In his room a short while later, Dad was sitting on his bed, saying he could see Doctor Brian in the corner of the room. But there was no one there. When he looked in the mirror, he laughed and said he could see Mum's underwear. He grabbed my arm again and said, 'They're coming. They're going to get us.'

The doctor came and checked him over. She said he was having a mental breakdown and needed to go to hospital straightaway. I said we would take him; I had already called Norman, and he was on his way. We took him to hospital, and they put him in a locked ward for his own safety.

I believe alcohol and the loss of his parents caused him to lose his mind. He was in hospital for two weeks, and we weren't allowed to visit. He was safer there than at home, and at least Mum had peace for two weeks: no drinking, no screaming; no shouting. For once in her life, she had time to herself.

Dad didn't drink for those two weeks, but as soon as he was home, he started again. He didn't remember anything he had said and done the day he went to hospital, and thought we were making it up.

Everything went back to the way it was, and it was like nothing had ever happened.

Norman was offered a job in Dunfermline, about an hour away from where we lived. It was a better job with more money. So, we decided to take the plunge and move away from Glasgow. We moved into a two-bedroom apartment above Colin White's men's shop in the High Street. It was a huge apartment with so much space. The window ledge was so wide, you could sit on it, look out over the High Street and watch the people coming and going.

One day I took Conor to feed the squirrels at the local park, a peacock saw the food in my hand and decided to chase me up and down the park. As I ran up the hill, he ran after me, so I turned and ran down. Still, he followed. Conor was laughing so hard, but I was terrified. I ended up throwing all the nuts and running as fast as I could for the gates.

Around this time, my sister, Wendy, gave birth to her first son, Braidon. We were over the moon for her and Josh. He was 8 pounds 6 ounces, and Wendy was so happy. I was happy for her.

Mum phoned me with the news that my grandad had died. They got the news from Dad's uncle. Exactly two years after his conviction. He served one year in prison and died after the second year in his hostel. He drank himself to death. I felt such relief. He could no longer hurt a child, and I was free. Yet, I couldn't rid myself of the nightmares. Both my grandfather and Habib haunted me every night. Why couldn't I fully move on? Grandad was dead, and I wanted to live my life free of his torments.

I went to Glasgow to visit Mum and Dad and stayed overnight. We had dinner, watched a movie, played some music. I had a few drinks too, so I was in a good mood. I put Conor down to sleep on Mum's bed, but as the night went on, Dad was getting too drunk. He asked me for £3000 to pay off his loans.

I told him, 'I don't have that sort of money.'

He said, 'Norman will have the money.'

I said, 'I won't ask him for it.'

He started getting angry. 'You fucking married Mr Money Bags. He's fucking rich.'

I said, 'He's not rich. He works hard for the money he earns.'

He seemed to think that because Norman had a car and wore a shirt and tie to work, he was rich. He started getting aggressive with me, and Conor started screaming. I phoned Norman around 12:30 a.m. and asked him to pick me and Conor up.

I told Dad, 'You keep this up and you will never see me or Conor again.'

He calmed down and apologised, but I needed to get out of there. I didn't want him to get aggressive around my son, ever. I don't know why I could never find it in myself to walk away from him.

When he was sober, he asked again for money. Mum said they were desperate, so I spoke to Norman, and he agreed to do it. I said we would help them out, as long as they never got another loan. They agreed to our terms, so we gave them nearly £3000.

I'd been naïve. They took out another loan that Christmas. I lost my temper with both of them and said we would never pay off another debt for them. We never got our money back, and I didn't speak to them for months.

We moved into a three-bedroom house in Rosyth, Fife. It was a nice house, two-storey and spacious. We had a garden, which was lovely for Conor.

I was really sick with the flu on our first Christmas there, but I wanted it to be special for Conor. We got him a small plastic train with animals and people. I wrapped them all individually, so he had a lot more to open up on Christmas morning. He loved opening the individual packages, revealing another animal or piece of track. I loved watching him play. He was such a happy little boy, and his happiness meant everything to me. He was going to get everything I didn't. Norman put the train track together, and the two of them played while I made breakfast.

Norman started working month on month off in Angola. I hated it when he was away; I was so lonely. I missed him so much, but we were hoping it was short term.

Our neighbour was a woman named Rachel, who had three boys. We met in the back garden while watching the kids play. Meeting in the back garden became our thing. We'd often meet out there with a glass of wine or vodka and coke. Her three boys loved my Conor and took him under their wings. They played with him for hours while we chatted in the garden. Rachel's friend Connie often visited. She had an animal rescue show on TV every Thursday evening that we watched. We all got on well. Norman had gone away to Angola, so having Rachel next door was a godsend.

Dad Was Arrested

One Friday afternoon in late 1998, I got a call from the police. Dad had been arrested for choking my brother, Colin. I was surprised by the call, but Mum had given them my number. She asked if I'd take him into my home until his court hearing. I said I couldn't, that I had a small child. She said there was nowhere else for him to go, so I said I had to speak to my husband first. She gave me a number to call her back. I told Norman what I knew, which wasn't much, so I phoned Mum and asked what had happened.

She said Colin and Dad had got into a fight and Dad had grabbed Colin by the throat and threatened to kill him. Mum had phoned the police because she was scared he would. She begged me to take him in.

After speaking to Norman and him agreeing, I phoned the police and said I would take him in as long as he didn't drink in my home. I said he could stay where he is if he didn't agree to that. She came back and assured me he wouldn't drink, and asked when I would pick him up. I said we'd be an hour or more.

We put Conor in his car seat and headed towards Glasgow in the pouring rain. As we drove past the Royal Infirmary Hospital, I saw Dad walking on the other side of the road. We turned around and pulled up alongside him. He climbed in, drenched and smelling of sweat. I said I would stop at Mum's and pick up his clothes, but I told him he couldn't get out of the car or go into the house.

Mum had a bag of clothes ready. She asked how he was, and I told her he wasn't good. I didn't realise he'd attacked Colin on the night before and stayed in prison overnight. Mum wanted to go out to the car to see him, but I told her not to. It would have confused everything.

We took him home, and I ran a bath for him. While he bathed, I made some tomato soup. He was quiet and didn't really talk at all. I gave him the soup and bread and put the TV on. He sat in silence, and afterwards I showed him to his room. I knew he'd have been struggling without a drink, but I said nothing. I went to the shop the next morning and rented some DVDs and got the paper and some magazines I thought he might like. He played with Conor and spoke a little about things in general. He was sweating although it wasn't that hot in the house, and he had the shakes. Later on, he asked if he could call Mum, but I said he wasn't allowed to as it was part of his bail. If Mum phoned us, I said that was a different matter.

Later that afternoon, she phoned to ask how he was, and I told her. She asked if she could speak to him. I said it wasn't really allowed, but it was up to her, so they spoke. I left the room for a bit, and when I came back, he was saying my house was like a prison, and he couldn't do what he wanted.

I lost it and didn't hold back. 'You ungrateful bastard. How dare you say that? All I've done is run around after you, and all you can do is complain. I'm happy to take you back to the prison, where you belong. You can leave whenever you want. I don't give a shit.'

He apologised and said he was just missing Mum. She agreed to come and visit him. This wasn't part of the bail agreement, and I wasn't happy, but Mum arrived with more clothes. They played with Conor for a bit and asked if they could take him for a walk around the block, which I agreed to. I thought the fresh air would lift Dad's spirits a bit. They were gone about an hour and, when he returned, he was holding an open can of beer with another 5 under the basket of the pram.

I took Conor and put him down for his nap. When I went back downstairs, I told him he could get the fuck out of my house. I said he could fuck off back to his own house or back to prison. I didn't give a fuck. I was pissed at Mum, too. She'd done exactly what he wanted, and that pissed me off.

Mum said he could go home, that Colin was dropping the charges. I can honestly say I was relieved; he triggered my past traumas with him, but I had to keep telling myself, 'I'm the grown-up now. I am stronger, I have a family. He can't hit me anymore.'

They caught a taxi to the bus station. I saw Rachel later that day, and she said she heard me shouting through the wall.

I got news that Dad's mother, Nannie, had died. It was on both her and Dad's birthday, 26th May, 1999. Not the best news to get on your birthday. Supposedly, she died of too much oxygen from her oxygen tank. I had no idea that was a thing, but that's what we were told. Dad phoned me with the news.

He said, 'I'll let you know when the funeral is.'

I said, 'I'm not going.'

He said, 'You should go and show face. You should come with me.'

So I went to the funeral. While I was sitting in the car with Norman, I looked out the window and saw a young girl standing with a lady. I recognised the girl straight away; it was Caitlyn. She was older, but it was her.

Tears filled my eyes, and I said to Norman, 'That's Caitlyn.' I hadn't seen her in almost 5 years.

At the chapel, I felt like the black sheep. No one looked at me. I sat holding Norman's hand. At the end, as we walked out, I saw Caitlyn at the back of the room with the same lady. She looked at me as I passed her. Did she recognise me at all?

We drove from the chapel to the crematorium with Auntie Grace. We spoke about random things—about how she, Uncle Robert and Joseph were doing.

Caitlyn wasn't at the crematorium. Auntie Grace said she was with a nun, who would have taken her back to school.

I was ignored at the crematorium, too; no one looked at me. I lowered my head and held Norman's hand. I wanted the whole thing to be over with, but I couldn't escape, because we had to take Auntie Grace back to Nannie's house. I wanted to leave, but Auntie Grace urged us to go inside. I had to see if Dad wanted to go home. We went into the kitchen for a drink. It was the only way I was getting through the day. My cousin poured me a large vodka and lemonade and gave Norman some water. I looked for Mum and Dad, but they were sitting outside with Dad's brother and sisters. I asked if he wanted to go home, but he said he wasn't ready to leave. Wendy and Josh were talking to some cousins. I stepped outside the front door, and one of my Nannie's brothers was there.

Uncle George said, 'You feel just like I do, honey, don't you? The black sheep of the family.'

I said, 'Yes, I do.'

Uncle George was disowned when he was younger. He was a drunk but had been sober for years. The family didn't like his wife either, so I knew exactly how he felt. No one spoke to him at the house, just like no one spoke to me.

Norman and I picked up Conor from Granny Fraser and took him back to pick up Mum and Dad. Auntie Grace and Uncle Robert played with him, throwing his socks to each other. Conor was laughing.

Auntie Joan asked to speak with me in another room. She said, 'I am so sorry for what happened to you. I was abused too. He abused me as a child.'

I was fuming. I said, 'Why did you go against me in court?'

She said, 'I had to think about Nannie.'

She was scared of her, just like everyone else. It made me wonder who else he'd abused, because they all started coming out after I spoke out. So many could have saved me, but they didn't. I walked out and told Norman we were going, picked Conor up and said goodbye to Dad. Mum came with us. A few of my cousins, Auntie Grace and Uncle Robert said goodbye and we left.

We took Mum home and stayed with her for a bit. A few hours later we got a call from Dad's sister saying they'd sent him home in a taxi. Fifteen minutes later, Dad arrived so bloody drunk, happy and emotional. Happy that he had his brother and sisters back, emotional because his mum was gone. About 20 minutes later the phone rang. I answered it to Auntie Joan.

She said, 'We think too much time has passed. We can't get back together as a family.'

I said, 'Please don't do this to him. I don't care if I never see any of you again, but don't do this to your brother. He's only just got you all back. He came home happy, don't take that away from him.'

I asked if Uncle Robert and Auntie Jane felt the same, and she said, 'Yes.' I hung up, not knowing how to tell Dad his siblings no longer wanted him. He was already asleep, so I told Mum. She was upset and didn't know how she was going to tell him. I went home and left Mum to break the news.

He took the news badly. 'Not only did I lose my mother, but I lost my sisters and brother all over again.'

He cried over them whenever he was drunk. He cried for his mother and said he couldn't wait to be with her. He was a selfish bastard. It was all about him and what he'd lost. He didn't look at what he had in front of him: his wife, his kids. He didn't think about me and what happened to me or who I had lost. This shit went on for years: him always crying over his mother.

Conor started playgroup when he was nearly 3—it was part of the naval base in Rosyth. He made friends easily and, after a few days, I didn't have much of a problem getting him to go.

I made friends with a few of the mothers: Melanie, Sharon and Helen. They were already friends with each other and lived two minutes from me. We met a few times a week for coffee, or tea for me as I've never liked coffee.

Chapter Nine

2000 – 2002

The next few years were reasonably peaceful. Norman was still working in Angola and coming home every other month. Conor was growing up too fast and was ready for kindergarten.

We got news that my brother's best friend, Ryan, had died. A group of boys had been drinking and crossed one of the bridges over the motorway. Ryan leaned over the railing and fell onto the motorway headfirst. Colin ran down and held his friend as he died. A week or so later, Colin carried his friend into the crematorium, where he was laid to rest. Two weeks after that, Ryan's brother, who I'd gone to school with, went to the same spot where Ryan had died and jumped off the bridge to his death.

Colin was never the same after that. He stopped drinking and became an angry person, picking fights with people for no reason. He was very distant and suffered from PTSD but wouldn't see anyone about it. He started hanging around with people who were into selling drugs. I don't think he ever took the drugs, but he was detached from the family.

Playgroup

I became the leader of Conor's playgroup. It was volunteer run but no one else was willing to take on the job, and I didn't want it to close down. Conor loved it. I had two group leaders and 16 kids. I was meant to report to the naval commander, but I only ever spoke to him towards the end of my time there. The playgroup ran smoothly. The parents were lovely, and the leaders were great.

However, there was one big incident. One warm day, one of the leaders opened up a side door to let in some fresh air, and one of the kids escaped. The boy was found climbing over the fence next to a main road. A few cars had to stop, and a lady brought him back. He said he'd wanted to go and get his mother.

The leader felt guilty and wouldn't stop apologising for leaving the door open. She didn't realise how easy it was for a three-and-a-half-year-old to escape without being noticed. I told her I was sorry, but I had to give her a final warning.

She said, 'There's no need, Sharon. I'm handing in my resignation. I couldn't have lived with myself if something would have happened to that little boy.'

I asked her to change her mind, but she wouldn't. She had been a foster carer for 35 years and worked at the playgroup for 15 of them. She made only one mistake—a very large one—but she felt too guilty to continue. Only a few weeks later, the naval officer decided to close the group.

I was sorry I had to close the playgroup, but Conor was old enough to go to nursery by then.

Norman started a new job in Angola. He worked one month on, one month off. I missed him desperately when he was gone—I felt so alone and lost. I was lucky I had Conor to keep me occupied, and I spoke to Norman as often as I could when he was away, but half the time he was on an oil rig.

I started studying an online psychology course to keep me busy when he was away. I loved it when Norman came home, and we could do family things together. Conor was full of beans—here, there and everywhere—and I started feeling tired all the time. I thought something was wrong with me, but I did a pregnancy test, which was positive.

I told Norman when he came home, and we just held each other. We were both in shock but really happy. We told Conor he was going to be a big brother, and he said he wanted a little brother.

The neighbours had a party to celebrate the pregnancy. Just like my first pregnancy, I drank alcohol. I wasn't drinking as much as before, but it was still troublesome. When Norman was away, the nightmares were worse—memories of being stuck in the van with Habib—and the intense internal pain I lived with daily. I had flashbacks and panic attacks. I couldn't escape my past; I couldn't escape the people. They haunted me daily.

I decided it was time for me to learn how to drive and to do it in Glasgow, where they had roundabouts and traffic lights. It meant I could see Rose while I was there. Conor and I caught the bus and took a taxi to the cemetery. I told her everything that had happened since the last time I had seen her. Sometimes I sat with her for over an hour, just talking while Conor played with his trucks in the long grass.

I took Conor to my tree and showed him how to climb it, but he was still too small. I would then walk to Mum and Dad's in time for my driving lesson. Mum and Dad looked after Conor while I had my driving lesson. Sometimes Wendy came, and she took over. She loved spending time with Conor.

I had a great instructor, and we got on really well, had a few laughs as we went. I felt very comfortable around him. Because Norman had been teaching me how to drive as well, and after my tenth lesson, he told me I could sit my driving test.

On the day of the test, I wore a jumper, and it was really hot in the car. The driving examiner told me to get ready to take off. I checked my seat belt, the rear-vision mirror and took off. I did a 'reverse around the corner,' three-point turn and a hill start. I was happy with how I went but a bit unsure with the 'reverse around the corner.' When we got back to the test centre, the examiner put his file in front of me. There was only one tiny mark on the sheet.

He said, 'That's one of the best driving tests I've ever seen. Just one small mark of where you reversed round the corner and were out from the curb a bit. But it was a perfect turn.'

I was over the moon because I'd been terrified and sweating buckets that whole hour. But I'd passed my driving test first time, and I couldn't wait to tell Norman. I was now able to use our car, so it didn't sit in the garage for months at a time.

I drove to Glasgow more to see Wendy and Braidon, and Rose. I'd always thought of her and talked to her from wherever I was, but I loved being able to spend time with her again, as I'd missed her.

Conor was a sickly kid. As a baby, he would bring up his full bottle, and he often caught viruses. When Norman got back from Angola, Conor had a temperature of 104ºF. He seemed lifeless, so we put him in the car and took him to Emergency. No one knew what was wrong with him, so they put him in isolation and started a drip. He lay there motionless, watching the cartoons on the TV. All he did was sleep and watch TV. He didn't speak much, and he didn't move. We were terrified, and I was grateful Norman was with me. It turned out Conor had an infection, so they pumped him full of antibiotics. After two days, he came home.

My brother, Colin, started visiting more often—I think, to get away from Dad. Colin had a son of his own by then—Stevie, who was two. He'd sometimes bring Stevie with him, and he stayed over when Norman was away, sleeping on the couch in the living room. One of the neighbours gave him an old car, so he tinkered with that most days using Norman's tools. He also liked Lindsay, one of my neighbours.

I knew I had to stop having wild nights and getting drunk. I was pregnant and about to have a second baby. I had to talk to Norman about him going away all the time. He had been doing it for a year and a half, and I needed him home.

When he came home, we sat down, and I told him I'd been struggling while he was away. Struggling with drink, struggling with panic attacks, struggling with flashbacks. We agreed he'd do it for a few more months to finish the project he was working on, and then he'd come home. He said another job opportunity had come up, and we could move to Norway.

I was shocked. 'Norway,' I said. 'That's too far away.'

'It's only an hour by flight,' he said.

He left me to think about it.

I stopped partying and just saw the girls out the front when the kids were playing. I told them I had to stop drinking as it wasn't good for the baby.

Catherine

Catherine was due on Norman's birthday, 23 May, 2001, but she decided to make her own birthday, on 25 May. I felt niggles in my tummy around 6:00 a.m., but nothing major. I went downstairs for a drink and lay on the sofa. As I lay there, I watched the clock, and noticed the contractions were every 4 minutes. Five minutes later, they were two minutes apart.

Norman had just arrived home the day before his birthday. I woke him and told him I was in labour. He got up and got ready, and I called the hospital and told them we were on our way and that the contractions were every two minutes, but the pain wasn't intense.

My bag was already packed and in the car, so everything was ready to go. I asked Norman to put my shoes on and tie them because I couldn't reach, and phoned my friend, Helen, to tell her I was in labour and that we would drop Conor off at her house.

But when I stood up and walked around the edge of the bed, my waters broke. I told Norman to take my shoes off again, as well as my trousers and pants, because Catherine was coming now.

Norman took Conor to a neighbour's to ask her to look after him, but she was so drunk from the night before she didn't answer the door. So he put Conor in front of the TV and ran back upstairs to me.

I was ready to push, so Norman phoned the midwife at the hospital, and she guided him through what to do. She told him to get a towel and, when he asked why, she said to catch the baby because I was standing up. I couldn't lie down, so I stood facing the bed, screaming as every contraction came.

Conor came upstairs and said, 'Mummy, I heard you screaming. Are you okay?'

I said, 'Yes, darling, I'm fine. Your baby sister is coming.'

The midwife asked to speak to me, and so Norman put the phone to my ear. She asked me to rate the pain, and I said it was eight out of ten.

She then asked me to put my hand down and see if I could feel the baby's head. I did as I was told, and I could feel her head. It was so special.

I said, 'Yes, I can feel her head.'

She said, 'Great! You're ready to push. You're ready to have this baby.'

So, I started pushing, with Norman kneeling on the floor behind me, ready to catch her.

I gave one last push, and she came, all gooey and gorgeous.

Norman asked me to turn and sit on the bed, and I had to lift my leg over the cord.

He handed her to me. She was beautiful and crying.

Conor was amazed but was really unsure of what was happening.

Norman picked up the phone from the floor and spoke to the midwife. 'She's here, and she's perfectly fine.'

The midwife told us an ambulance was on its way and a midwife was coming, too. The paramedics arrived first, and one of them said, 'I've never been to a home birth before. Can I cut the cord?'

Norman said, 'Go ahead. I've done the hard part.'

The midwife arrived, took the baby and wrapped her ready for a bath. The paramedics left, and the midwife said, 'It's time to deliver the afterbirth.'

I lay on the bed, and she put her hand on my tummy and the other around the cord and told me to push one more time. As I pushed, the afterbirth came away. She took it into the bathroom and put it in the bath, then came back and checked me. She said I was fine, that I didn't need stitches, and everything looked good. So she got a damp face cloth, and I washed myself as best I could, while she took Catherine for her first bath.

When she came back, she put Catherine in her crib and told me she was 6 pounds 7 and a half ounces.

They stripped the bedding to be washed and replaced the sheets. The midwife washed the floor, where my water had broken. I climbed into bed, and then she gave me Catherine, but I struggled with breastfeeding, so I bottle-fed her, too. The midwife said I didn't need to go to hospital because everything was fine, and she left.

Norman looked after Catherine while I had a hot bath and changed into some fresh pyjamas. When I climbed back into bed, Conor sat on the edge of the bed watching. The phone rang, and it was Helen wondering where I was with Conor.

I said, 'She's here already.'

She said, 'Who's there?'

I said, 'The baby. The baby's here. Catherine's here.'

She screamed and said, 'I'm on my way.'

My neighbour Maxine had seen the ambulance and the midwife outside and wondered what was going on, so she came over too. She ran past Norman, up the stairs and into the room, so excited to see the baby had arrived.

She said, 'That's a first. I've never seen that before in my life. It's so exciting.'

Helen came in all excited and said, 'You'll never believe what your son just said in the middle of the street. He said he had seen his baby sister coming out of his mum's bum!'

By this point, everyone was out on the street and would have heard him. Bless him.

The midwife who talked us through the delivery on the phone rang that night. She congratulated me and said she was happy for us all. She wanted to speak to Norman and told him if he ever needed a new job, he could get one as a midwife! She said he did an amazing job and that he should be so proud of himself.

Norman had to go to work to pick up a few things, and his employees had put a package together: the biggest bunch of flowers I'd ever seen, a Marks and Spencer voucher for £100 and a toy medical kit for Norman. It was the best present he ever got.

Catherine was a content baby. She didn't cry much, and never took the dummy.

Mum, Dad, Wendy, Josh and Braidon came to see the new baby, and they all held Catherine, even Braidon. Josh took Conor out front to play some ball, but didn't take his own son with him. Wendy said he never played with Braidon like that.

Mum was besotted with Catherine, and for the first time ever, when she hugged Conor, she told him she loved him. She never did that with us, never hugged us, never told us she loved us. I felt cheated, heartbroken, jealous even.

Norman had to go back to Angola twice more. It was hard with two kids. Conor started primary one. He loved school, had lots of friends. At least I had a break during the day while he was at school, only having to look after Catherine. But when he came home, we had to do afternoon tea, cartoons, homework, baths, dinner and bedtime. It was exhausting, and I longed for the day Norman came home to stay.

When Conor was five years old, he went out to play around 4:00 p.m. with Dawn's son one afternoon, but when I looked out the window, he wasn't there. I stood outside the door shouting his name, but he didn't answer. I banged on Dawn's door, but she didn't know where they were either. Catherine was sleeping and I couldn't leave her, so Dawn sent her daughters out to look. The neighbours all came out to see what was going on and went in all directions looking for the boys. I stayed at my front door in tears, feeling powerless because there was nothing I could do.

It was dark outside by then, around 8:00 p.m. and still no sign of Conor. I went to phone the police, but I heard Dawn shout, 'They found them, Sharon. They found them.'

Five minutes later, they came around the corner, not a care in the world. They'd been playing in the field across from the houses. I ran, knelt down in front of him and held him so tight. I told him how mad I was, but how much I loved him, and how scared I was that he was gone.

I don't think he fully understood what he put me through that day, not even now. Every bad thing possible went through my mind when he was missing, maybe more so because I was abused as a child. It took me back to my childhood and when I got lost in the elevator.

I grounded him for a week.

Colin came to stay for a few weeks. He got the old car working and was using it to drive back and forth between Mum and me. He started seeing Dawn's daughter.

One night, Conor got sick—he was burning up and crying and lay beside me for two nights. I called the doctor out, who said he just had a bad cold and gave me some paracetamol. Conor hated the medicine.

He didn't get better, so I took him to the hospital. Colin drove me, even though he didn't have a license at the time, while I held Conor in the back seat. Colin's girlfriend came too.

They took us all into a small room at the hospital. A nurse came and checked Conor over, then a doctor. After he left, Conor looked at me. I stood up, took his hand and held his head. In an instant, he went limp, unmoving. He stopped breathing, and I screamed, 'Get the fucking doctor. He's not breathing.'

Colin ran from the room and came back with the doctor. The doctor started giving Conor CPR, and again I stood there powerless, not knowing what to do for my son, my baby boy.

He started breathing, and I cried. God, did I cry. I couldn't hold back my tears. I held Conor's face and kissed him.

He stayed in hospital for three days and, yet again, no one could tell me what was wrong with my son. They put it down to a viral infection. That's all they ever said—he had a viral infection.

Norman finally came home to stay, and was I grateful. He had a month off, and it was nice having some help around the house, and help with the kids, too.

We spent Christmas in England with Norman's parents. We drove for nine hours through the night, and the kids slept in the back seat. When we arrived, Norman and I slept, and his parents took care of the kids.

Norman's parents were healers, and his mother was a psychic medium. People would talk through her in their own language or accent. Vinnie and Holee were the main characters that came through. I found it scary at first, but when I got used to it, it was beautiful. Vinnie and Holee both gave messages of hope.

On Christmas Day, Conor got a bike, but Catherine was too small to enjoy her presents. I went into the garden for a smoke one afternoon around sunset and was chased by a bat. I was terrified, but everyone inside was laughing as I ran back and forth in the garden.

It was always hard to say goodbye to Norman's parents, and his mother always got emotional.

My dad had a scab on his leg that he picked at and made bigger. It became septic, and he had an operation in which a chunk was cut out of his calf. It didn't stop him from drinking. One afternoon, I walked in when he was lying on the sofa and Conor had the can of beer to his mouth.

I screamed at him, 'You do not give children alcohol.'

He said, 'It's only a little bit of beer. There's no harm in it.'

Conor said, 'Braidon had some too.' Braidon was two years younger than Conor.

I took Conor, and we left.

One day, Mum and I went to Glasgow City Centre to go shopping. The rain was torrential and, just after 12:00 p.m., we got news from one of our neighbours that something had happened in the graveyard.

As soon as we got the news, I walked the 2 minutes from Mum's house to the cemetery and looked over the wall. They now lived on the south side of the graveyard, and there was a brick wall surrounding that part of the graveyard. There was a white tent about 10 meters from the wall and yellow tape everywhere. I asked one of the neighbours standing next to me what had happened, and she told me there was a missing boy. She said she saw the ground open up and swallow him whole. The hole was right beside my tree, the tree I felt safe in, the same one I had slept in after a beating from Dad. Rose's grave wasn't that much further away. I was worried that something had happened to it.

I think I stood there for about an hour, hoping they would bring the boy out alive. After a while, everyone went home, including me. There was nothing we could do by standing there, and I was soaked through.

It was on the two o'clock news: the boy was the caretaker's son. He had been walking his dog when a hole opened up due to the amount of rain in the grounds of the graveyard. The dog disappeared into the hole. The boy went to rescue the dog and disappeared himself. A specialist mine rescue team recovered his body five days later, 50 yards from where he'd disappeared.

I could no longer visit Rose after that day as the public were no longer permitted to enter that part of the graveyard because it was too dangerous. Most of the gravestones in the area had fallen over, and many graves were lost. The ground was uneven and boggy. My tree was gone, lying on its side. I could see it from the roadside. I couldn't believe my safe place was gone. The thought of it always being there was a comfort to me. I believe Rose's grave was no longer there either, but I can't be sure. A good part of the lower graveyard was destroyed. Trees, graves and stones gone or lying flat on the ground. No access was allowed, so I couldn't see the extent of the damage. This broke my heart—I could no longer visit her, and I felt I had lost her. I cried on and off for weeks. My heart was torn in two.

I should have known then I didn't need to visit a grave to talk to her, to feel her presence. She was with me all the time when I needed her: I just spoke to her, and I didn't need to visit a gravestone to do that. I still had all my childhood memories of being in the graveyard with her. I still talk to her and feel her around me even today. She will always be a big part of my life. You still can't access that part of the graveyard after all these years, so I have no idea if Rose's grave is there.

Norway

Norman was offered the job in Norway again, so he decided to go for a month, and I would stay for the first two weeks. I left the kids with my sister, and we flew to Kongsberg (Kingstown), a small town in the south, about an hour's drive from Oslo. We stayed in the Grand Hotel. It was a stunning hotel right by the river in the middle of town. The room was big and spacious with the most amazing view of the west side of town.

It was January and the temperature was around -10º Celsius. I spent my days walking around and exploring, sometimes swimming at the pool, while Norman worked, then we'd meet for lunch, usually in the hotel. The people were friendly—most of the young people spoke English, but the older ones only spoke Norwegian. We ate at the local Chinese most nights; the food was amazing. One morning, we woke up to a foot of deep snow, which was picturesque.

After two weeks we flew back to Scotland and picked up Conor from my sister and took him back to Norway with us, leaving Catherine for longer with my sister. Conor had never seen snow like that before, and he loved it. To be honest, I'd never seen snow like that either. Snow in Scotland is nice for two minutes and then it's all slushy and horrible.

We bought Conor toys that he could enjoy in the hotel with me all day while Norman worked. He picked a collection of animals and farm equipment and played with them for hours—on the window ledges, on the bed, all over the floor.

During this time, my nightmares were really bad, and I hated it because Conor was also in the room. At least, he was a good sleeper.

We fell in love with Kongsberg and decided we'd move there. After a few months of organisation, we moved to Norway, leaving my past behind. We lived in a two-bedroom apartment on the west side of town, facing an old church. It was fully furnished, because our furniture would take time to arrive from the UK. The sofa was pink and knitted with matching armchairs—the most hideous thing I'd ever seen. Catherine's cot was in the main room, and Conor had his own room.

The first night in the apartment, I woke around 1:00 a.m., clawing and scratching at myself. Something had irritated my skin, and I was red raw and blotchy. I took a shower and went back to bed to try sleeping again. I woke around 2:30 a.m., clawing myself apart so I showered again. I had 3 showers that night. In the end I was in tears. Norman spoke to his workplace and, apparently, the girl who'd stayed there before us had 3 Siamese cats. They took all the bed sheets and curtains, and someone cleaned the sofa and chairs. At last, I could sleep a little. Nightmares still took over half my night but being able to sleep the other half was a godsend.

We made great friends quickly. Norman and Lorraine were an older couple from Aberdeen in Scotland who'd been in Norway a few years. Norman worked with my Norman, and they had known each other for some time. They lived not far from us, close to the ski slope. Lorraine gave me tips for the best shops and places to take the kids. They also told us about a great Norwegian tutor, Ellen, who was in her 80s.

Norman loved Laurel and Hardy and Charlie Chaplin and, one night, when we took the kids over for dinner, Norman showed Conor his collection of DVDs. Conor spent the rest of the evening engrossed, watching Charlie Chaplin and Laurel and Hardy. To this day he still loves those old movies and has his own collection. My kids looked up to Norman and Lorraine like grandparents.

After about 8 weeks in the apartment, we moved into a house with a garden. We bought a huge trampoline and got tickets for my parents to visit. They loved watching the kids outside on the trampoline. It was around June and the weather was beautiful. Dad only drank at nighttime when the kids were in bed, which I didn't mind as long as he kept his temper in check. We took them to Oslo to see the statues in the big park. Oslo is an interesting city, but I loved Kongsberg because it was a small town. Mum and Dad stayed 10 days that first time and there was no friction between us. As Dad aged, he seemed to be changing. He was calmer, more mellow. He had lost so much weight, and his complexion was grey, he looked old, not the monster I remember.

Wendy and Josh arrived in July. It was hot and summery. I'd missed my sister, and it was nice to see her. We visited Oslo and did all the touristy things you do when family and friends come to visit. We went to the Kon Tiki Museum and the main attraction in Oslo, the park with the statues. It broke my heart when my sister had to leave, but she had to go home to her children, a son and a daughter.

After eight months, we moved into a bigger house with three storeys. It had a big balcony and an absolutely stunning view. We could see the hills and the ski slopes all lit up at night.

There was an attic on the third floor, which I used when I needed time out. I'd sit up there and do a jigsaw puzzle or draw pictures; it was like my art studio.

In Norway, kids start school at six years old. Conor started Grade One at a primary school around the corner from us in Gamlegrendasen. It was a beautiful school, all open with the forest behind it. On his first day, we met his teacher and teaching assistant. His teacher, Inar told us we had to get Conor a knife.

I said, 'You're having a laugh. No way am I getting my son a knife.'

She said, 'All the children have a small pen knife or flick knife.'

She told us they teach them how to use them. On a Thursday in winter, they ski out to the woods and build a bonfire. They cut a branch from a tree and show them how to use the knives to shape the branch so that they can cook marshmallows and hot dogs on the fire.

I still felt uncomfortable about this, but we went with what they said. We bought him a pen knife from the Kon Tiki Museum in Oslo, wrote Conor's name on it and put it in his school bag.

When the winter came, the place was thick with snow. Conor skied cross country to and from school. It ran from 8:00 a.m. until 1:30 p.m. Monday to Friday. They were shorter days, but they packed a lot into those hours. I tried cross country, but it wasn't for me, and I was too scared of heights for going downhill.

One day while shovelling snow from the driveway into the garden, I stepped too far and fell through the snow. I was about 4 feet down and covered in snow. I couldn't grab anything to pull myself out and I screamed and screamed. It wasn't too long before my neighbour came and threw a rope down to me. I grabbed it and he pulled me up. When I think of it now, it was terrifying. If my neighbour hadn't heard me scream, I don't think I would have survived. It would have been about -10º Celsius.

We were living a good life and, for the first time in my life, I felt safe and happy. No one could hurt me where I was. I had Norman, I had the kids, and I had friends. That was all I needed.

I joined the International Women's group. It was made up of women from all over the world: America, Canada, England, Scotland, Italy. Vanessa led the group, and we met at a different person's house each time. So, we would have an American night, a Canadian night, and so on. At Christmas, we all got together at Vanessa's house. Everyone made a batch of cookies, and we'd swap so we went home with a different batch of different cookies for Christmas.

Lorraine and I hosted a Scottish night. I had been back to Scotland and my sister, who was a chef at the time, gave me haggis to take back to Norway. I made haggis, nips (turnips) and tatties (potatoes) and black pudding. I didn't tell anyone what was in the haggis and black pudding until the end of the evening, and I only told those who asked.

Catherine was speaking more and more Norwegian. She came home from barnehagen (day care) one day saying, 'Mama, kan jeg ha brod skiver med syltetoy?' ('Mama, can I have bread with jam?) I had to ask her to show me what she wanted, and she took my hand, led me into the kitchen and showed me the bread and jam.

An International School opened in Kongsberg, and the principal and his wife interviewed interested parents. I told them I was willing to work there, if they needed someone.

The kids began attending Kongsberg International School: Conor in Three and Catherine in Kindergarten. A few weeks before school started, they offered me a job working in the before- and after-school club, and I took it, because I thought my kids would enjoy playing before and after school. But I didn't realise how long their day would be.

The week before school started, I met all the staff, and made two good friends that day: Jen, from England, and Hege, from Norway. Both were teaching assistants in kindergarten, so I got to know them well. Jen's husband, Andy, taught at the school, and Norman and I became good friends with both of them. Jen started learning Norwegian from my Norwegian teacher. She picked it up faster than me.

Hege and I became best friends, and Conor played Pokémon with Hege's son, Tinius, who was a few years younger. We met up at night, too, and had a few drinks. I still didn't know how to control my intake and would overdo it at times, and get emotional. I told Hege a little about what happened to me as a child. Not for sympathy, but for her to understand why I was the way I was. She hugged me and said she was sorry. It didn't change the way she was with me. She introduced me to her friends Ziza and Beata, and we all met up every now and then for drinks. Beata was larger than life, a big personality, but we got on so well, and I was out every other weekend with the girls drinking.

Once a month we would drive two and a half hours to Sweden to do our food shopping. It was a lot cheaper, and we would buy in bulk, and then drive the two and a half hours home. The two-and-a-half-hour drive took you through the countryside and it was picturesque, but not as nice as Norway. Every now and then, we'd go through a bit of land where they grew the Christmas trees, and you could smell the pine. The air was pure and clean, and everything smelt much fresher there.

Norman was working really hard and very tired. I didn't realise how tired until one night when we to a family-friendly pizza place for dinner. I was busy feeding Catherine and when I looked around, Norman's head was lowering into his pizza. He was exhausted and needed to do something about it. It was hard working full-time, looking after the kids and keeping house in a foreign country.

Winter arrived again and the snow returned. One day, when Norman dropped me in town to do some shopping, I bumped into my Norwegian teacher Ellen. She drove me back to her house for tea. God, could she drive! For a woman in her 80s, she wasn't scared of driving, especially in snow. She lived on a hill and the road curved into the garage. She drove up the hill and turned that corner like it was nothing, straight into the garage. I was terrified. But she'd been driving that road for at least 50 years, so she knew every curve and every turn.

I loved spending time with her and listening to the old stories. She mixed Norwegian and English, still trying to help me learn the language. But it didn't matter what she did, I still struggled. Even after all this time, I still only had the basics, but I could get by. Most of the young workers were trying to learn English, so I didn't need much Norwegian. It was only the older generation who would speak Norwegian.

As Norman's two-year contract was coming to an end, we had to decide if we were going to stay or return to Scotland. I didn't want to go back to my ghosts, and I was happy with my job and friends. Norman loved his job, too, and the Norwegian lifestyle. He'd also made friends and went to the pub with them at weekends.

We decided to stay, so we sold our house in Scotland and bought a house in Kongsberg. While we were in England visiting Norman's parents, I saw a medium who told me we'd buy a white house with a white fence with the number 5. It came true: we bought a house that was white with a white balcony, and it was number 5.

So we had a place to call our own in Norway. Everything was falling into place, and I was happy. I had a beautiful family, a beautiful home, an amazing life. But my past was still haunting me, and I was still having panic attacks and nightmares, seeing Grandad and Habib in my dreams. I drank at weekends to try to block them out, but that only made them worse. I was the life of parties, the one that played the fool. But I was crumbling inside, a time bomb waiting to go off.

My beautiful house

We lived on a hill and had views right down the valley. Sometimes we'd sit out on the porch, and it would suddenly cloud over, and we'd look down the valley and see the rain or snow coming. It gave us plenty of time to pack up before it hit.

We had a housewarming, and I invited all my colleagues from school. I got the karaoke out and a few of the girls sang all night to Abba. We opened the doors to the balcony, and people sat outside. In the summertime. Kongsberg never really gets dark, so we sat outside until 11:00 p.m. We held a party every few months, and they always ended with everyone singing to Abba. They were epic parties, I was told.

We were spending more time with Jen and Andy and their dog, Misty, a gorgeous Weimaraner. Norman worked with me and taught me spiritual healing when we first got together, but I didn't use it often, but now I was doing healing again. It gave me comfort. So Jen and I met once a week, and she gave me healing one week, and I gave her healing the following week. This went on for months. I would place my hands on her shoulders and head and feel energy flow from my hands. The healing helped me sleep and eased the panic attacks. Norman still gave me healing, too: we'd sit on the sofa watching TV, and he'd put his hand on my head or my back, and I'd lay my head on his knee. It was so comforting.

Being spiritual gave me a sense of being and probably saved me in many ways. I believe our loved ones who have passed over are all around us; guiding, protecting and loving us. I believe that when we are ready to go, they will guide us home. I believe in the healing touch, and I believe that if I didn't have that belief I wouldn't be here today. My husband saved me in so many ways, and I don't think I can ever express to him just how much.

Conor and Norman took lessons in downhill skiing. Every afternoon, they'd ski to the barneslope (children's slope), and meet Norman's friend, Gavin, and his wife, Stina, who were there for support. One day on the chair lift, Conor slipped off, and Stina grabbed him by the trousers and hauled him up her knee. When I was told this story, I laughed at the image of 6-foot tall Stina with tiny Conor on her lap.

The children picked up skiing quickly and moved onto the bigger slope. They skied every other day over the winter. We bought Catherine a pair of little cross-country skis—she skied around the garden for hours and loved it.

In addition to the before- and after-school clubs, I started working with a couple of kids who needed extra help. One boy was 7 and struggling with maths and English. I helped him for about 10 hours a week. He got frustrated when he didn't know how to answer a question, but he worked really hard. I worked with him for three years, as well as with his parents and Ruth, the school nurse, who was connected to all children that had difficulties. He was diagnosed with autism and had problems in the classroom setting and with his studies.

Ruth was also my son's nurse after Conor was diagnosed with ADHD in Grade Four. He was a lovely boy but struggled with keeping his attention focused. When he came home from school, I'd ask what he had for homework, and he'd tell me he didn't have any. But when I spoke to Mari, his teacher, the next day, she'd tell me what homework he had.

We decided to have him tested, and it came back as ADHD. I struggled with this because Conor wasn't violent or aggressive, nor angry or frustrated, so I didn't understand how he could have it. We were told that in order for him to qualify for help in the classroom, he needed to be on medication. We refused at first, but we knew Conor needed help, so in the end we agreed to the medication. He started on Ritalin, but within a week, I found him on top of his bed (one with a desk underneath) with a belt from my nightgown around his neck, ready to jump. I talked him down by telling him we loved him and that we would stop the medication. My heart was pounding in my chest and tears welled up in my eyes. I had so many things going on inside my head. If he jumps, he could break his neck, he could hurt himself badly. I was terrified.

I ceased the Ritalin straightaway, and told the doctor there was no way he was going to stay on it. We were encouraged to try Strattera; told it would be better and would keep Conor's focus in class. I was reluctant, scared of the same thing happening but tried it. Then Conor got an assistant for six hours a week. He became calmer, more focused. I was relieved but watched him like a hawk. I never stopped worrying about him.

Christian

Christian was a boy in Grade Five and had ADHD. I was the Special Needs Assistant working with him. He struggled in class and was destructive by winding other students up when he didn't understand the questions or what was going on. He found it hard to keep his attention on what was happening in the room, and he'd become disruptive by throwing pencils. pens, anything he could get his hands on, or he would grab at other students' shirts, so I had to take him out of class and work with him one-on-one.

On a good day, he was the perfect student. But some days, I'd have to take him into the playground and let him on the climbing frame to get some of his pent-up anger out. Sometimes his frustration was so intense, he'd break something or hurt himself. I quickly learnt how to hold him when he lost control—I'd stand behind him, wrap my arms around him and drop to the floor while holding him tight. Sometimes that was the only way to calm him down.

Christian was lovely, very caring except when he was upset. One day I got called away from another student to Christian's classroom because he was holding a boy up against the whiteboard with the scissors in his hand. It took me only a few minutes to get there.

When I got there, I told the teacher to move the kids to one end of the classroom. I stood near the door and tried to wave at Mike, the principal, whose office faced the classroom, while I talked calmly to Christian.

'Christian, can you give me the scissors, please? Why do you want to hurt Konrad?'

He said, 'He's a lying fucker.' He said he was telling lies about Christian's mother.

I kept waving my hand out the door, hoping that Mike would see. I could hear whispers behind me, so I knew someone was there. I kept going.

'Christian, please don't do this. You really don't want to hurt Konrad. Please hand me the scissors. We can go outside into the sunshine, sit on the climbing frame and talk about it. Would you like to do that, Christian? Would you like to go outside?'

'Yes,' he said.

'Hand me the scissors and we can go outside.'

The teacher and all the students were crouched in the back corner of the room. I stepped closer and put out my hand, asked again for the scissors.

Christian let go of Konrad's collar, took a step back and handed me the scissors.

I felt like I could breathe again.

Mike and two of the teachers, Andy and Andrew, were standing outside the door, and the three of them stepped back when Christian gave me the scissors. I took his arm, gave the scissors to the teacher and walked him outside.

We went to the playground and sat on the climbing frame and talked about what had happened.

Christian said Konrad had called his mother a slut, and said he should go and jump in front of a train and kill himself. He said, 'Maybe that's what I should do. Jump in front of the train. Maybe I should do it after school.'

I related to Christian so much when thinking of my own past.

I told him he was loved by his mother and brother, and that I loved working with him. Afterwards, I spoke to his nurse, Ruth, as I needed to know I had done everything I could. Christian was suspended for 3 weeks.

One day, I took Christian out of class to work on maths. We went into one of the classrooms on the top floor of the building. Christian was in a mood that day—it was like he was two different people: one was very playful and the other tormenting. At one point, he got up and stood on the window ledge, holding on to the frame and leaning out. He started saying, 'Look, Sharon, I'm going to jump. I'm going to jump now. My head is going to splat on the ground, and I'm going to die.'

I stood, but I didn't want to go too close to him in case he felt threatened. I said, 'Why do you want to jump?'

He said, 'No one would care if I jumped. No one cares about me.'

'That's not true, Christian. You have many people who care about you. Your mum, your brother, Philip, Mike and me. We don't want you to jump. Why don't you come inside, and we'll sit down and talk? Come in and sit down, Christian.'

Then he started saying, 'I'm going to do it, Sharon. I'm going to do it. I'm going to jump.'

This went on for 10 to 15 minutes. Then I told him I was leaving the room and when I came back, I wanted him sitting at the table ready to do some work.

I left the room, dropped to the floor and started crying, thinking, What the fuck have I done, what have I done?

I shouted downstairs to Mike over and over again. He eventually came to the stairwell, and I told him he had to get outside that Christian was threatening to jump out of the window.

He ran, and I turned around and looked at the closed door to the room. I put my hands on the doorknob and prayed that Christian would be sitting on a chair when I entered. My heart was pounding through my chest. I turned it slowly and gently opened the door. Christian was sitting at the desk, ready to do his work.

I thanked him for doing the right thing and carried on with the day like nothing had happened. I had a meeting with Ruth, Mike and Christian's mother later that afternoon. It was agreed that Christian should have more testing done.

Summer holidays came around fast. We had a lovely summer break. My parents visited. Dad was looking fragile—he'd lost a lot of weight, and the years of drinking made him look old. He didn't get angry like he used to; he was much calmer. Not what I'd expected. He had a small cut on his head, like a spot that had been burst. Every time he knocked it, blood would spurt from it. I'd never seen so much blood from something so small. He would wake up during the night with blood spurting all over the walls, sheets, floor. It looked like someone had been massacred. He looked yellow, too, like jaundice. All in all, though, the trip went well.

The summer break came and went quickly, and it was time to go back to work. I met with Christian's mother, Mike and Catherine, the deputy principal. Christian had been diagnosed with Tourette's and schizophrenia, on top of his ADHD. He had a lot to deal with and, on top of all that, I had to pass the reins to someone else. He needed a male assistant as I couldn't support him the way I used to. He'd grown over the summer break—taller than me—and there was no way I could restrain him.

He cried when I told him and, I must say, I had a tear in my eye too. He was a great kid. We managed to get a really good male assistant to work with him.

Chapter Ten
2002 – 2005

I arrived home from work one night around 4:30 p.m. to find Norman lying on the floor in the living room. He didn't usually get home until about 6:00 p.m., but he said he'd hurt his back and was lying flat on the floor to stretch it out. I ran him a hot bath and started preparing dinner when I heard a loud crash. I ran to the bathroom to find him on the floor. He had got out of the bath and collapsed. I dried him. He crawled to the bedroom, and I managed to get him onto the bed. I wanted to call an ambulance, but he insisted he would be fine. I got him dressed into his pyjamas and pulled the covers over him.

When we woke up the next morning, he said he needed to go to the bathroom but couldn't walk. He crawled, and I helped him onto the toilet. When I went back, he was crawling along the floor, and at that point I decided we needed an ambulance. Again, he said he would be fine, but I disagreed.

I took the kids to school and phoned for an ambulance. They told me to take him to his doctor. I called the surgery, and they told me to call an ambulance back to take him there. So, I had to call an ambulance again, which took him to the doctor's surgery.

The doctor came down to see him, climbed into the ambulance and shut the door. Two minutes later he came out and said, 'You have to go straight to the hospital.'

At the hospital, they did lots of tests but had no idea what was going on. They put it down to a viral infection, and he was in hospital for five days. I didn't go to work but stayed at home to look after Norman and the kids.

I returned to work part-time, working half the week before school, half the week after and two out of five days in the classrooms. I needed to be at home more for the kids and Norman.

Norman completely recovered and went back to work like nothing had happened. But seeing him so helpless had terrified me, and I was scared I was going to lose him. I didn't know how to express that to him. I struggled with seeing him so helpless, and I wanted to be there for him and for the kids. The thought of losing him didn't bear thinking about.

My Thirtieth Birthday

I held a party for my thirtieth and invited everyone from school. It was summer, and the weather was beautiful, so I opened up the balcony door and let the fresh air in. We had music blaring, and the karaoke on as usual. Everyone was having such a good time. Then two guests, Mari and Shani, disappeared, and no one seemed to know where they had gone. Someone suggested that Mari had gone home, but she was the singer and entertainer, so I was confused why she'd left.

Caroline suggested that I go to her house, just down the hill. By this time, I was pretty tipsy but took a glass in my hand and set off. Everyone else followed, so it looked like we were taking the party to Mari. When I arrived at her house, I opened the door and called to her but got no answer. So I climbed the stairs, and, as I reached the living room, the music started. The whole band was there: Caroline and Mike on guitar, Shani on drums and Mari singing *I Will Walk 500 Miles* by The Proclaimers.

I laughed so hard. It was the best birthday present ever. I worked with a great bunch of people, and I loved them all.

The Cookbook

The library was in desperate need of new books and needed a facelift, so we were looking to fundraise. We decided to put together a cookbook, and I asked all the kids and staff to give me their favourite recipe and a photograph of the recipe. While they worked on that, I got to working on famous people. We wrote letters to the royal family in the UK, to all the chefs and comedians we knew. The royal family replied, telling us that they had their own charities and wouldn't be giving to ours, which was quite disappointing.

But John Cleese replied with a breakfast dish:

Cornflakes Recipe by John Cleese:

1 packet of Cornflakes

1 pint of milk

Method:

1. Buy a packet of Cornflakes.

2. Open the cardboard box.

3. Open the sort of plastic packet inside the box.

4. Pour the contents (sort of yellowy brownish bits of things) onto a plate.

5. Buy a bottle of milk.

6. Take the top off the thin end of the bottle.

7. Invert the bottle gently over the cornflakes making sure that the milk does not go over the edge of the plate.

8. It's very simple to make and delicious. An alternative is to use Coca-Cola instead of milk.

Add basil as required.

We also received recipes from celebrity chef Ainsley Harriet (Akee and salt fish served with cornmeal muffins), the former mayor of Kongsberg (stuffed cabbage), the mayor of Kongsberg (Vidar lande, which is old-fashioned pea soup), and celebrity chefs Gino D' Acampo (Double chocolate mousse with pistachio nuts) and Delia Smith (Chocolate drop mini muffins with red noses).

We had 92 recipes in total, including breakfasts, starters, main courses, desserts, bread and cookies. We put it all together at the school over weekends and nights in order to get it all printed off. The cookbook was called Cooking Around the World with K.I.S. (Kongsberg International School), named by Christian, who I worked with. The kids entered a competition to design the front cover, and a Grade Six girl won the competition.

It's a project I've been proud of all these years, and we raised so much money to buy books for the library and do it up. The mayor of Kongsberg came to the school and signed copies for everyone. Newspaper reporters came too. Conor stood beside the mayor for the photo. One friend, Alison, said her daughter should have been in the picture, too, and thought I'd chosen the child to stand with the photographer, but I hadn't. Our friendship ended as a result, which was sad.

I still use my copy of that cookbook to this day.

Meanwhile, by the summer of 2003, things weren't that great between Norman and me. We had been drifting apart for months. He was working long hours, and I was out most weekends drinking with Beata and Hege. We hardly saw each other. His parents came to visit, and we drove to Oslo for the day. We stopped at the big park to see the statues. There's a statue of a boy standing on the bridge with his arms in the air and screaming. It's one of the most famous statues in Norway because it was stolen and, finally, returned.

Norman's mother and father took the kids further on, but we stayed by the statues. I said things needed to change, or we needed to split up. Neither of us wanted this, so we had to find a way of coming together. I said I'd only go out with the girls every third week, and he said he'd try harder with work. We committed to spending more time together as a couple because we both loved each other and wanted it to work. We made it work, and we spent more time together.

One day Norman called me and said he had a job opportunity either in Singapore or Australia. My first reaction was that they were both too far away, on the other side of the world, but we'd talk about it when I got home.

We went over it and over it and over it and, in the end, decided it wasn't a good idea. Norman's parents were getting older, and my dad was really sick, and we wanted to stay close to them, so we decided against it.

My friend, Beata, was carefree and fun—one snowy night, she stripped off and jumped on the trampoline naked. For her fortieth, Hege and I went to an adult shop and bought her a dildo and some sexy knickers. By the time we got to her party, she'd already been drinking and was in a good mood. When she opened our present, she took out the dildo, put one leg up on the chair and pretended to use it.

I wish I had it on video. We always had such fun together. I had amazing friends.

Chapter Eleven
2005 – 2010

My work Christmas party in 2003 was held in a fancy hotel—the Bolkashoi. A band made up of teachers was playing, Mari was singing, and I was having a great time dancing with Norman, but I felt eyes on me all night. Alison, the woman I'd made the cookbook with, still held a grudge and, on the way back from the bathroom, she approached me in the hallway.

'Why the hell did you choose your son for the picture with the mayor?' she said.

I said, 'I didn't choose him. The photographer chose him.'

She said, 'I don't fucking believe you.'

'Tough shit,' I said. 'Believe me or not, I don't care anymore. I know what happened, and that's enough for me, so I'm sorry if you feel that way and don't want to be friends anymore, but I'm not gonna accept this horrible attitude from you.'

I walked away. I felt too old for this sort of pettiness—it doesn't get you anywhere.

I'd been thinking about Norman's job offer for weeks and called him to come into my work at 4:00 p.m. one day. The kids were out playing in the snow, and I brought them in to watch a cartoon. Norman arrived, and we sat on one of the desks and talked.

I said, 'Maybe moving is a good opportunity for us to start anew, to find each other again.'

Within 30 minutes, we'd decided to move to Australia. When the kids had gone home, we wanted to tell someone to make it real. Jorunn was in the office, so I told her we were leaving for Australia. She couldn't believe it but said congratulations.

It was real; we were moving to Perth, Australia.

Hege and Beata were shocked because we hadn't spoken about it. Jen and Andy were sad that we were leaving but happy for us.

We decided we had to have one last party before we left. We held it at the Bokishoi Hotel. Everyone from work came, and my sister and her three friends flew over from Scotland. Jen bought me a cowboy hat, and I wore a waistcoat and jeans, trying to look Aussie. People danced all night, and it was the best party we'd ever hosted. I'd made amazing friends in Norway, and I was going to miss every one of them. But it was time for a new life, a new us, a new me.

Conor and Catherine's classmates held leaving parties for them. Toril gave Catherine beautiful little books about *Spot the Dog*, and Conor's teacher gave him *Holes* and *Small Steps*. His classmates wrote him beautiful letters and cards.

We met for breakfast at the Grand Hotel before leaving for the airport. My workmates came and Ellen, my Norwegian teacher, who was like a grandmother to us. It was an emotional farewell—I was crying as I hugged everyone, and they all waved as we headed away. We had been in Norway for five and a half years.

It was a sad but also a happy day. We were heading for our new life in Australia.

Perth, Australia

We landed in Perth, Australia, in April 2007. It was glorious weather, and we were wearing shorts and T-shirts because we'd just come from a country with snow lying on the ground. The Aussies were in long trousers and jumpers because it was autumn and cool for them.

We stayed at the Peninsula Apartments on the south side of the city. You could see the city across the river from our apartment. A ferry ran to the city every 20 minutes and Norman caught that to work. He just had to walk across the grass and he was at the ferry dock. Every now and then, the dolphins would swim alongside the boat.

Conor asked if he and Catherine could go to the park one day. Having come from Kongsberg, the safest town in the world, where you could leave your front door and car unlocked, where everyone knew everyone else, and your kids were safe everywhere, I let them go play in the park. About 20 minutes later they came home with two strange men.

Catherine said, 'Mummy, they've come to play you some music.'

I was in shock but let the men in. They played the mouth organ and sang for us.

Afterwards, they said you have lovely kids, to which I said, 'Thank you.' They gave Conor a mouth organ and Catherine a small tambourine. After they left, I had a big chat with the kids about bringing strangers home and talked to them about strangers in general. My kids' innocence changed that day.

We looked for a house and school and decided on Karrinyup Primary School. The interview with the principal went well and both kids started after the Easter holiday. We moved into a small house in Karrinyup that faced a golf course, had a swimming pool and a big back garden. It was perfect.

One of the first things I did was go to Jackson's Art and Craft store. I bought an easel and canvas, paints and brushes. I had always been an artist and drawn pictures and portraits of people, but I'd never painted before. I always wanted to have a go. It was new to me, but I loved it as soon as I started. Even today I love painting—it's the one thing that calms and grounds me. Below is my very first painting. I guess the child is me and the adult is taking me to safety.

The First Day of School

Catherine started Grade One and Conor Grade Six. As we stood in the playground waiting for the bell, a woman walked along the verandah who I felt I had known. Of course I didn't; I'd only just arrived in Australia. It was just one of those feelings you sometimes get.

The woman was Catherine's teacher, Robyn. Catherine took off her outdoor shoes and put on her indoor shoes, like she had done hundreds of times in Norway, but Robyn said, 'You don't need to do that here.' We had a few things to learn.

After a few days, we met with Robyn, who said Catherine wasn't ready for Grade One, that she needed to be a kid a little longer. So we put her into pre-primary, the grade below. Conor loved his teacher, Mr. Milligan—he was able to capture Conor's imagination.

Beata and Roy came out just after Christmas. Gosh, I'd missed my friend, and it was so good to see her again.

They spent all their time in the pool with my kids. We took them to Whiteman Park, and feeding the kangaroos was the highlight of the outing. We took them to the chocolate factory, and they went on a wine cruise because Roy's business was catering. They went on a few wine tours, but that wasn't my thing, so I stayed home.

On the 1st of January 2008, Mum called to say my father was sick, and it wasn't looking good. Apparently, he wanted to talk to me, so I called Mum's mobile. He asked to speak to Norman, so I passed the phone. He apologised for the way he had treated him and said he was proud of the way he was with his family.

He didn't apologise to me; he didn't talk to me much at all. I kept thinking, What about me?

The next day, on 2nd of January 2008, Wendy called to say he'd passed away. I sat on my bed, not sure how to feel. My father had just died, and I felt lost, not grief-stricken.

I told Norman and the kids and spoke to Beata and Roy because I had to fly back to the UK for the funeral. Beata and Roy stayed with another friend, and I booked a flight back to the UK for the next day.

My brother picked me up from the airport and took me to Mum's. I climbed the stairs, and Mum met me in the hallway. I gave her a hug, and she said, 'Do you want to go in the room and see your father, or do you want to go into the living room and see your aunt and uncle?'

I didn't want to do either. I wasn't ready to go in and see my father's body, and I hadn't spoken to my aunt and uncle in more than ten years. I decided to take my case into Mum's room and take five minutes to myself.

I went into the living room, and Auntie Grace and Uncle Robert stood up to hug me. They apologised for leaving the court all those years ago and not getting in touch. Supposedly, they went out for a smoke with Grandad, and my Auntie Grace had asked him again, 'Did you touch Sharon?'

Finally, he broke down and said, 'Yes.'

This was before the court case, before I had to give evidence, and they'd said nothing. I didn't know how to react, whether to be pissed off that I'd gone through three days of hell on the witness stand, or relieved that they both knew, and it had come from his own mouth.

Dad was lying in the other room in his coffin, and I had to go in and see him. I walked in expecting to feel something, but I didn't. For a moment I was a small child again, and all I felt was relief. Relief that he couldn't hurt me anymore, couldn't talk down to me anymore, couldn't harm me anymore.

My brother took me to the alcohol shop, and I bought enough drink for everyone. Colin then gave me a huge roll of money to give to Mum. When I asked him where he got it from, he said he had been doing a lot of homers (painting and decorating jobs) recently.

I gave Mum the money and asked her if Colin was a drug dealer. She said, 'No, he's been doing a lot of homers.'

I said, 'Don't lie to me.'

In the end, she said, 'Yes, but I have nothing to do with it.'

I was disgusted he could do something so awful. So much had come out of the woodwork already, and I was grateful I lived in Australia.

On the day of the funeral, the house was full of family and neighbours. Dad's sister, Joan, turned up, which shocked me as she wanted nothing to do with him. Robert and Grace were there, too. Lots of Mum's family. I hadn't seen any of them for many years, and they felt like strangers to me.

At the crematorium, Wendy and Josh sat together, and Colin held Mum. I was at the end of the pew feeling lost and alone. As everyone left and they shook our hands, I felt chills down my spine. I had to leave the hall and stand outside—I couldn't handle all the hypocrites.

We went to the pub afterwards, very fitting for someone who'd died of alcohol abuse. About 20 people went to the pub, and I had an open tab for food and drinks. Everyone was talking about the good old times. I guess they were talking about the parties, which all used to end in fights.

I sat out of the way with my sister and Josh. When I went up to the bar to pay the bill, the bar manager said it had already been paid. I asked her who paid, and she pointed to my cousin Andrew, the one who'd slashed

Norman's tyres and beat Dad with a baseball bat. Andrew was one of the biggest drug dealers in Scotland and probably rich, but I wanted to kill the fucker. I walked over to his table, jumped over it and hit him in the face. I grabbed him by the shirt and hit him over and over again. Uncle Robert and Colin pulled me off him. Auntie Grace called a taxi to take us back to Mum's. I was so fucking angry, and everyone was telling me, let him pay; he deserves to pay, but I didn't want his drug money. I didn't want anything to do with him.

I later found out Mum was close to her sister again, after everything she did, even saying she hoped my grandfather got away with it. I could have screamed. What was wrong with these people? Or was it me? Was I the one in the wrong? I wished Norman was there—I needed to hear his voice—but it was after midnight in Australia

We put all the furniture back in the spare room, and I slept in with Mum that night. She said she was happy I was there. We didn't talk about what had happened earlier in the day. I think we were both too exhausted.

The next morning, I brought it up.

She said, 'Just let him pay for the meals and drinks.'

I said, 'What the hell is wrong with you? Don't you remember what he did?'

She told me that Andrew had visited them quite a bit before Dad died, and he was friends with Colin.

I screamed, 'Of course, they're friends. What the fuck, Mum? What the fuck is wrong with you all? Have you lost your minds?'

I couldn't wait to get home to Norman and the kids, but I still had a week left. We went through all Dad's clothes and bagged everything up for the charity shops. Mum gave me Dad's watch for Norman and some of his model cars for Conor. I spent the last few days with Mum and Wendy, and it was really nice. We didn't talk about the funeral. I decided that Mum and Colin could see and do whatever they wanted; it was none of my business.

Wendy and Mum took me to the airport. As I said goodbye, Mum said, 'I love you.'

I said it back.

I had never heard Mum say she loved me. I thought about those three words all the way home, and how much they meant, coming from her. I had waited all my life for those three words.

Returning home to Norman and the kids was like heaven. I had to let what happened in Glasgow go, or it would eat me up. At home with my family, I felt immense peace. I'd missed them desperately.

The next year, Conor went into Grade Seven, where he struggled. We met with the principal and told him Conor had ADHD and was on medication. We also told him Conor didn't want the other kids to know. Unfortunately, his teacher didn't get the memo and told the class, allowing the bullies to come out of the woodwork. They cornered Conor in the bathroom, pushing his buttons by telling him he was stupid because he had ADHD. Conor snapped. He picked up a bin and hit one of them over the head.

When we arrived at school, Conor and the other boys were sitting outside the classroom. Conor told us what happened, and I believed him. Conor wasn't a violent kid. It all came out in the classroom; they'd pushed Conor, wanting him to snap.

I was angry at his new teacher, and he was told not to mention Conor's ADHD again. Conor was bullied all the way through high school by one of those boys.

Catherine started Grade One with Mrs. Stewart, (Robyn) and I offered my assistance in art. I told Robyn I was a self-taught artist and a special needs assistant when in Norway. I worked alongside Coral, one of the classroom assistants, and we got on really well. I started out volunteering there one day a week, but that quickly turned into two. I was happy to work in the classroom again, and I also got to be with my baby girl. Catherine loved Grade One and her teacher.

I was there one day when a blue-tongue lizard casually strolled across the classroom and into the storeroom. I remember Catherine's face, scared but amazed by this creature, as was I. The other kids were not fazed at all and just carried on with what they were doing. According to Robyn, we would see these creatures often.

In the mornings, we took the kids onto the playground and let them run a few laps before heading into the classroom for work. I showed Robyn Brain Gym, which is a movement-based program using the brain, senses and body. The kids repeat simple movements using symbols, like drawing the infinity sign with their fingers or thumb in the air, or around their eyes like the number 8. The programme helps improve speech, reading and thinking skills, and can also help in reducing stress. Robyn decided we could teach it, so I taught Brain Gym to the children.

By the end of the year, I was working with Robyn two or three times a week, and I stayed working with her after Catherine moved on to Grade Two.

I also organised an art exhibition for the end of the year. The teachers put together a big painting for each class, and each child did their own drawing or painting, too. Some grades made T-shirts with paintings on them. Jacksons gave us a discount on canvases and paintbrushes, and we bought the paint from Bunnings.

I worked with a few classes on their pieces. I split the big canvas into six and got the kids to paint six different pictures.

I had lots of help in the run up as well as on the night of the exhibition. Carine Senior High School let us use their hall. On the night, 90% of the paintings sold, and the rest went back to the school to be hung. A number of local artists donated three paintings each, and 30% of the selling price went to the school. I sold two of my paintings, which I was extremely happy with.

The whole night was a huge success.

On September 10th, an old friend, who was a nurse at a hospital in Scotland, let me know Caitlyn had died. Caitlyn was 21 and had been in a coma for a few weeks. My friend got in touch with me to send her condolences, but it was the first I'd heard.

I remember standing in shock, not knowing what to say or do, wondering why no one had told me. Maybe they didn't know where I was or, more likely, they didn't want to get in touch. I was always the black sheep, the one that was always in the wrong, the one that could do no right.

But this was Caitlyn, and she was part of me, too. I had lost someone, someone who was always on my mind, someone never far from my thoughts. I always had a dream of Caitlyn being blissfully happy and living a full life. I never thought of her life being cut short because of her disability. I hadn't seen her since that day at Nannie's funeral, and I'd imagined her living a normal life.

I didn't know how I was going to grieve the loss: Norman didn't know about Caitlyn, and neither did my kids.

I cried hard that day. When I went to school, I bumped into Coral, who asked if I was okay. I broke down and told her about Caitlyn. She took me into the classroom, and, when the kids left, I told Robyn. Now two people knew my secret, one that I thought I would take to the grave.

After school, I picked my kids up and went home. I never spoke to Norman about it.

I started working with Robyn three, sometimes four, times a week. But I decided to go back to college and get my certificate as a teaching assistant again, because what I had from Norway didn't stand in Australia.

I went to college twice a week and studied in between. Within six months I had my certificate. Terry, the new principal, gave me a job working with the other Grade One teachers, Chris and Jill, in the classroom next door, as well as Robyn.

Jill wanted to raise money for wheelchairs for kids, and so we decided to make Angel cards. Each child in the class came up with a saying and designed a picture on a card. We made 50 copies and sold most of them.

One day in class, Robyn read a book to the kids called Flat Stanley, about the adventures of Stanley Lambchop, a little boy who is squashed by a bulletin board while sleeping. He survives and decides to make the best of being flat. He discovers he is able to enter locked rooms by sliding under the door. Stanley decides to go on lots of adventures.

I spoke to Robyn about getting the kids to draw Flat Stanleys of their own and posting them to a school in Scotland. She loved the idea, so I found Kelvongrove Primary School in Scotland and we got the kids to draw their own Flat Stanleys. They all wrote letters to the Scottish students, telling them about themselves, and we posted them off.

About two months later, we received a package in the mail from Scotland. Inside were Flat Stanleys and letters to each of the kids. We helped them read the letters, and then we sat and discussed them. It was a great experience for the kids.

For Book Day that year, Robyn dressed as Flat Stanley's mother, Mrs. Lambchop. We laughed and had difficulty working out how to attach a full-size painting of Mrs. Lambchop to Robyn. We laughed so hard Robyn ended up on the floor.

That was one of my favourite days. I don't think I've ever laughed so hard.

Chapter Twelve

2010 – 2015

Terri sent me on a course to become a Rainbow Facilitator, in order to work with small groups of kids who are going through grief or abandonment—like a death in the family or divorce and remarriage of their parents. I read books on grief and loss, and we played games, worked on printed sheets, did exercises and quizzes that branched into specific areas of interest.

I enjoyed the course a lot, but it was confronting, and I felt triggered by my own past. But I'm glad I did it, as it showed me I could be there for children going through a tough time in their lives. The further into the course I got, the more I realised there was no one there for me as a child—no adult to talk to, no one who understood or believed me. The only person I had in my life who listened to me was Rose.

I still have a card I used to give to the kids. It came from the Rainbow website. It says:

I'm Thumbody
I am me!
There's not another person,
In the whole world like me.
I have my very own thumbprint.
I am special.

Leonie

Norman and I realised both of our kids needed extra help in maths and English. One of the mothers told me about Kumon, a learning method that allows the student to study at the level right for them.

Leonie was the facilitator, and I took them Tuesdays and Thursdays after school. The kids hated it, of course, but I pushed them to go because I thought it was good for them.

One day while sitting outside waiting for the kids to finish, Leonie came out and asked if I was okay. It was around the time Caitlyn died, so I was struggling more than a little. I broke down and told her what had happened. She told me she was a spiritual healer and would come to see me. I invited her to the house, told her about my past and how I struggled to talk to people about it. I told her my head was exploding because I had no one to tell it to.

We met once a week or once a fortnight over a two-year period. We sat and chatted, then Leonie gave me Reiki healing. It helped so much to calm my mind and body. Being able to talk to someone helped, too. I was broken. I felt like a time bomb waiting to go off. I was drinking, but knew I needed to stop. I knew, too, that if the healing was going to work, if my mind was going to be clear, I needed to stop drinking.

The kids stopped going to Kumon, but I kept seeing Leonie for chats and healing. She became one of my closest friends. During this time, I became very spiritual. I had been spiritual for a number of years, but at that time I had an awakening. I could see and feel more, maybe due to what I had gone through as a child, or maybe I needed more at that time. Either way, I felt calmer than I had felt in years thanks to Leonie.

I started painting again. It also cleared my mind and helped with the healing. I gave Leonie the first painting I made (see earlier).

We visited Norman's aunt Doreen and uncle Gordon and cousins Janet and Pauline in Sydney. We finally met Janet and Pauline and saw Auntie Doreen and Uncle Gordon again. They took us sightseeing around Sydney—it was nice but way too busy; I love the quieter life in Perth. Catherine loved Pauline, because she made ice cream with crushed Maltesers. Janet was a chef, so the food was amazing. I loved having a real family for the first time in my life.

Hege, her mum and her two kids came to Perth in the summer of 2008. We visited Whiteman Park and fed the kangaroos and patted the koalas. We took them to the chocolate factory, and my two and Hege's two queued for handfuls of chocolate again and again. I was sure they would be sick in the car. Hillary's boat harbour was their favourite place. The kids loved the beach, and I'd leave them there with Hege and go back to collect them later—sunbathing isn't my thing.

It was a sad day when we had to say goodbye. I missed Hege so much, still do.

The Murals

Terri, the school principal, called me one day and asked if I would join another artist, Ros, and paint murals around the school. I hadn't done anything on that scale before. Ros and I got together and worked out how to do it. We asked each student to paint an image, then gathered them all and placed them over the floor of a demountable. Ros, Terri and I then chose which images we would transfer onto the walls to be painted.

Bunnings supplied some paint, and for every 3-litre tin that we bought, we got a 3-litre tin of jellybeans. We had so many jellybeans, we held a raffle to count the number of jellybeans in the jar.

We held a busy bee over one weekend, and staff and parents prepared the walls with white undercoat. Every child in the school got a chance to paint something on the walls, but Terri wanted it to look professional, so we had to go over some to pretty them up. Terri was constantly looking over our shoulders, saying, 'Have you missed a bit?' 'Maybe just check this over here?' 'Is that supposed to be there?' It drove Ros and me crazy.

One Saturday morning when we were working on the murals, we heard Terri's shoes clip-clop down the verandah towards us. I remember thinking, God, here she comes again, just as I heard her say, 'You need to go deeper into the holes, Sharon.'

I thought, *Terri, just go back to your bloody office.* She proceeded to check Ros's work and went back to her office. Then we heard an almighty scream, and Terri came running out saying there was a blue-tongue lizard inside. We got the lizard out, and she shut the door so it couldn't get back in, locking it without realising her keys were inside.

'Bugger, bugger, bugger,' said Terri. We all laughed so hard. We phoned the office manager, who brought over some keys.

From that day on, whenever Terri said anything, we would say, 'Bugger it,' and laugh.

One day when we were talking about the murals with Terri, she suggested changing something.

Ros said, 'I'm going to take you to the ground.'

The three of us burst out laughing, and Terri said, 'Am I that bad?'

Ros and I replied, 'Yes,' at the same time.

We worked many hours, during and after school and over weekends in the blistering heat to get the murals finished, and they looked great. I wrote a poem for Terri to thank her for that wonderful six weeks, and called it 'Journey of the Murals with Terri'. I read it aloud at the Christmas work function. I ended by saying:

I would like to thank the boss for an adventurous 5 weeks and present her with the Amazing Bugger Award for 2012.

I gave Terri her trophy of appreciation.

Vietnam

In 2014, Norman was offered a position in Ho Chi Minh, Vietnam. We were happy in Perth, but I could see Norman was ready for a change. I was the one who was scared of change, but I said yes for him. The kids didn't want to leave their friends, but they accepted the move. Catherine was in grade 6 and Conor was in grade 12.

When we landed, the plane door opened, and I felt the rush of hot air hit my face. I hate humidity—I feel like I can't breathe. I thought, I'm going to hate this.

Norman's company rented us a large, five-bedroom apartment in District 2, next door to the International School where the kids would go. It was a perfect location for everything—school, shops, the city, where Norman worked. The apartment was in a compound, with a coffee shop, a grocery store, a gym, tennis courts and a restaurant that made the best Vietnamese food I'd ever had. It was actually two apartments, so we set the kids up in one and Norman and I in the other.

We had our own driver, who took us anywhere we needed to go. The car was cool, but stepping out nearly killed me. The kids walked next door to school.

While Norman was at work and the kids were at school, I was alone in the apartment. I struggled to find things to do all day. My easel, paints and canvases arrived, but I didn't want to paint all day. There was a language barrier, so I didn't want to go anywhere. And there was the heat and the busyness of Ho Chi Min City.

I was lonely, and depression kicked in quickly. Within three months I was in so deep, I couldn't see anything positive in life. One day, I got the driver to take me to the liquor shop, where I bought vodka and Baileys. In the afternoon when the kids came home from school, I'd give them afternoon tea and set them up to study, then go to my apartment and drink until Norman got home. I tried to disguise the smell of the alcohol by brushing my teeth or eating mints, but he could still smell it. He didn't mention it for a few weeks, and when he did, I got defensive and agitated. I told him I needed it to get through the day.

After a disagreement with Norman one night, I climbed the stairs to the roof of the apartment building. It was raining, but warm. I looked over the edge, thinking I could jump to my death and that would solve everything. No more nightmares, no more panic attacks, no more hurting my family. I was on the third floor—what if I jumped but didn't die? What if I ended up a paraplegic or quadriplegic, and Norman and the kids had to look after me for the rest of my life?

I cried out and fell to my knees in the pouring rain, defeated. I needed help and soon, or I wouldn't survive the hell I was in.

We made an appointment at the International SOS Medical Centre in our district with a female doctor. I told her what had been happening for the past three months, and a little about my past and how it was impacting my life and family. I also told her I was suicidal, and I didn't want to put Norman through anymore. She was really good but said there was no real help in Vietnam. She thought I needed EMDR (Eye Movement Desensitisation and Reprocessing), but that was not available in Vietnam. The two options were the UK or Australia.

I knew then that I had to choose between therapy or my family. If I chose my family, I knew I would lose them all with my depression and drinking. So I chose myself and therapy. I knew I couldn't return to Scotland and my ghosts, so I chose to go back to Perth and see a psychologist there.

It meant leaving Norman and the kids in Vietnam, which was one of the hardest things I've ever had to do. The day I said goodbye, I cried so hard. Catherine struggled to say goodbye, too. She held onto me so tight and cried, not wanting me to leave. I promised to video call them every day, twice a day if I could.

I organised to stay with my good friend, Judy, and her family. She had a room with an ensuite at the back of her garage. It was just what I needed. I ate dinner with the family at night, then went to my room and called Norman and the kids. Sometimes I called Catherine after school, as she needed me more at twelve and I felt guilty for not being with her at that crucial age. She wanted to talk to her mum about things like boys, life and everyday living. I missed them desperately.

Dr Yajna

I looked up EMDR online, and it sounded a lot like hypnosis. It's designed to work with traumatic or distressing memories and is an evidence-based treatment for trauma. First, you must identify the distressing memory or negative experience, and during the therapy, you focus on that traumatic memory while your therapist directs you to move your eyes in various directions using her finger or fingers. It helps weaken the emotion connected to that memory and helps you feel more detached from the memory.

What is EMDR?

EMDR stands for Eye Movement Desensitization & Reprocessing. It is a therapy proven to help reduce symptoms related to:

- DEPRESSION
- PHOBIAS
- ANXIETY
- TRAUMA & PTSD
- ADDICTIONS
- OTHER EMOTIONAL PROBLEMS

How does EMDR work?

EMDR has a direct effect on the way the brain processes information, releasing emotional experiences that are trapped in the nervous system.

1. Your therapist helps you recall an upsetting memory, thought, or feeling.
2. Then, your therapist activates both sides of your brain by using Dual Activation Stimulation (DAS), which is something you see, hear, or feel on both sides of your body. It's like watching a ping-pong game.
3. The upsetting memories are REPROCESSED by the brain, resulting in painful memories and thoughts being replaced by more RESOLVED.

I felt anxious sitting in the waiting room because I had no idea what to expect. Before I went to the appointment, I'd looked up my doctor, Dr Yajna, online. But when she walked out of her office into the hallway, I was shocked. My first thought was, She is so young, and my second was, She looks like a Disney princess in her stick-out polka dot dress.

I wasn't sure the therapeutic relationship would work, but I knew I had to give it a go. I sat across from her, and she asked me why I was there. I told her I had left my family to receive help, that I was desperate. Then she asked about my past, and I found her very easy to talk to. We discussed EMDR but decided we needed a few sessions of talking therapy first, as she wanted to get to know my past so we could pick a point in my history to start the EMDR.

After a few weeks, I didn't see Yajna's age anymore. She was a professional, and I started viewing her as one. I found it easy to talk about my past. She found a point in my past that troubled me most: the nightmare of my first time with Grandad and the bloodied sheets.

I was terrified of starting the therapy, of having to go into the image of that night, of remembering the details while awake and not in my nightmares. We sat facing each other, Dr Yajna just off to my right. She held her hand in front of my face and moved her pointer finger and middle finger side to side, asking me to follow with my eyes. While following her fingers, she asked me to go into the image of my grandfather in bed with me. It was like watching a film reel playing out. I felt the fear rise in me, and I broke down—it felt too real. I did this once a week, sometimes twice a week, for months.

I hadn't painted in a long time, but after my first EMDR session, I felt I wanted to paint again. I painted a memory box for Yajna. She interpreted this as the holding environment in our relationship, which was important for me to open up and feel safe in.

It was intense work, and I became suicidal. Yajna called me when I didn't have sessions, just to check up on me. The twice-weekly therapy sessions, the phone calls and the voice recordings she made for me were to provide the holding environment I needed at that time to prevent hospitalisation. Her simply being there was one of the most helpful parts of therapy. As I learnt to feel comfortable and safe with Yajna, I started to let friends and family closer to me, too.

Eventually, the intensity of the image of my grandfather was no longer there. In fact, after many months, that nightmare stopped completely. I remember waking up thinking, Did I have the nightmare? I was the happiest I'd been in years. I texted Yajna with the good news. The second day without it, I woke and cried with joy. When I saw Yajna, I cried, gave her a hug and said, 'Thank you for everything.'

But that was just the start. We still had work to do, but Yajna got pregnant, and we had limited time.

Yajna said, 'It was such a privilege to work with you intensively to the point that the nightmares you had for over 30 years stopped prior to my maternity leave.'

I called Norman a few nights, but he was at the pub. When I eventually reached him, I asked why he was at the pub so much. He said he needed some time out, some time to himself.

As the nightmares had stopped, I flew back to Vietnam and saw Norman and the kids for a week. We were sitting in the restaurant, Blue, one night. and Norman was looking at his phone and smiling. I asked why he was smiling, and he said. 'No reason.'

Catherine said, 'He's smiling at his girlfriend, Mum.'

I asked Norman what she meant by that, and he said nothing, so I asked to see his phone. At first, he refused, but then he gave it to me. I asked who the girl on his screen was, and he told me it was the bar manager.

I said, 'What the hell is going on?'

He said, 'Nothing. We're just friends.'

He told me she had a boyfriend and that they only spoke at the bar about me and the kids. I asked him why she was sending him messages, and he said they were friends.

I couldn't get this friendship out of my head. I didn't understand why he would talk to her and not call me instead. I told him how much I needed him, told him how hard therapy was, and how I was doing it for him and the kids.

He said, 'You need to be doing it for you, not for us.'

I was angry. I didn't want this woman knowing my business, and I especially didn't want her knowing my husband. As the days and weeks passed, I grew more and more insecure and, once back at Judy's, I would still phone the kids each night. I phoned one night and asked to speak to Daddy.

They said, 'Daddy's not here.'

I asked where he was, and eventually, they told me he was at the pub. I asked why they didn't want to tell me, and they said, 'Daddy said not to make you upset by telling you.'

This made me paranoid. I called Norman's phone over and over again, but he didn't answer.

I decided I was going to kill myself, but I didn't know how to do it. I was living in a little room. I didn't have any knives. I had limited medication and no belt to use. I was at a loss. Instead, I cried until I fell asleep.

I didn't tell Judy; I didn't want to burden her. She was doing an amazing thing by allowing me to stay, and I was grateful.

I finally spoke to Norman, and I told him how I felt and what I felt like doing.

He said, 'Please don't do that. She's just a friend, nothing more. Sometimes I need someone to talk to, so I sit at the bar and chat about anything and everything. She has a boyfriend, and they're planning on moving to England together. There's nothing to worry about, Sharon. I just go there for the company. Nothing more.'

He said he loved me, that I was just to look after myself, and that he wasn't going anywhere.

For months I struggled with that relationship. I saw a photo of her one day, with Catherine and Norman. It was National Day, and they were wearing national dress. It made me feel sick. I had to talk to Yajna about it. I had to keep my feelings in check. I had to know in my head that Norman wasn't cheating on me, that they were just friends.

I realised I needed a house of my own. I couldn't stay with Judy for 18 months. Norman and I found a two-bedroom house in Karrinyup. I bought a green Suzuki Swift that I called my little green bug. It gave me independence. I started working with Robyn again at the school, just part-time because of my therapy. A few nights a week I cooked dinner for Robyn and her husband, Rob. It kept me busy when not doing therapy. The kids came for 6 weeks over the summer break. I'd missed them so much. I flew back to Vietnam with them and spent August there because Conor was turning 18 and I wanted to be with him on his special day. We went out for dinner, then to the rooftop bar, where I danced with my son. We then went to a bar to listen to a friend of ours sing *Happy Birthday* to Conor.

The next day, Catherine asked if I would go to Blue with her for a drink. As we sat talking, I could tell something wasn't right. I asked, and she said she went on my laptop to leave me a message and decided to open up one of my messages that said, 'Letter to Mum'. She thought it was a letter she had written to me because she used to do things like that—leave little notes or drawings on my laptop.

Catherine leaned over the table and said, 'I know about Caitlyn, Mum.'

I was in shock. I didn't know how to answer her. 'What do you mean you know about Caitlyn?'

'I read a letter to Nannie on your laptop. I thought it was a letter I wrote to you. I want to know about my big sister. I want to know what happened to her.'

I told her about Caitlyn. About how young I was. About my grandfather. I told her about Caitlyn's disability too. I also told her Caitlyn had a good mum and a good upbringing, and that she was happy. I then told her that Caitlyn had died, and that's when she cried. She said she would have loved to have met her big sister. I told her I hadn't spoken to anyone about Caitlyn, that she was my secret and what I'd written on my computer was private, that I had written the letter as part of my therapy. I also told her that I was glad that she knew, and that I would tell Conor and Daddy.

I organised a drink at the local coffee shop in the compound. We sat outside where it was quiet. The air was warm. I looked at Norman and Conor with tears in my eyes.

I said, 'There's something I need to tell you both. I had a baby when I was 13 years old. She died a number of years ago. I had to tell you both about her as part of my therapy.'

Conor said, 'I'm so sorry, Mum.'

Norman said he already knew about Caitlyn, that I'd told him a number of years before when drunk, but he'd never brought it up again because he didn't know how I felt about it.

From that day on, I felt relief—relief I'd told my family about Caitlyn. Relief that I no longer had to keep the secret. I was now able to celebrate her birthday, 14th February, every year, and I was able to celebrate her death in September every year.

I had to deal with all of my abandonment issues. One day, Yajna bought me the story of the Velveteen Rabbit, by Margery Williams. It's a tiny book about a tiny stuffed rabbit whose desire it is to become real. She read the story to me and asked if I related. I said, 'Yes.'

In the story, the oldest and wisest toy in the nursery, the Skin Horse that was owned by the boy's uncle, tells the story of toys magically becoming real due to love from children.

'Real isn't how you were made,' he says. 'It's a thing that happens to you when a child loves you for a long, long time, not just to play with, but really loves you, then you become real.'

I was used, abused and battered all my childhood, but finding Norman and having my kids, I became real just like the Velveteen Rabbit.

Yajna was going on maternity leave, so I decided it was time to join Norman and the kids again after 18 months apart.

Yajna gave me the book *Oh, the Places You'll Go!* by Dr Seuss. She wrote inside:

'Dear Sharon,

Step by step, you can do it, and my strength has my belief behind you!

Yajna.'

Norman had three months left on his contract when I returned. I was in a good place: I wasn't drinking, I was nightmare-free and ready for the next chapter. I felt stronger and better able to cope with what lay ahead. I don't know if that's because I'd been away for so long and was feeling better in myself or if the weather had changed, but the humidity wasn't as intense.

The first thing I had to do was spend time with my children. It was good being back together properly. I also spent a lot more time with Norman, going out for meals or to Blue in the evening for a drink and chat. Those three months were very special.

My 40th

For my fortieth, Norman booked a trip to a Vietnamese island. We walked on the beach with the kids, ate at the restaurant, took rides on a little golf buggy, had massages and relaxed. The whole place was romantic, and we decided to renew our vows in front of the kids and with the beach behind us on the morning of my birthday. Catherine took a number of pictures of me and Norman and then one of the staff at the complex took pictures of the four of us.

This second wedding was my favourite because it had all my favourite people, Norman and the kids. Norman booked a surprise birthday dinner in a private room at the restaurant, with a glass window to the kitchen. We could see the chefs make our food. We ate Pho (soup) followed by Vietnamese salad and a beef dish with lemongrass and ginger. We had chocolate cake, and everyone sang happy birthday to me. It's my best birthday to date. I felt like I had the best husband and kids on this planet. I didn't want the trip to end. I wish I was back there now.

My 40th

For my fortieth, Norman booked a trip to a Vietnamese island. We walked on the beach with the kids, ate at the restaurant, took rides on a little golf buggy, had massages and relaxed. The whole place was romantic, and we decided to renew our vows in front of the kids and with the beach behind us on the morning of my birthday. Catherine took a number of pictures of me and Norman, and then one of the staff at the complex took pictures of the four of us.

This second wedding was my favourite because it had all my favourite people, Norman and the kids. Norman booked a surprise birthday dinner in a private room at the restaurant, with a glass window to the kitchen. We could see the chefs make our food. We ate Pho (soup) followed by Vietnamese salad and a beef dish with lemongrass and ginger. We had chocolate cake, and everyone sang happy birthday to me. It's my best birthday to date. I felt like I had the best husband and kids on this planet. I didn't want the trip to end. I wish I was back there now.

Newcastle

I'd expected to return to Perth but, instead, we packed up and moved to Newcastle, England, into an apartment near the city centre, then a large house in the countryside. Our neighbours were sheep, and it was blissful. Catherine caught the train to school, and I knew she was safe because a lot of other school kids were on the train with her.

Mum lived two hours from us, so I visited her often. The kids didn't go back as much as me—they weren't as close to Mum as my niece and nephew. I prepared dinner for the kids and Norman, then drove the two and a half hours to Glasgow to see Mum. We'd go out shopping and spend quality time together. We were closer now that Dad was gone, and she was more open with her affection. I think it took for him to die for her to show this. She told me she loved me and that she was proud of me. She even said I made a good choice with Norman and that she wished she'd found a man like him.

The only thing I hated was that Mum never left the area I grew up in, where I was raped and abused. There were too many ghosts. I had to walk past Nannie's old house, which reminded me of what Grandad did to me. I went to the graveyard, stood at the wall and looked at my tree. It was dead but still lying on the ground because it was too dangerous for anyone to remove. Rose's grave had gone, too. I said a prayer to her, wondering if she was still with me. But I needn't have wondered because I could still feel her close. I still talked to her when I needed to.

My nightmares returned. I think I was re-traumatized by passing the house where I was raped. I shouldn't have gone back, but Mum didn't drive. She caught the train to see me a few times, but mostly I travelled to her.

Our garden in Newcastle was huge, and I had to cut the lawn because Norman had allergies. We put up a bird feeder and watched the woodpeckers feed from it—it was magical. As the weather changed from summer to autumn, and the leaves of the trees turned orange and yellow, it was stunning. Of a weekend we'd walk up a country lane, and the horses would stand by the fence and watch us as we passed. Catherine loved this and wanted to go horse riding.

Autumn turned to winter, and snow came. We hadn't seen snow in many years, so a white Christmas was perfect.

After Christmas, I started to struggle, so I contacted Yajna and told her I needed help. I didn't want to find someone in Newcastle as I didn't want to tell my story all over again. Yajna started calling me once a week over Messenger. It wasn't the same as seeing her in person, but it was a connection, and a connection that I needed. I missed Perth—I missed my friends, and I was struggling with going to Glasgow and with my connection to Mum. I loved seeing Wendy, my sister, and her partner and daughter when they visited. I missed her desperately when away. We were close and still are.

At the end of our year in Newcastle, we had to make a decision about whether we stayed in England and went to Bristol or headed back to Perth. We decided to go home to Perth.

We visited Norman's parents in Ireland to say goodbye. We spent lots of time with them and at his sister's house with her kids. I struggled with the Irish accent as it's very strong, and the kids' accents were broad.

Two days before we were due to leave, Catherine called my phone from the next room. I answered and she asked if I would go to her bedroom. When I went to her room, she was sitting on the bed crying. I asked her what was wrong, and she told me Granddad had done something to her. He kept trying to kiss her. He kissed up the side of her face and bit her ear, leaving teeth marks there. She said he kept grabbing her to him for a cuddle and rubbing himself from side to side against her. I was furious. I wanted to kill him. It brought back too many memories for me.

I was in shock. I'd known this man for many years. He was a spiritual man, yet he had done this to my daughter. I held her tight and told her I was there for her. Norman needed to know, so I said we had to tell her dad. Norman was in our bedroom, so I took her by the hand and walked her along the hallway. Norman sat up, and I said Catherine had something to tell him.

Catherine looked at me, tears in her eyes, and I knew she couldn't say anything. She didn't want to hurt her father. So I told him. Norman took Catherine, held her tight, not letting go.

We dressed and went downstairs. The plan was to tell Norman's mother what had happened. She was outside hanging out the washing, so we waited at the dining table, but Norman's father came into the kitchen. Catherine grabbed my hand, and I took her out into the back garden.

Norman came out, and we sat with his mother at the outside table and told her what happened.

She said, 'I'm sure he didn't mean anything by it,' and it was left at that. It was mentioned that he possibly had early dementia. I hoped that was the reason, because I struggled to believe the man I knew would do that to my daughter, especially knowing what I had been through as a child.

We returned to Newcastle, and I went through to Glasgow to say goodbye to my family. Mum had tears in her eyes as we said goodbye and said, 'I look forward to coming and visiting you in Australia.'

Moving Back to Perth

I struggled with what happened to Catherine and going back to Glasgow and seeing my old ghosts. Mentally, I was all over the place. My nightmares were back and taking over. I was exhausted all the time. I quickly made an appointment to see Yajna again, and we soon got back into a routine: doing imagery, talking and EMDR. It was like I'd never had 15 months away.

The nightmares gradually stopped, but I was struggling with what had happened to Catherine. As her mother, I'd promised to protect her, and I felt I'd let her down because I didn't see it coming.

Then the news came that Norman's father had killed himself by drinking weedkiller. He did have dementia and wanted to end it before it advanced. He died a horrible death. His internal organs shut down one by one. He was in excruciating pain. We chose not to tell Catherine. She just knew he died.

Norman travelled back to Ireland for the funeral and missed Christmas with us. Catherine was angry about that, because her father was going back for the funeral of a man who'd hurt her, and it was Christmas. She felt like her father was taking sides, which he wasn't, of course. He had to go back for his mother and sister. Dementia can make people behave in ways they wouldn't normally.

Catherine saw a psychologist of her own, Shanti, in the same offices as Yajna. She got on really well with Shanti and managed to open up to her, and still sees her to this day, even though Shanti is in Tasmania. They Zoom call once a month.

Yajna told me she was pregnant again. I was really happy for her but wondered how I would manage when she went on maternity leave. She suggested a few psychologists that 'babysat' some of her clients, but I didn't feel comfortable, so decided against it. I wasn't ready to share my past with anyone else. I told her I'd wait until she got back. By the time Yajna left for maternity leave, I was in a stable place. I was still having nightmares, but they'd calmed a bit. My grandfather wasn't haunting me anymore.

I got a job working in the school canteen. It was faster paced, which I managed, but I clashed with management. My boss liked to be in control of everything. She tested and double-tested everything I did. No matter how well I had done it, she would check it. We laughed it off in time and put it down to a love-hate relationship. I loved working with the kids again—I was just seeing a different side to them. They were more in play mode and not in work mode at break time.

I'd been working at the canteen for 6 months when I started bleeding constantly, and was feeling tired and weak all the time, struggling to keep up with the work. My GP referred me to a gynaecologist, and I had a hysterectomy. After the operation, the gynaecologist asked if I had been hurt before because I had extensive internal scarring. He was surprised I'd had my kids normally. I had to go back to have a polyp removed and the scarring cauterized. I was in a great amount of pain for a while afterwards.

I returned to work, but I wasn't the same after the operation, so I handed in my resignation. I was sad to leave the school, but I was having horrific nightmares about Habib; they were encroaching my everyday life. I was having panic attacks and flashbacks, and my bulimia was so out of control. I couldn't keep anything down. I had control over it for a few years, but it was taking over my life again.

Chapter Thirteen

2015 – 2017

Danielle

I sought help for my bulimia. I told my GP, and she referred me to a psychologist named Danielle. This was in May 2018, and I didn't know what to expect after seeing Yajna for 4 years, but she made me feel comfortable straightaway, and I found her easy to talk to.

She asked me when the bulimia had started, and I said I was young but was unsure of the age. She believed there had to be a reason for me starting around the time I did. Did something happen to me then? I told her about Habib, and she said, 'I think we have a lot more to discuss before we deal with the bulimia. We can't deal with bulimia without first working with the reason for it.'

I thought I'd dealt with my past with Yajna, but I was wrong, so wrong.

We started from the beginning, and over the next few sessions we skimmed over my past. I can honestly say that talking about it again helped bring the intensity down.

We then got to talking about Habib ejaculating into my mouth and how I threw up immediately following. That's when the bulimia started: I couldn't keep food down after that day.

We also discussed the possibility that bulimia wasn't my biggest issue at that time. I also needed to deal with my nightmares, flashbacks and panic attacks, as well as issues I had with my parents. I had a lot to work on, but we had to take it one step at a time.

It took a few months to go through everything from my past. It was tough going over everything again, and I was mentally and emotionally exhausted. I carried so much guilt and shame about it all. Did I wear the wrong outfit? Did I wear my hair a different way? Why did I get in the van with Habib? Did I look at him a certain way? So many questions.

Seeing Danielle helped so much, because she helped me understand that it was nothing I did or didn't do that made anyone mentally or physically abuse or rape me. I did nothing to deserve the way I was treated. Until then, I used to think I walked around with a sign on me saying, 'Abuse me anyway you want.' I used to believe I was cursed, that I deserved what I got. But no-one deserves the sort of pain I went through all my childhood. Everyone deserves respect and love. Everyone deserves peace and a loving upbringing.

Perth Clinic, January 2019

I'd started self-harming around June 2018, cutting my arms, and I was suicidal. I sat with all my pills at one point ready to take them, but Norman came home early that day. I had hit a low point; the nightmares with Habib in them were consuming my waking day and night. I was in my office and had my craft knife in my hand one day and thought what it would be like to cut my arm. The feeling got the better of me. and I cut up my forearm. It gave me instant relief, but I was shocked at the blood loss. I hadn't thought it through properly. I didn't have anything to mop up the blood, so I took my T-shirt off and wrapped it around my arm. I held it there until the blood had stopped, cleaned the arm as best I could, then bandaged it up. Norman saw it when he got home from work and asked what had happened. I said that my craft knife slipped. He put butterfly stitches on it and bandaged it up. After a discussion with Danielle and Norman, I decided to go into Perth Clinic for a few weeks. I must say I wasn't keen on the idea at all.

Norman took time off work to take me in. I was terrified—I'd never been in a mental health hospital before and didn't know what to expect. I was assigned a psychiatrist on admission. The reception and administration staff were lovely, and I was taken through into a small room and asked a number of questions. We went through some paperwork, I had my picture taken, and I was shown to my room. Unfortunately, I was sharing a room with a young girl, and I was quite anxious about this because of my nightmares. I was told it would only be for a day or two and then I would have my own room.

Norman sat with me for a while, then one of the nurses came in and took my height and weight, and asked questions about why I was staying at the clinic. She asked what I needed from them while I was staying there. I said I needed support to get through each day, that I needed something to help me sleep at night because I suffered from nightmares. I apologised to the girl staying with me, and I only hoped I didn't keep her up all night.

When I met the psychiatrist, Dr So, I panicked because he sounded like Habib. He looked nothing like him and, in fact, he was a nice man, but I couldn't get over the way he sounded. The doctor asked lots of questions about my past and present and increased one of my medications from 20 milligrams to 100 milligrams per day.

After he left, Norman stayed until about 4:30 p.m., then he left, too. I felt so alone and confused, unsure of where I was or what I was doing there. The nurse came back and sat with me for a while and explained the different groups. She told me I would be attending Purple Group the next day. Purple Group is for mood management, people experiencing depression and anxiety. Norman and Catherine came in for a short visit in the evening. It was nice to see them because everything felt so foreign.

I had a rough night and didn't get much sleep. I took something around 2:00 a.m. to help me sleep and got up around 5:00 a.m. and had a cup of tea. I finally got back to sleep only to wake up with my alarm at 7:00 a.m. I showered and dressed, and the nurse came around with my morning medication. They were weaning me off my antidepressant and starting another.

I had Purple Group, followed by art therapy. I wasn't sure if art therapy was for me. I knew I was an artist, but the structure didn't appeal to me at all. The art therapist was nice though. I then went to 'senses' in the evening. I had to take my pillow and blanket and lay on a mat on the floor. One of the nurses then read out a meditation and played music. It was relaxing, but I couldn't quieten my mind enough to truly enjoy it.

I was then booked in for DBT (Dialectical Behaviour Therapy). It taught me about mindfulness, distress tolerance, emotion regulation, interpersonal effectiveness and planning for distress.

I kept my appointments with Danielle twice a week. Her office was within walking distance from the clinic. We talked about trying to change my psychiatrist to a female because of the triggers. I was very tired because of the nightmares, and I felt groggy and had a dry mouth due to the new medications.

When I returned to the clinic, I went straight to therapy with the Occupational Therapist, Laura. She spoke about anxiety and flashbacks. I felt my anxiety rise, my heart race, and I felt nauseous. I asked Laura if I could go back to my room. My nurse gave me some Nurofen and Panadol, and I tried to sleep it off.

Once I got my own room upstairs, I felt more comfortable. My friend Helen came for a visit. She was glad I was safe. A night nurse named Kim was an absolute angel, and I wished she was my mum. She would do her rounds at 9:00 p.m., just before bed, was so friendly, and made me feel like a special human being. I looked forward to the nights she was on. Cathy was another nightshift nurse who cared about my welfare. They'd talk to me, comfort me, when I'd had a really bad nightmare.

Norman arrived just after 6:00 p.m. and I would order dinner for him, too. The chefs at the clinic were outstanding, and the meals were 5 star. They were friendly and kind, a great bunch of people.

Mum called me on Messenger, and I was unsure if I wanted to answer, but I did. I told her where I was and that it was because of my past. I told her it was haunting me, and I was suicidal.

Her answer was, 'You must put it behind you. Put it in the past where it belongs.'

I said, 'You were raped. How did you cope with that?'

She said, 'You put it behind you and get on with your life. Think of Norman and the kids.'

They were all I thought about. If I wasn't in a good place, they would see that every day; that's why I needed help. I was doing the right thing, wasn't I? I needed to believe I was.

My nightly routines were the same: medications, shower, and sleep, waking twice, sometimes 3 times, with nightmares. Taking more medication and going back to sleep. I was a walking zombie.

I was allowed leave at the weekends, so I went out with Norman and the kids for brunch or lunch. I'd then gather up art materials from home before heading back.

On Australia Day, some of the patients went out to see the fireworks. They sat in the park across the road, in their pyjamas and dressing gowns. My room faced the front of the building, so I was able to see the fireworks from my room. There was a water feature outside my window. Every now and then, someone would put a family of tiny plastic ducks in the water, which made everyone smile. One day I saw a kookaburra bathing.

My sister and brother sent me messages saying, 'Get well soon.' Wendy told me how much she loved and cared for me. It was a long journey, but I was going to make it out the other end, and I did through group therapy and counselling. I attended group therapy every day and saw my psychologist twice a week.

When Dr So came to see me one day, I started having a panic attack. My nurse came in and, once I'd calmed down, I said I needed my nurse to be present when Dr So was visiting me.

So it was arranged he would only visit when accompanied by a female nurse so I felt safe.

Kim, one of the nurses, noticed a pattern to the nightmares. I seem to wake up around the same time every night.

Friends visited, and I made them cups of coffee, showed them some of the earrings and bracelets I was making, trying to keep myself busy in between therapy sessions. Making the jewellery helped me get through the day. Group therapy finished at 12.20 p.m. so I had a good 9 hours left in my day. As I saw one friend out, they joked that an alarm would go off if I stepped beyond the gate. I said, 'Should I try it?' Of course, there is no alarm—you're not held within the walls. It is a safe place.

I started reading *The Happiness Trap* by Russ Harris, about how to stop struggling and start living. The book helps break self-defeating habits, reduce stress and worry, and create a rich, full and meaningful life. I found it really helpful.

The sixth night was my worst. I woke from the nightmare around 2:00 a.m. in a panic and pressed the bell for the nurse to come. It was dark, and I was distressed. A male nurse with a beard came into the room, and I panicked even more. I cried out for him to leave. He tried telling me he was a nurse, but all I could see was Habib. I went into a horrible, terrifying panic attack. A female nurse came in and gave me some medication.

When I woke in the morning, I wasn't able to get out of bed for breakfast. I felt so drained by the panic attack. Norman took me out for a bit, and we walked in nearby Kings Park. He took me home for a while, so I could spend time with the kids, even if it was only for a few hours. I sat with Catherine in her room with her for a girly chat, and we fell asleep together—I was so exhausted from the night before. Norman woke me up to say we had to return to the clinic.

I felt anxious going back to my room, but I had an understanding nurse. She said it would only be female nurses attending to me from now on. I felt calmer and more at peace.

Diary Extracts

The following are extracts from my diary at the time:

29/1/19

I started DBT primer. Last night I had the nightmare, falling out of my bed and hitting my head on the bedside table. Kim gave me some meds to help me sleep again. I woke in the morning with a black eye—a great start to my DBT therapy. I had a banging headache, so had to take some painkillers. DBT started at 9:00 a.m., and I had to fill in the health and well-being questionnaire, but I don't think I scored very well on that. Having too many negative thoughts; it's really tough being positive at that moment. We discussed mindfulness in depth over the three hours and being in the here and now. I felt I'd covered a lot of that with Yajna and Danielle, so I was quite comfortable with the discussion. My head and my eye were throbbing though.

Conor came up to see me this afternoon. It was nice spending one-on-one time with him. He stayed for dinner, and we sat outside and ate lamb shanks. We had a chat, and it was nice having no distractions around.

30/1/19

DBT, we discussed emotion regulation today and talked about various types of emotions and how to acknowledge them.

31/1/19

In DBT, we worked on interpersonal effectiveness. Identifying priorities in our relationships—getting what we need but preserving our relationships.

Some close friends and Catherine went to a carers/supporters meeting tonight. They said it was helpful and gave them an insight into mental health in general. While they were at the meeting, I spent time with Norman.

1/2/19

In DBT today, we did Planning for Distress and looked at crisis survival skills.

- I found the course overwhelming, as there was so much to take in and having to practice it daily – be mindful, live more in the moment and not in the past. It will be really tough and challenging, but I will succeed.

- I have to!!

End of diary entry.

I got back to sleep after a nightmare only to be woken by the fire alarm. God, it was loud and went off for a good half-hour. Going off like that in the middle of the night is a nightmare in itself. The head nurse came round to tell us it was a false alarm and to try and sleep.

I spoke to Mum, but it wasn't a great connection. I told her I was doing well in the clinic. I never told her how bad things were or when I was struggling.

I talked to Dr So about the nightmare meds as I was having pains in my chest and feeling sick and dizzy. My blood pressure was also high.

I was back in Purple Group with Laura, and it was nice to have normality again. We covered lots on stress management, anxiety, goal setting, helpful rewards and good goals.

I had a creative day making bracelets and earrings while watching a movie on YouTube.

I walked to see Danielle for my 1:30 p.m. appointment. We decided to try EMDR, and focused on the pipe before Habib used it in me. We worked on just letting it be and putting everything else in the chest I had imagined. It was a really tough session. I drew in my book all afternoon. Drawing always takes me to another place in my mind, a calmer place. I draw my emotions, angry, frustrated, peaceful and calm. It helps me deal with my past by producing art pieces that show my emotions, it kept me positive.

Next time I saw Danielle, I was struggling. I was saving up my meds, not taking them, and I had a bag of pills in my bag that I planned on taking on my way back to the clinic.

Danielle asked me what was wrong, but I couldn't tell her. Eventually, I told her that I planned on doing something on the way back to the clinic. I said I'd had enough, I was tired.

She spoke to me for a good 30 minutes before I broke down and told her what I was planning. She asked if I would give her the pills, but I held the bag.

She said, 'I can't tell you not to do it, Sharon, but I'm pleading with you not to. You deserve to live and live a full life with Norman and your kids. You deserve so much more in this life. Please give me the pills. Sharon, I don't own your choices, and I can't stop someone that really wants to, but we need to keep you safe. I can't let you tell me that you are at risk and not do anything about it.'

I hesitated but finally gave in and handed her the bag. She thanked me and took the pills and called the clinic to explain my risk.

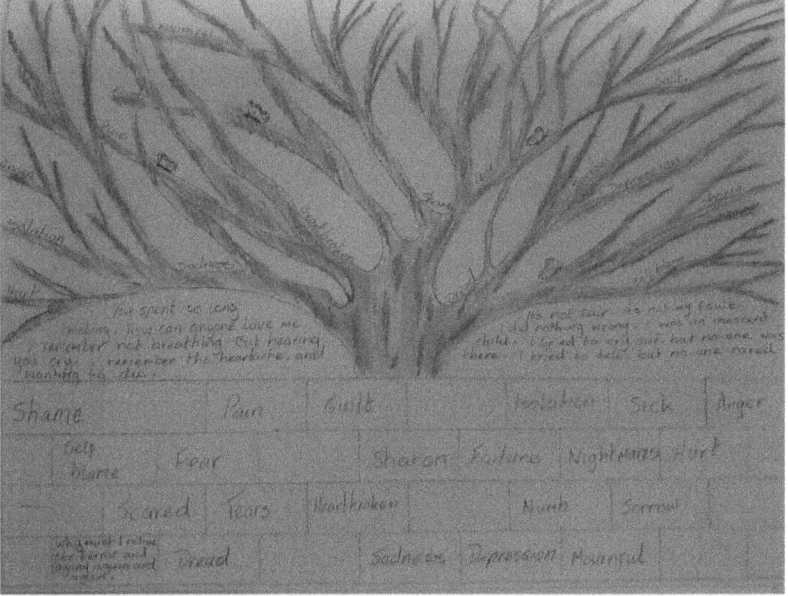

In a later session, Danielle wore the bracelet I'd made a few days before. It meant a lot seeing her wear it. We worked on EMDR again, and focused on the end of the image, when Habib left me in the fetal position in the van, in pain, with blood everywhere.

Every session of EMDR is intense, but some are more intense than others. This was one of those sessions. When I go into the images, sometimes I feel, taste and smell everything. It's exhausting, but I know it works and hope that one day I will be nightmare free.

I wrote in my diary what I had taken from therapy this week:

- To be more in the here and now.

- I accomplished accepting mindfulness, accepted being in the clinic, accepting help when it was offered to me.

- I was grateful for being in a group with nice people and I was grateful for Laura the OT.

10/2/19

When Norman visited, he looked so tired. We had dinner together outside in the courtyard, then went to my room and lay on the bed hugging. I had missed that so much.

Kim was my night nurse again. I'd made a Tree of Life keyring and gave it to her when she came in to say goodnight. She loved it and gave me a big hug. I still wish she was my mum.

12/2/19

My next appointment with Danielle was very emotional. We focused on Habib and the pipe that he used to rape me, and then taking me to the apartment and raping me again. When he had finished with the pipe, he threw it down by my head. All I could see was the blood. The pain was excruciating, and I felt it inside and out. I just wanted to die. I wanted him to kill me. He told me I had to drink the vodka if I wanted to go home. I remember the bath filling with blood as I tried to clean myself.

Throughout the session, I could feel the pain again. I returned to the clinic an emotional mess. I don't know how I managed the walk. I went to my room, curled up on the bed and cried myself to sleep. I woke at 3:40 p.m. with another headache. My nurse gave me some Ibuprofen and Panadol, and said if I needed to talk, she was there to listen.

14/2/19

Valentine's Day would have been Caitlyn's 30th birthday. I was feeling really low today, and the topic in Purple Group was stress. I didn't speak much. I didn't bother with breakfast or lunch, so I grabbed a scone in the afternoon and ate it in my room. I left therapy at 12:00 p.m. because my friend Helen was coming to take me out for a few hours. We went to King's Park, but it was so busy we couldn't find a parking space, so we drove back to the clinic, parked the car and went next door to the café. I just had water, and we talked about Caitlyn, therapy and how I was feeling. When I went back into the clinic, I rested on my bed and dozed for a while. Catherine arrived in the afternoon. We lay on the bed and hugged. That special time between mother and daughter is like nothing else. She stayed and had some dinner and Norman arrived at 7:40 p.m. to pick her up. He stayed for 10 minutes, and I walked them both to the gate and hugged them goodbye.

I made a number of Trees of Life keyrings and handed them out to some of the nurses. They attached them to their lanyards.

I woke through the night with a fright, and hit my head on the bedside table. I had a huge egg on my head. Kim gave me some ice to put on it. I woke in the morning with a huge headache. I asked my nurse for an extra pillow which I put between me and the bedside table.

In Purple Group, we worked on self-esteem. I struggle with self-esteem, self-confidence and self-care. Laura gave us some paper and asked us to write something positive to any of the other 6 people in group. I gave one to everyone and received 5 notes in return:

1: I think you are a very strong, beautiful lady with so much to give.

2: Hugs, keep strong.

3: You are an amazing artist. The kindness you show to others is beautiful, be kind to yourself, you deserve it.

4: You show courage and strength each day, you are kind and supportive. You work incredibly hard, be kind to yourself.

5: Sharon, you are such a wonderful strong woman, who despite your struggles still manages to bring light into all our lives. Don't stop being your insightful, talkative self (with that sweet accent).

I got quite emotional when I read their words. Every message and every word touched my heart.

15/2/19

Helen picked me up and took me home to see the kids because Norman was at competitions for skating. He is a figure skater—on wheels, not ice. Catherine skates, too, but it was her Year 12 ball, so I took her to have her hair and makeup done. She looked beautiful in her dress. I took her to Nannie and Poppy's (Kay and Nev's), we put music on, and Poppy danced with her. It was so graceful. I then took her to Helen's, and she had photos taken with Helen's daughter, Elysha, as well as with Norman and me.

We dropped Catherine at her pre-ball party with her friend Michelle. All the kids looked amazing—the boys in their suits and the girls in their ball gowns. I remember thinking, My baby is all grown up, and feeling sad about that. Conor took me back to the clinic.

I had a lovely day. I was so proud of my kids. They are both amazing human beings.

19/2/19

At my next appointment with Danielle, we did EMDR, working on seeing the bloodied pipe. As I got to the end of the scene in the van, I was able to picture Danielle by my head. She placed her hand on my head, and I felt safer for having her there. For the first time, I felt like I was going to get through it. I couldn't picture her at the apartment—that was too graphic. She told me to write the memory, then write it again with a different ending.

It was so bad that we went between processing, to having a break and biting off any chunk we could, but sometimes we didn't have a choice and it was all there in the room. We tried to use ways to help me not go into reliving the memory, so I could process it while knowing I was also safe in the present and in the room. I found hearing Danielle's voice in EMDR really helped me to remember where I was, so she made sure she kept speaking calmly so I knew she was there. During these times, I often felt like I was the age I was when the trauma happened.

We wanted to help the nightmares as I was getting injured and exhausted. We tried for me to be in the scene in a more powerful way, but that felt scary. It felt better to imagine I wasn't alone. The memories were so intense that we tried different ways of helping me tolerate processing them. The nightmares were severe. We tried to write the dream with a different ending, but the vividness of the trauma was so strong, Danielle said it was just going to take time and that once the intensity was less, it might work better.

I tried to imagine what happened after the bloody bath. I imagined myself in my room and pictured Danielle with me. In my imagination, she put my pillow on the floor and placed a blanket over me. She sat beside me, putting her fingers through my hair as I cried myself to sleep.

I told Danielle I placed her in the van as I lay there bleeding and scared, and in my room afterwards. She was happy that I connected her to the image. She said she had goosebumps.

Back at the clinic, I was exhausted and emotional. I spoke to my nurse, Thelma, about how I was feeling. She sat with me, listening for a good 20 minutes and told me if I needed to talk again, she would be there for me.

I found a lump in my neck, so the doctor came to see me. She checked it and ordered blood tests and an ultrasound. The phlebotomist came and took two vials of blood, and Thelma booked an ultrasound. It was all done pretty quickly. It came back normal, but it gave me a scare. I remember thinking, What else can you put me through? Have I not had enough?

20/2/19

In Purple Group we spoke about support, barriers, advantages and disadvantages, and good supports. We spoke about taking the mask off that we always wear to keep us safe. We spoke about being open to help and being honest with ourselves and others. We then spoke about resources, like GPs, psychologists, psychiatrists, Lifeline and Sexual Assault Resource Centre (SARC).

Dr So put me on a higher dose of night-time meds. That was all I prayed for—sleep to come.

I continued EMDR with Danielle. We worked really hard on the part of the nightmare where Habib threw the pipe down beside me. I told Danielle I had dreamt her into the dream. and I now felt confident that EMDR would work. She gave me a high five and said, 'We did it!'

Knowing Danielle was in my dream was one way for me to know I was not back in the past. If she was there, I could learn I was having a dream, as my body tried to process the trauma, and was not back in the past. We hoped that eventually I could process the trauma, so the dreams were less intense, and how to ground myself in the present when I woke up in a sweat. We also worked on ways so that in time we could change the outcome of the dream.

I was desperately missing Norman and couldn't wait to be back home with him, but I knew that I was in the right place. I needed to be well. I had to go home a different person, one that wanted to be here, wanted to live. Before going into the clinic, I was so close to ending it all. I felt I was a burden on Norman and the kids. I was so depressed and wanted to take my pills to end it, but Norman had my medications locked up in his office.

The EMDR was working, and I was beginning to tolerate the image rather than the image controlling me.

One day, I went to Red Group instead of Purple Group, which was art and crafts. I drew a picture in my visual diary and, in my room afterwards, I did some crochet.

I met with my doctor and when he asked me how I was going. I told him we had had a small breakthrough with the EMDR. I told him I could now visualize Danielle in the van with me, calming me by putting her hand on my head and telling me I will be okay, it will all be over soon.

He ordered bloods to check my iron because I was still purging, but not all the time. I purged more in the evening after dinner. I'd been trying to keep my breakfast and lunch down, because I was taking my meds before those meals.

In Group we were given articles from magazines of positive sayings and told to pick a few. I picked, 'When you recover or discover something that nourishes your soul and brings joy, care enough about yourself to make room for it in your life.' by Joan Shinoda Bolenc.

I spoke with one of the nurses about the session on the senses, and that I'd cried most of the way through. I found it difficult to love myself, believe I'm a good person. I didn't believe those things. I wouldn't give up though.

One night, I told my nurse that I struggled with positive affirmations, hearing positive things about myself. Things like, I am worthy, I am loved, I am a good person, I am caring. The nurse asked if I'd tried looking in the mirror and saying those things to myself. I told her how much I hate seeing myself in the mirror and she asked if I'd try just a few seconds each day and say something positive to myself. I promised her I would.

During EMDR with Danielle, I found myself getting frustrated and angry towards my family. My mum and dad were both in the bedroom drinking when I got home after the rape. Mum didn't come and see if I was okay; she just accepted it was me, and that was it. I was hurting and in pain, and I needed my mum—God, I desperately needed my mum—but she wasn't there, not properly. I was ignored, as usual. Drink came first. As we processed my trauma, more started to come up about my parents' lack of response and help. This started to bring up more and more of the trauma of how I was neglected/treated/abused by them. We spent a long time on family trauma once this came up.

To visualise Danielle in my nightmare had given me some comfort. It had got me through the last few weeks.

8/3/19

Today is my last full day in the clinic. I have mixed feelings—I feel anxious, scared, what if I messed everything up? I need to focus on my mindfulness. Dr So arrived at 7:30 p.m. to sort out my medication for going home. He asked if I was intending to attend groups after I went home, and I told him I was on the list for a 12-week DBT course and that I would also attend Purple Group a few days a week with Laura.

9/3/19

It was a worse night than usual—I don't know if it was because I'm going home today. My nurse gave me my morning meds and took the rest with her to bag up for me to take home. I packed everything up and went for breakfast. I cleared my room and then headed downstairs to wait for Norman. He arrived just after 10:00 a.m. It was a strange feeling going home for good.

At home, I felt a bit lost and struggled to function. Norman made dinner—pork mash, peas and corn. It was really nice.

We had a family meeting and put a crisis plan together. I wrote down all my meds and phone numbers for my supporters: Norman, Conor, Catherine and Helen. We agreed that Conor would hold my meds. We bought a 7-day medicine holder and filled it with my medication.

I have such an amazing family; they are all so supportive and caring. I was in bed by 8:30 p.m. It was a strange feeling getting into my own bed and not being in the clinic.

I woke up through the night and forgot where I was.

The next day when Norman and Catherine came home from skating, we had some lunch. I walked into my office, saw the mess, walked back out and closed the door. Before I went into the clinic, I had become manic, and my office looked like a bomb had hit it. I would start a project and not finish it before moving onto the next. When starting a new project, I would go out and buy the materials, but I would buy too much. I started making books, so I went out and bought the card, leather and binding materials. I then went on to buy wooden boxes to paint as gifts. I ended up with over 50 at one point. The floor in my office floor would be covered to the point I couldn't work on any one thing. I bought 40 canvases and have only painted on a handful.

I woke up bright and early to work on my office again. I wanted to get some quality time in there, and I needed to clear the floor. At that moment, I couldn't get from the door to my desk without falling over something, so I needed to keep going.

It took me four days to go through my office, clear everything out and actually sit at my desk and do some work. I felt better.

That night, I made toad-in-the-hole (sausage and Yorkshire pudding) with the help of Norman and Catherine. We then sat outside and had dinner. I knew it was going to take a little bit of time to get back into a routine at home.

I dropped Catherine at school and then drove to see Danielle. We decided we wouldn't do EMDR that day because I was too wired, I couldn't concentrate because of the dexamphetamine I was prescribed a week before. I was prescribed them to keep me awake through the day because I was napping. We put together a weekly plan. I needed everything in writing at the moment because I was forgetting too many things. I wrote a crisis plan for Helen and met with her to give it to her. It was nice seeing her outside the clinic.

I attended the clinic a few days a week for Purple Group. I started taking the train into town and then catching the red Cat bus to the clinic.

I was struggling to get into a routine at home. I was too used to the routine I had in the clinic. I had been there for six weeks by that point.

Helen picked me up and took me to see Danielle. I was swearing a lot, and Danielle said I was too wired to do EMDR.

I felt so much anger—anger at myself for being weak all those years. Instead of feeling compassion or empathy towards that younger me, I was angry and frustrated at her. I was also angry at my granddad, angry at Habib, angry at Khalid, angry at Dad, Nannie, Aunt Joan, Ronald, Angela, Andrew, etcetera, etcetera, etcetera. The list went on and on.

I struggled to get out of bed and function. I had been home just over two weeks by then. I called the clinic and cancelled my group session because I couldn't cope. Instead, I tackled my office, but I felt like I was going round in circles. I had piles of things I wanted to give away and things I wanted to work on.

I went in to work with Robyn and took a box full of small rocks with me, one for each of the kids and Robyn. I also gave them a small box that they could put their rocks in. I showed them a rock on which I'd written a positive word and decorated. I told them to do the same to their rocks. They could decorate the rocks with feathers, diamonds, paint pens, glitter, anything they wanted to. We helped them write words on the rocks like: Be happy, Be caring, Love, Peace.

I taught them how to meditate using tummy breathing. I got them to lie on the floor and put their rocks on their tummy and watch how the rock rose and fell with each breath. I got Robyn to do the meditation with the children every day, and it was very successful. The kids were a lot calmer and clearer in their reading.

Yajna phoned me to tell me she was going back to work after maternity leave. She said her door was always open for me. I loved working with Yajna, but I had come a long way since then. I felt I had opened up more to Danielle over the past year, and a lot more had come out, things I'd never spoken about before.

Norman gave me some healing in the evening when I needed my mind to be at peace. I'd lay on the sofa with my head on his lap, and he'd place his hands on my head. I could feel the warmth coming from his hands. It was grounding and calming. I loved those spontaneous healing sessions—I felt so much calmer afterwards.

One night, I woke from a nightmare shouting, 'No, Danielle.' I'd dreamt about being in the van and pictured Danielle next to my head saying, 'I am here, Sharon. You will get through this; it will stop. Be strong Sharon. I'm here for you.' She'd placed her hand on my head. But he was raping me while she was there. His eyes were bulging, and he was so angry, and I didn't want her seeing it. I couldn't cope with seeing them both in the van at the same time.

I ran into Dr So as I was leaving the clinic. He said he'd spoken to a few female psychiatrists and asked them if they would take on my case, but they'd said my case was too complex and they wouldn't take it on.

I felt broken, upset and confused. Am I that bad? Is my case that bad?

The following week I was on a lunch break from a session at the clinic when I got a message asking me to go to Reception. I grabbed my lunch and returned to the clinic. They told me Dr So was no longer my psychiatrist and I couldn't attend any more groups.

Again, I felt upset, lost, worthless, heartbroken. I threw away my lunch and walked to Danielle's. She was furious. We didn't do EMDR because I was too upset. I didn't see the point in living anymore; I thought there was no reason.

The next morning, I woke feeling lost. I should have been getting ready to go to the clinic, but instead I had to stay home because I wasn't allowed back. It felt unfair that Dr So had stopped seeing me without telling me.

Dr Robbins called to check up on me, which was really nice of her. She was also angry with what happened. With the help of Norman, I put together an email to the clinic.

The clinic apologised for what had happened and arranged for another psychiatrist to see me, Dr Sue, but the appointment was four weeks away. Dr Robbins said I could see her in the meantime if I needed. The manager at Perth Clinic also called and said she was disgusted at the way I was treated. She arranged for me to still attend Purple Group and the 12-week DBT course. I was grateful to her and to the clinic for their support.

I returned to Purple Group with Laura. There were lots of new faces and only two people I knew from before. Norman was heading to Scotland, my doctor was no longer my doctor, and it felt like the only constant I had in my life was Danielle and the clinic.

23/4/19

I finally confronted my mother. She'd put in for a council house near my sister but changed her mind at the last minute. She'd also told Colin that Wendy hated him because of his drug dealing, and told Wendy that Colin hated her man, Craig, because he used to be a police officer. Mum didn't like Craig because he had OCD and loved to clean. God, I would love a man who loved to clean my house.

I told Mum that I didn't want to know what was going on with Wendy and Colin, to stop stirring things up between them and that she seemed to enjoy seeing them at each other's throats.

Then I accused her of abandoning me when I was young. For continuing to work at the shop after Habib raped me. She said she needed the money to pay for Dad's drink.

When I told Danielle, she was angry, especially because the money was to pay for alcohol, not something essential.

I also told Danielle that Norman and I had made love on Sunday night. I'd had a flashback, and he'd held me as I cried. He'd said I didn't need to be sorry, that he loves me, and that's enough. We don't need to make love to show our love. It had been 19 years since we last made love due to the flashbacks and panic attacks. It was too hard to be intimate. We still held hands, hugged and kissed but didn't make love. I wanted to try again because therapy was going well, so I thought I was well, but I wasn't.

It was nice to connect lovingly with him. I do love him and want to give him all of me one day.

I'd taken Norman to the airport in the morning, and Conor and Catherine were in their rooms as usual, so I was alone with my thoughts and feelings. I'd had the thought of hurting myself for weeks and, as I was packing my art materials away, I came across the craft knife. I sat with it for what seemed like a lifetime. Then I cut my wrist, just deep enough to feel the pain. It took my mind away from my internal pain for a while. Some days, it was too much to bear.

I now remember everything that happened 31 years ago in that van and apartment. I remember it all. Every single detail and it is hurting and haunting.

For the first time in a long time, I felt like giving up on life. I felt that I couldn't keep putting a mask on for everyone and pretending I was fine when I was actually falling apart.

At my appointment with Danielle, we spoke about my memories. I hadn't felt like ending it at all in such a long time, but the thoughts, images, flashbacks and panic attacks were so intense. I was exhausted. I came so close to having a drink. I hadn't cried that openly in a long time, and my heart was breaking.

I was readmitted to the clinic.

I cried all the way back to the clinic, signed in and went to my room. I left the door open a little. I just felt safer with it open. I went to the park across the road and listened to the birds above me in the trees. It was the only thing that would calm me down—I find the sounds of nature calming. I phoned Helen and told her everything had come back to me, and I was heartbroken.

I stayed in the clinic for 4 weeks. I told Laura about writing my book. It's something I have thought about for years now. She thought it would be very healing for me. Laura left the clinic the same day I left. What could I say? She'd been part of my journey for the past six months. As a group therapist and as an individual therapist.

Why?

Why me? Why so many times? Why so many people? Why over so many years?

I prayed, prayed to God, prayed to anyone that would listen.

I cried myself to sleep night after night.

No-one came, no-one heard my prayer, no-one cared.

I was alone, no-one to talk too, no-one to tell, no-one to help me get through this hell I'm living day after day, night after night.

My heart aches, so much pain, so much sadness, so much anger, so much frustration.

Why?

Mum

Wendy's son had been living with Mum for the last few years. He was hanging around my brother a lot, not working, just sitting at home. Wendy was concerned that he was selling drugs for Colin. I called Mum to find out what was happening.

We were in the middle of the COVID pandemic, and they were in lockdown. I asked Mum why she wasn't insisting that Braidon get a job, but then I got angry about Colin. It was a day for saying everything that I wanted to say, and it all came out.

I knew my brother was giving Mum money to put together his drugs in her house, and I knew she loved receiving the money and spending it. Mum was never one for conflict, and I think she just accepted what Colin was doing. I don't know if she liked it or not; I never asked her.

I asked Mum about Habib and Grandad, about the money they gave her. She told me Habib had given her £3,000 as a down-payment for me to marry his cousin. She was supposed to encourage me to marry him, but even though I refused, she spent the money and couldn't pay it back. Habib raped me a few weeks later, and I wonder if it was payback.

Grandad gave Mum and Dad money every week. I thought it was debt, but it was to pay for me. So much came out in that argument, what happened with Grandad, Habib and Ronald. I saw a different side to her, but I still loved and cared for her—I just didn't like her very much.

I told her that Braidon and Colin had to stop going out because they could catch COVID. I was worried for her health, as she was taking strong inhalers and other medication for her back. She was never a smoker, but her lungs were bad.

After the fight, I deleted Facebook and Messenger, so Mum couldn't contact me anymore.

Only 4 weeks after the phone call Mum did get COVID.

Next is a series of texts between me and Danielle.

Danielle had always told me to be gentle to my younger, anxious self, love her if I could, even when I was overwhelmed. I tried to imagine myself caring for that lovable, anxious and challenged little girl:

Me: *Mum has COVID and I don't know how to feel. Wendy said she's very ill, but I don't know how am I supposed to react? Do I call her? Do I ignore it or do I let her die hating her? Am I a bad person for wanting her dead? Fuck! I'm so confused Danielle and I don't know what I'm doing.*

Danielle: *Oh dear. You are not bad for wanting her dead. She caused you so much pain, it's natural for you to wish that pain would go away. I don't think you need to decide tonight, let it settle. You don't have to make contact* *with her. I guess there is the reality that she won't make it, but she might, so you don't need to get drawn back in. One option would be to send something you want her to read, or just to write to yourself if you feel there is anything to say. It is okay not to have any contact. You can also say you know she's had her own trauma, and you don't want her to suffer. Any of these things are okay. Try to sleep tonight and we'll chat. You didn't cause the rift – her actions did. You're not responsible.*

When I slept, all I saw was her taking the money from Grandad. I saw the exchange of money between her and Habib. It was so clear in my mind.

I have many different feelings: the protective child, wanting to protect her; the lost and confused child, who needed their mother; the angry child who was used, abused and sold by their mother, again and again.

A large part of me wanted her to die, wanted her to suffer like younger me suffered. Another part of me hated the fact that I was angry enough to want that to happen. Then, I was that confused child again.

Me: *I really don't know how to feel, Danielle. It's like there's a bomb in my brain that's going to explode any moment. I am lost and tired and broken.*

Danielle: *I'm so proud of you for being able to give all your beautiful and deserving parts a voice. To make your decision, you need to listen to them all and hear their concerns as valid. Think of it as a round table meeting with your parts. Let them speak, and adult Sharon gets to decide.*

I affirm your decision to stay away, but I know these life moments are not always clear, and there will be consequences whichever way you decide. You have to go with the choice that most meets your needs at this point. You don't know how you will feel if anything happens. That's in the future and we don't know that until we arrive. It's about making a best guess for what you can manage right now and what you'll be able to manage in the future. Consider not just what you should do, but what you can do and what you want to do, and your ability to manage that choice. Even if there are regrets, it doesn't mean you made the wrong decision. There was no great choice. If anything happens, understand your reasons for choosing that path. I will support and assist whatever you decide. Although Norman can't help you decide, he'll be a good ear. If you choose not to even engage with the idea or concept of contact, we'll support you 100%. You're not broken; you're in pain.

Me: *An ambulance has been called for her. She can no longer breathe on her own.*

Danielle: *Aww, I'm sorry this had to happen now when things are already so challenging. Your choices are: One, accept things as they are. You were very hurt and you don't need to say anymore. She had her chance to apologise and change things, and she didn't take it. Two, you can decide to make contact, either directly or via someone else.*

I'm sorry for what you're going through. You may regret not communicating, but you may also regret communicating. You might regret that you tried and made it worse, or you might do it and be pleased you did. You might feel too triggered to communicate at all. But you're allowed to choose based on what you want to do. You'll get through to the other side, and work through whatever is left after this crisis is over.

Me: *I spoke to Wendy and Mum is getting worse each day. She had a fall and can't go to the bathroom anymore. They have upped her oxygen to the highest it can go. Her body is getting too weak to fight. It would take a miracle now for her to survive.*

Me: *Mum is deteriorating rapidly. They have started to turn her onto her stomach to help her lungs take in more oxygen. She can't talk properly anymore and she's not eating much, so they are trying to get fluids into her.*

Danielle: *Okay. Hold steady. She's where she needs to be, and they are doing everything they can. Think of that. Try not to think in detailed imagery. It's a psych trick so we don't get traumatised by people's stories.*

Think of her being in the best place she can be right now. Imagine them help her to go more peacefully. I know how hard this is. You'll get through it.

Me: *It's hard, Danielle. She's dying and not peacefully. Wendy just phoned. She's talked to the doctor. They've put Mum on an IV drip and the oxygen is as high as it can go. It's just a matter of time. They don't think it will be much longer now. They said it would take a miracle for her to live. I feel useless. I can't hold my sister and tell her it's going to be okay, because it's not. I feel numb and lost, too many emotions to name.*

Danielle: *All the parts of you will be unsettled as the tension is high. Speak to them, care for them. They'll settle in time. You're doing what you can. You can't control everything right now.*

Me: *She has pneumonia now and might not make it through the night.*

Danielle: *Thinking of you.*

Me: *It's Caitlyn's birthday today.*

Danielle: *I'm so sorry. I hope she's resting in peace. Beautiful soul.*

Me: *It has been an emotional day. I don't think I've cried this much or this hard in a long time. My head is aching and I'm so tired. My heart is torn in two I want/need Mum to hold on a bit longer. I don't think I could cope with her passing today, not on Caitlyn's day.*

I phoned Mum tonight. I needed to ask her to hold on. It was hard to understand her, and she cried when she heard my voice. I could only make out a few words, but she said she was sorry over and over again. Her words, 'I'm sorry, Sharon, I love you.' She repeated it many times. She said she was scared.

Danielle: *I hope part of you is comforted by her apology. She sounds very unwell. You're very brave to engage with her. I'll chat with you tomorrow. Take care until then.*

Me: *I am so tired, Danielle. I need it to be over now. She needs to be let free. It's wrong to prolong it. I can't have any more contact. I won't speak to her* again. It's too hard to keep going there. I can't forgive and forget. I have done all I can. I have taken her apology. I can't take any more medication to help me sleep without going too far. I've had a few dizzy turns today. I forced myself to drink a smoothie and, yes, I managed to keep it down. I think I needed the sugar for energy.

19/2/21

Me: *Mum died at 2:16 a.m. I was waiting on the call for the last couple of days and, when it finally came, I wasn't shocked. She's gone. My mum is gone. How do I feel? Lots of different emotions. I still loved her – after everything, I still loved her. I got in touch with the hospital. There will be no embalming, because she died from Covid. There will be no open casket. It will all be done quickly, within the week. I have contacted the funeral parlour about the cremation, and I've contacted the crematorium. Only 20 people can attend. That, in itself, will be war amongst the family. It will be live-streamed for us to see the service.*

Norman said I should think of myself at this time. But I feel lost. Fuck, I don't know how to do this, Danielle. The meds are not doing their job. I need time out. I have been asked to write the eulogy and choose the music and flowers. Wendy and Colin don't get on – in fact, they hate each other, so they are not going to deal with it. I don't know how I'm going to write this eulogy. All I know is I have to, otherwise nothing will be written, and Mum will leave this world not knowing what people thought of her, and there were many people that loved her.

Danielle: *Hi Sharon, it would indeed be heart-wrenching. I totally understand your emotions. If you need to write your feelings down to get them out in your journal, do so. If you need to rest and let the storm settle, do that. If you need to walk and talk with Norman, do that. Your Mum is at peace now, and you have all the time in the world to process it all. You don't need to do it now and no matter how hard you try you won't be able to. We'll process together in the coming weeks. To the parts that cared for your mum, I'm so sorry for your loss. To the parts of you that are confused and angry, I totally get what you have suffered and why you feel the way you do. Take care.*

Me: *I don't know what I need or want at the moment. My brother offered to fly me home, but I said, 'It's not happening.' As much as my younger parts are struggling and mourning, I would never accept this offer. I have to try and do what's best for me now. I'm too tired to think straight at the moment but I know Mum is in a better place and is no longer in pain. I think I need to go for a walk.*

Danielle: *You have to look after all your different parts at this time, Sharon. That 8-year-old, 12-year-old, 14-year-old, 17-year old. You have to think of all of them and take care of them as best you can. They will be feeling lots of different things towards your mum. Most of them had a lot of love for her. That younger you looked after your Mum, cared for and protected her.*

I wrote the eulogy, chose the songs and picked red and yellow flowers with the help of Wendy. They were her favourite colours. I phoned my brother and told him he needed to take the reins, as I was burnt out. I did all I could from Australia.

My sister offered to help with everything, but Colin wouldn't talk to her, which was selfish. Everyone was hurting, not just him. I was sick of going back and forth between them. Colin needed to grow up and do what was right. I was done in and ready for the whole thing to be over. Mum needed to rest in peace, whatever that meant for her.

Me: *My head is on fire; I am on the brink of losing my mind. I can't take it anymore. I thought it all would end, Danielle, but it fucking hasn't. Maybe it's because I said I wouldn't care if she got Covid and died? Maybe I'm being cursed for that? Maybe I'm not meant to have peace? I was the outcast – I am the outcast – and now I have proof. I can't take anymore. I'm done.*

My brother showed me some paperwork – I don't know if it was because he's dyslexic, or if he was taking his own drugs, but he had no idea what he had in his hand. He said he would post the medical papers to me, along with a copy of the death certificate, and other things he didn't know what to do with.

It seems my dad wasn't my dad. The paternity test was done when I was three years old. Now that I look back, after that, things changed. That's when my dad would get aggressive with me. I always wondered why me, why I was the one. Now I know. I seem to give you more and more shit, Danielle. I'm so, so sorry. Is it going to take me the rest of my life to work through everything? God I want a stiff drink.

Danielle: *Turn off your phone and have a stiff iced water or tea. Put a wet cloth over your head and lie back, listen to relaxing music and take yourself there if you can. Rest your weary head, nothing else matters. Block it out and protect your overwhelmed parts. Give Norman your phone. You may be the outcast in that family, but you are the centre of your chosen family and you are a perfect child of the universe. I wish peace for you.*

Me: *He's not my Dad. He was never my Dad. He used me as a punching bag because I wasn't his child. That's why Wendy was the love child. They made her together. I don't know why they did a test in the first place, I wish I knew.*

Danielle: *My heart breaks for you, Sharon. I admire how strong you are and I know you'll get through this.*

27/2/21

I picked up my baby girl today. She is gorgeous: 10 weeks old, and I named her Mia. There is something special in all this chaos. She will bring light into my life.

Mia was just what I needed. She got me through one of the toughest times. The love that poured from her was genuine and pure.

Colin fought hard to have mum embalmed. He wanted her body brought home to her house, and the coffin opened for people to view her body. I found this disturbing, but I told him he could take over as I had to pull back. I let him get on with it. I couldn't be there for the funeral, so I let him do what he was going to do. Due to her having COVID, the body had to lay in state for two weeks. The funeral was organised for the second week in March, and they were bringing her home and opening the coffin. He had organised a white coach to carry her body and two white horses to guide her to her final resting place. I don't know if this was for her or for his stature in the community. Either way it was going to be the funeral of the century.

I thought surely no one would attend because of COVID, but I was wrong. I called Colin on WhatsApp the night before, checking to see she got home okay. He looked exhausted; I think the whole thing had taken a toll on him. He said she got home safely, as he walked from room to room in the house. He put out a cigarette in the kitchen and walked into Mum's room, where she lay in her coffin. Before I could say stop, he turned the camera on, and I was looking at her body in the coffin. She was purple, not pink, because she had no oxygen left in her body when she died. I broke down and cried because that wasn't my Mum lying in that box—it wasn't her.

On the day of the funeral, my cousin called me on WhatsApp so that I could watch it. I saw the coffin being brought out of the house, and six men lift it onto their shoulder. Two of those men were my brother and my nephew, one was my cousin Andrew, and three others were drug dealers. Basically, everyone who carried the coffin was a drug dealer. It looked like something from the olden days, with the gangsters, the mafia and the drug lords.

They placed her in the coach—the horses were beautiful. They had yellow feathers coming out the top of their heads, Mum's favourite colour. The street was crowded with people, all social distancing with masks on. I spotted a few cousins at the far end of the street, and neighbours standing across the road watching. The coffin was carried around the streets where she had lived most of her life and then taken to the crematorium.

I watched the service itself online in my theatre room. The eulogy went well—I'd managed to get something from each member of the family, and I didn't forget anyone. Only 20 people were allowed inside the crematorium, and they had to be socially distanced. There was a crowd standing outside, listening to the speakers, and many more listening at home, like me and my family.

It was hard to watch—it didn't feel real. I was sure that at some point Mum would phone me and apologise for all the mistakes she'd made, and we'd move on. But that was never going to happen—not now. I was never going hear her voice again. All I had now were pictures and memories. But I still loved my mum, no matter what she had done.

Mum had three death policies that my brother took after she died. He phoned me and told me that one was for Wendy, one was for him, and one was to pay for the funeral. He said there was nothing in my name. I wasn't surprised—I didn't expect to have anything left to me.

When Wendy went to cash the policy, the bank told her it had been cashed already. Colin had forged her signature and taken her money along with his own.

Of course, I had a disagreement with Colin about that, and he cut me off. I wanted nothing more to do with any of it, so I decided to delete my new Facebook account again. I needed to start afresh, and the only way was to erase my family, everyone except my sister. I still talk to Wendy every week. I love and miss her desperately. After seven years apart, we'll see each other again next year when she comes to Australia on holiday.

Colin and his girlfriend threatened me on WhatsApp, so I decided to delete that, too. My cousin called, telling me she was told I was dead. I thought at that point it'd be better off if everyone believed that, and I could just live my life in peace. So, I changed my phone number, too. I became a ghost. I'm happier for doing those things—I have Norman and the kids, my beautiful dog, my sister, niece and my friends and therapists, and I don't need anyone else.

After Christmas and New Year, I went back to Perth Clinic for Red Group. I'd tried art therapy before, but it hadn't gone well, but the previous art therapist had retired, and a new one, Ingrid, had taken her place. She was bubbly and humorous, and I joined the group. Being an artist, I have a certain way of doing things and like to show my emotions in my work. The layout of the room was more welcoming, and the group seemed friendly. Ingrid gave us photos of paintings by an artist and asked us to create our own piece of art using whatever medium we wanted. I chose paint and created a really dark piece because my head was in a dark place at that time.

I was doing EMDR with Danielle, but Dr Sue had left the clinic, so I was without a psychiatrist again. However, I was allowed to keep attending Red Group and art therapy until I found a new psychiatrist. I needed stability in my life and the clinic played a major part in that.

Dr Liana, February 2023

I managed to get a new psychiatrist, Dr Liana. I couldn't say her surname, so she let me call her Liana.

When we first met, I thought it wasn't going to work. She seemed against admission into the clinic. I knew that while I was doing EMDR, I needed extra support, and I'd self-harmed the week before, cutting my leg quite deeply. I hadn't cut for a while, but everything was falling apart, and I needed some release. I also told her that in the space of two years, I'd lost two psychiatrists when I needed support the most. I said too that I was concerned about having to tell half a story again to another doctor. I shared part of my life story, told her about the nightmares and about EMDR with Danielle and how I would like to start doing it again.

She sat in silence while I spoke and took great care in listening to what I had to say. I hadn't had that before. She asked to meet Norman at the next meeting and had a lot of questions for him—wanting to know how I was at home, if I was safe. Norman said he had my medication and gave it to me weekly. I put the medication into a pillbox, and he locked it up until I needed it again. He also had all my craft knives, and I was only allowed one when I showed him what I was using it for. We still do this today.

Dr Liana was happy with the meeting went and said she would get me into the clinic as soon as she could so I could start EMDR with Danielle.

I was admitted in February 2023. I was so surprised by her care—I'd never had anyone hear my story, hear my past. She visited every Monday, Wednesday, Friday and Saturday, and would sit for an hour listening to me talk about my past. She took such care with her questions and made me feel heard. Danielle was the only person who knew my story. I had never told another soul everything, but she wanted to know everything, and I felt comfortable enough to tell her. She didn't want to feed me medications and leave me there. She wanted to treat me as the person, and that's what I felt. We looked at my medication and kept it to a minimum, which was great. I didn't feel like a zombie. I felt like a normal human being.

While in the clinic, I attended Art and Crafts and Art Therapy with Ingrid. I really looked up to her and was able to relax in her company. She brought out a side of me that I had hidden for way too long. I showed my anger, frustration, love, and so many emotions through my art. The groups changed a little each session, with new people joining, but a few of us were regulars, and it was nice to get to know each other a little.

EMDR was exhausting, but I was getting through it, and knowing I was going back to a safe place helped me so much. The nursing staff, as always, were amazing.

Before I left the clinic to go home, I organised to see Ingrid one on one for art therapy, which I began in March 2023. When we first started working together, my drawings and paintings were dark.

She asked, 'How are you feeling?'

I said, 'Sad and angry.'

'What would that look like?'

I said, 'Blackness.'

She gave me a large sheet of paper and asked me to show her. I picked up a black pastel and started gently scribbling on the page, but I could feel the anger rise in me. Ingrid could see this and told me to let it out. I started scribbling faster and more furiously, covering the sheet. Ingrid replaced it with another piece, and then another. I went through a few pastels. I was exhausted and crying openly by the end of the session. But I felt good for having released my anger and sadness.

As I started coming out of the darkness, it felt like I was climbing a hill, and the light was in the distance ahead of me. I hoped to reach the light sometime.

It took time, but I am finally in the blue—still on the rocks, but I'm getting there.

Ingrid asked if I would like to create something with plaster, so I decided to replicate my tree, the tree that was my safe place in the graveyard with Rose. I used wire and foil to create the shape, then plaster to form the tree. I created the leaves out of sponges, then painted it all. I created Rose's gravestone and miniature me from polymer clay. I then added fake grass and little stones surround the entire structure.

The whole process was huge and a mixture of emotions. I cried a lot, but I am so proud of the outcome. Art therapy is amazing for PTSD and trauma.

EPILOGUE

It is now May 2024, and I am in a good place, the best I've ever been. Life feels great. Both my amazing kids have flown the coop, which I thought would be hard, but I see more of them now than I did when they lived at home. I am the proudest mum alive. Conor works for a concreting company, and Catherine is a massage therapist.

Norman and I enjoy spending quality time together. He tells me he sees a huge change in me. The kids do too. This is great for me to hear.

I still see Danielle and Ingrid once a week, and my psychiatrist once a month. I see a Somatic Psychotherapist every few weeks. Because of them, I am in a great place. My nightmares are no more. Thanks to Danielle, EMDR and my medication, I am free and sleeping soundly at night. I look forward to bedtime now. As of just over a few months ago, I have been able to keep food down. I think it was due to the EMDR with Danielle.

I still have panic attacks now and then, but they are nowhere near what they used to be. I had an incident at the dentist, because the assistant was leaning over my face and had facial hair and spoke like Habib. It triggered a panic attack, and I did EMDR with Danielle, and spoke about what happened and the fact it wasn't him. A day later, I kept my food down, and I'm still managing to do so.

Don't get me wrong, it's bloody hard some days. I still have the urges depending on what I eat. I know it's going to be something I constantly need to work on, but I'm willing to do so. Keeping my appointments keeps me on track. I have the best support group around me. My medication is also stable.

After picking this book up and putting it down so many times over the last four years, I have finally finished it, and I am proud of myself for writing my story and everything that's happened. It's not going to the grave with me. It's no longer haunting my everyday life. I am finally free of it.

I still have days where I struggle, days when I ask, Why me? I guess I will always have days like that. I still carry baggage, but it's a lot lighter than it used to be. I believe I will need some sort of therapy for a long time yet, maybe for the rest of my life, but I know it will become lighter and lighter.

I pray this book helps someone see that there's life beyond the trauma. Just reach out. There is all kinds of help out there for you. Believe me!

Love Sharon x

Afterword

Sharon,

I joined on your long journey after the experiences of your early years had shaped the burden you would carry. I have seen you try to blank the many memories in multiple ways, including tears, alcohol, pain and medication, to name a few. Many masks have been worn and discarded over the years. No one will know the full extent of what lies behind a mask, but always the simple wish to be seen as normal was the strongest.

Lived experiences never leave you, but they can be diminished by the addition of positive achievements and memories. Despite the many low points, there have been successes, the biggest being to stay ahead of the demons trying to take over and finish your journey, closely followed by having a close-knit family. There have been many people who have crossed your path and offered a nugget that has helped you, and you in return, have equally touched many people to help them on their journey.

The breadth of your life story is immense and to many, likely unfathomable. An everlasting wish you held is that nobody else should have to experience what you went through. This book started as a task to help process and manage your thoughts, but it soon became something you hoped would help others; even helping one person, would make the pain of going through memories worth it. Now, with the ending of this book, it is time to reflect on your achievements and to work out what the next chapter in your life is going to be. I'm so very proud of you Sharon.

Luv Norman

Dear Mum,

Looking back over the years, and all the times we used ti sit down, and you would tell me about your past and how you were struggling. I would be lying if I said it wasn't hard to sit there and try to keep a straight face when faced with the sad truth of your past.

But I always tried my best to be the rock there to comfort you in your times of need and an ear for you to open up to, as I know it always makes things a little lighter when there is someone willing to listen.

The hardest part about it all was being able to put faces to the trauma and not being able to think about those people the same again and being unable to confront those people and feeling powerless as it was all in the past. Though saying all that I have seen tremendous growth in you, and you have built quite an amazing support group with people who care for you and love you. You have come a long way, and I see little improvements every day and it makes me so proud to call you mum.

As I have seen time and time again, Family can be the biggest blessing but also the worst of enemies, but the best families are usually those we create and not we share blood with, but in the case of immediate family we have I could not be prouder and happier.

I love you so much mum,

Love your amazing son

Conor

Dear Mum,

I remember being so confused, angry, and worried when I was younger. I didn't understand what was happening – your panic attacks, how your mood could change so quickly – it was all so hard to make sense of.

Then one day, I found that letter you wrote to your mum. Suddenly, pieces started to fall into place. But at the same time, I felt so many emotions – anger at your family, sadness for everything you'd been through, and hurt that I hadn't known sooner. Looking back now, I understand that I was to young then to really grasp it all.

As the years went on and you began to open up to me, everything started to make sense. It was like finally being able to see the full picture after years of missing puzzle pieces.

There were some really scary times. Times when I was so afraid I might lose you. I remember waking up every day wondering if you'd still be here tomorrow. I remember the fear when we were told to hide the sharp objects, and when you came home but couldn't be left alone. Those were such hard times for all of us.

When we were in Ireland, and that moment happened to me, I knew I could come to you. I knew that you would believe me. I was so scared to tell Dad, but you sat beside me and helped me through it. You've always been there for me, through every difficult moment. I know I can tell you anything, and you'll listen without judgement.

You've come such a long way, Mum. Over the past few years, we've all seen such an incredible change in you. You're brighter, happier, and so much more confident. You bring light wherever you go and somehow make friends with everyone you meet.

I know there are still hard days – but you always find your way through them. You're still here, after everything you've faced, and that says so much about your courage, your strength, and your heart.

You are my best friend and one of the strongest people I know. I'm so proud of you and so grateful that you're my mum.

Love your best friend and your favorite child

Cat xx

Dear Sharon,

I vividly recall you saying that telling your story at our sessions felt scarier than being a young girl in the courtroom, too small to even reach the glass of water, testifying against your perpetrator. Despite this, you came, gradually built a trust, and opened up more and more, until you started to enjoy the depth and closeness of our therapeutic relationship.

Your strength, dedication and determination to heal were truly admirable. I was deeply moved by your bravery in entrusting me with your deepest emotions, especially considering the numerous betrayals and hardships you had endured. Together, we put our hearts and souls into ending over 30 years of nightmares. I was immensely relieved when you shared that you were finally able to sleep peacefully, without nightmares.

It has been an absolute privilege to work with you, observe your incredible transformation, witness the deepening of your relationships with Norman, your children, and your 'friends like family.' It is truly heartening to see you flourish.

I hope you stay well and continue to find joy in your art, and cherish the moments with Norman and your children and friends.

Warm wishes always,

Yajna

Dear Sharon,

We all carry trauma with us from different times in our lives. Most of us bury these experiences in the deepest part of our consciousness and call ourselves strong for it. You have shown me that true strength is standing within the fiery pits of the most complex of traumas showing that brokenness is not weakness. You are an inspiration to women who do not yet exist, and you represent the combined strength of those who cease to exist because of their trauma. You are the unashamed voice of all of us, screaming, 'I am still here,' even as the storm of your past bellows, trying to silence you with a pain that never gives you reprieve. I know that after reading this book, many women will have the courage to stand within their own fiery pits. We will stand beside you in the storm, hands raised like the branches of the tree of life, and together we will be thunder that shakes up the sky.

'We are still here.'

Thelma

Nurse, Perth clinic

Dear Sharon,

I want to offer my whole-hearted congratulations on your remarkable achievement in completing and sharing your book, 'The Girl in the Graveyard'. Your willingness to delve into the depths of your own personal trauma and bring it to light is nothing short of extraordinary. Your journey from those painful experiences to becoming an author is truly amazing, and I have no doubt that your courage will serve as a symbol of hope for anyone who has faced life-altering traumatic events.

Writing a book about your trauma is a deeply meaningful act of self-expression and resilience, and demonstrates your unwavering strength and dedication to your personal path of recovery. Through sharing your experiences, you've not only given a voice to your own pain and conveyed the emotions of your younger self, but you've also extended a hand of hope to others struggling with their own haunting past traumas.

Once again, congratulations on your incredible achievement of writing your first book, and I hope you find comfort in the knowledge that others who have endured a lifetime of trauma may read it and find a way forward.

With very best wishes,

Dr Nikki Cummings – Credentialled Eating Disorder Dietitian

I met my dear friend, Sharon, when our girls became close in high school. After forming an immediate connection, we were able to feel comfort and ease in sharing our deepest traumas and darkest thoughts. Sharon has a gorgeous ability to laugh. Her devotion to family and friends is beautiful. Her strength to keep fighting for healing and forgiveness is profound.

Thank you for trusting me, Sharon. You are an inspiration and true friend.

Big love and hugs always,

Helen

Sharon first came to me saying her trauma had been resolved and she was ready to focus on her bulimia. Little did we know, she would soon have a consultation with her gynaecologist, and his comments on her internal scarring would precipitate a cascade of memories to be shared over years.

The story is harrowing, the pain heavy and, at times, unrelenting. It could not be contained and it kept coming. There was no way out but through.

Each session, I began to feel Sharon's true spirit more. She knew deep inside what relationships and love were supposed to be, and she had a yearning for a relationship like that herself. Sharon's conversations with Rose in the graveyard were an antidote to loneliness and neglect, a space for connection, to exist, to have someone listen. Caring for her siblings, Rose, the hedgehog, the mouse, kept parts of her heart exercised, loving and soft, in the face of endless violence, hardness and neglect.

Consequently, Sharon has manifested much beauty in her life through creating and giving, via her art and painting, or helping children in need. The girl in the graveyard became the most loving and proud mother. Her marriage to Norman has endured many shades and colours because of the depths of trauma and recovery. Yet it remains strong, loving, spiritual and supportive. This is a testament to the capacity of both to connect, accept, respect, support, and heal at the deepest level.

Sharon has not only survived but created a haven for her family, where her children could experience the safety and nurture she was not afforded.

This book shares her story, the writing of which has been a challenging but healing journey, aided by her remarkable and detailed memory. She is wise, funny, potty-mouthed, generous and spiritual. Sharon has bravely shared her story with me in the therapy room. We have sat in the darkness, we have seen the light, we have laughed and, at times, we have even shed a tear together.

Now, through her courage and determination, on these pages she shares her story with the reader, honouring and giving voice to the parts of her that held these memories unshared for many decades. She has told a truth that the adults around her denied her, time and again.

Trauma doesn't disappear. If it is not screaming, even as it heals it has echoes. Sharon will continue to work and grow, and her healing journey will continue, weaving throughout her life, along with many other rich life experiences as future chapters unfold.

I have seen and admired Sharon's remarkable spirit, and now the reader, too, can see how, even in the face of the worst, bright light can shine and live, and there is always hope.

Danielle

Clinical psychologist

I have had the privilege and honour to work with Sharon who truly is one of the most brave and courageous souls I have ever encountered. There are those who are born into the most horrific trauma and endure the most horrendous and heinous attacks at the hands of others, who then choose to never allow anyone who crosses their path to be harmed as they were. Sharon is that person. She allows love to guide her over and over again, as she could never stand by and allow another soul to ever experience the harm that has befallen her.

In being brave enough to face her extraordinary pain, tremendous terror, and fear with enormous courage, piece by piece like a laborious mosaic, she is not only healing herself, but stands in strength in her quest to protect others.

On the one hand, Sharon has the roar of a lioness within, who stands with courage and conviction in her truth, and a desire to protect all those who are blessed to know and be loved by her. Yet, she also has a soul with butterfly wings that touch this earth ever so gently, with love and compassion for all of life.

Megan

Somatic Psychotherapist

I first met Sharon and her daughter, Catherine, in 2007, when I welcomed a new group of excited Year Ones into my class for the first time. The family had moved from Norway the previous year, and were adjusting to a new country as well as school.

Sharon is an amazing artist and readily volunteered her time to help in our art classes. She was creative, well-organised and extremely generous with her time and resources. She was calm and positive, empowering children to 'have a go' and be proud of their successes. They adored her and couldn't wait for the 'Mrs O'Rourke's Art Days'.

Over the years, Sharon and I developed a close working relationship and friendship. She continued to volunteer her time with the children in my class each year, even after her own children had moved on to secondary school. There were many laughs along the way and lots of fun preparing for assembly backdrops and performances. The book character 'Mrs Lambchop', will always hold special memories for us.

Sharon loved to cook and prepared the most amazing meals for my family. My elderly parents loved her as their own and she was always welcome at family gatherings. We spent many hours talking about her earlier life in Glasgow. She appreciated being able to share her thoughts and stories, and we wished we could have done more to help her.

Sharon was feisty, fun, and appeared happy. However, her struggle to deal triggers, anxiety and constant nightmares were very real challenges on a daily basis. She would often just put on a 'happy face' to mask her inner turmoil.

It was during these years that Sharon sought professional help to tackle the trauma that continued to haunt her from her childhood. She was incredibly strong, brave and committed to the tasks set for her in order to improve her life.

Over the years, we watched 'little steps' become bigger goals in her quest to heal. The seed for writing this book was planted long ago.

AFTERWORD

Congratulations on writing your book, Sharon, and 'sharing your story'. It is going to 'make a difference' and help others to navigate their own journey. We are so incredibly proud of your efforts and know that you will be a 'shining light' for others to follow.

With love,

Robyn Stewart

I first met Sharon when she attended the open studio (Red Group) at Perth Clinic. I won't forget seeing her walk in quietly, keeping very much to herself, she would sit silently at the table and paint. Sharon would respond politely to people when they spoke to her, but what really struck me was how much this quiet lady carried the 'weight of the world' on her shoulders.

Looking back now, it must have felt that it was 'too much' to share or put onto others, that she was walking with heavy inner demons that she didn't want to inflict on anyone else, and that she was wrestling with how to contain them within herself.

Since then, I have had the privilege of working with Sharon for several years, and getting to know all the complex, intelligent, witty and talented aspects of her, as well as getting to know some of those demons she was wrestling with. I feel we have laughed and cried on this Art Therapy journey together.

Writing this blurb for her book was so challenging for me in many ways. I even asked Sharon if I could say it in an art piece instead (to which I was given a clear …'no') My hesitation has not been one of not wanting to support her in the writing of her incredible story, it is simply that I feel there are very few words I have access to that can truly put justice to the journey I have been privileged to be a witness to.

Ultimately, I would say that after 30 years or so of working with people with mental health issues and trauma, Sharon stands out as being the bravest, most authentic and resilient person I have worked with.

As you read her story, you will get to understand the experiences of trauma that she had to bear, persistently, from such a young age, not just one betrayal, but many, cruel and traumatic events. Many people, probably myself included, would cave, would give in or give up, when dealing with not just the emotional and physical wounds of the initial incident, but a life of pain and flashbacks and nightmares and panic attacks, day in and day out.

Sharon has survived this, although coming close at times, has never given up. She has held the love of her family as guiding beacon before her to encourage her to get to the other side, despite never having experienced such love herself as a child. She has consistently lived her life as an honest, genuine and compassionate person, despite this never being role modelled for her.

She is forever an inspiration to me about bravery and 'keeping on going' even when you can't even imagine the other side. She reminds me that we can laugh, even in the midst of pain. She humbles me in that she has overcome such huge odds set against her, without ever losing sight of love, kindness and the goodness in people.

I hope in reading this book, you get to see some of this woman's strength and courage and gain some hope from it.

Ingrid

Art Therapist

Perth Clinic

www.ingramcontent.com/pod-product-compliance
Lightning Source LLC
Chambersburg PA
CBHW061725070526
44583CB00024B/3013